Children's Emotional Lives

PETER LANG
New York • Washington, D.C./Baltimore • Bern
Frankfurt am Main • Berlin • Brussels • Vienna • Oxford

SANDRA LEANNE BOSACKI

Children's Emotional Lives

Sensitive Shadows in the Classroom

PETER LANG
New York • Washington, D.C./Baltimore • Bern
Frankfurt am Main • Berlin • Brussels • Vienna • Oxford

Library of Congress Cataloging-in-Publication Data

Bosacki, Sandra Leanne.
Children's emotional lives: sensitive shadows in the classroom / Sandra Leanne Bosacki.
p. cm.
Includes bibliographical references and index.
1. Child psychology. 2. Cognition and culture. 3. Children—Language.
4. Social perception in children. 5. School environment—Psychological aspects. I. Title.
LB1117.B67   370.15'34—dc22   2008003857
ISBN 978-0-8204-8896-7

Bibliographic information published by **Die Deutsche Bibliothek**.
Die Deutsche Bibliothek lists this publication in the "Deutsche
Nationalbibliografie"; detailed bibliographic data is available
on the Internet at http://dnb.ddb.de/.

The paper in this book meets the guidelines for permanence and durability
of the Committee on Production Guidelines for Book Longevity
of the Council of Library Resources.

© 2008 Peter Lang Publishing, Inc., New York
29 Broadway, 18th floor, New York, NY 10006
www.peterlang.com

Printed in the United States of America

To my Mother, who taught me to read people's
eyes behind their smiles.

Contents

List of Tables

Acknowledgments

Throughout the researching and writing of this book, I have had the invaluable support of numerous individuals. I owe a debt of gratitude to my home institution, Brock University for providing me with a rich opportunity to further my inquiry and dialogue concerning children's emotions. I thank all of my colleagues and friends at Brock University for their kind support during the book preparation process.

I wish to thank the all those involved with the schools in which I have conducted my research studies on adolescents' and children's thoughts and emotions over the years including the children, parents, teachers, principals, and school staff. Throughout the years, at the Ontario Institute for Studies in Education of the University of Toronto, Brock University, Dalhousie University, and the University of Illinois at Chicago, I have had the pleasure to work with numerous friends, colleagues, and graduate and undergraduate student research assistants on various research projects and I thank them all for their assistance and support. I thank Spogmai Akseer, Mandy Frake, Pam Klassen-Dueck, Brianne Litke, Shelley Smith, Katie Sykes, and Amanda Varnish for their assistance on the longitudinal research study discussed in the book. I thank Larry Nucci, University of Illinois at Chicago, Chris Moore, Dalhousie University, Bruce Homer, New York University, and Kang Lee, the Ontario Institute for Studies in Education of the University of Toronto, for inviting me to their home institutions to spend a portion of my sabbatical leave year 2005-2006. I am sincerely grateful for their support and encouragement as these sabbatical visits made sustained thinking and writing on the topic of children's emotions possible. I also thank Janet Astington, Janet Boseovski, Jerome Bruner, Robert Coplan, Andrew Dane, Karen Drill, Judith Dunn, Esther Geva, Stacey Horn, Kristin Lagattuta, Zopito Marini, Tanya Martini, David Olson, Janette Pelletier, Linda Rose-Krasnor, Ken Rubin, Victoria Talwar and Judith Wiener for furthering my thinking about shyness and children's social and emotional development.

Throughout this project, it was a pleasure to work with the editorial and production team at Peter Lang. I appreciated the timely response and constant encouragement, guidance and support from my editor, Chris Myers at Peter Lang. I also thank Phyllis Korper, consulting editor at Peter Lang, and the anonymous reviewers for taking the time to review my manuscript. I also thank the members of the production team at Peter Lang including Sophie Appel, Heather Boyle, Valerie Best, Patricia Mulrane, Brittany Schwartz, Bernadette Shade, and Set Sokol for their time, guidance, assistance, and patience.

Background research and reflection underpinning the ideas and data presented in this book was supported, in part, by funding from various grants and scholarships received from Brock University, Dalhousie University, Ontario Institute for Studies in Education of the University of Toronto, the Social Sciences and Humanities Research Council of Canada Postdoctoral Fellowship and Standard Research Grants #410-2003-0950, and #410-2006-0361.

Early versions of portions of this book are published in the *Culture of Classroom Silence*, (p. 131), Bosacki, 2005. Grateful acknowledgment is herby made to copyright holders for permission to use this material. This material was reprinted by permission of the publisher. All rights reserved.

Most importantly, I thank my parents and sister for their unconditional loving kindness while I devoted my time and energy to this project. Their emotional support has made this book possible.

Preface

My first experience of the complex emotion of what is referred to in the Polish language as "tesknota" or a sense of nostalgia with sadness and longing, remains engraved in my heart and mind forever. I was no older than four years and our family lived close to a Royal Canadian Legion Hall where Scottish Pipe bands would sometimes practice. I remember as a child, when I first heard the odd sounds emerge from the bagpipes, I was standing in our backyard on a warm summer's early evening. This haunting, unfamiliar music evoked such sudden, strong feelings of "tesknota," that I soon found the inner turmoil too unbearable to remain silent and I began to weep uncontrollable tears. My Mother who was standing close by, upon seeing me cry, asked me why I was sad, and I claimed it was because I was listening to "sad music."

The foundation of this book began during that night, and similar childhood experiences when I would listen to my Mother sing songs in Ukrainian to my sister and I. "How do you say sad in Ukrainian, how do you say love in Polish? What does this mean in English?" Growing up in southern Ontario, Canada, as a young child, I often bombarded my Polish-Canadian father and Ukrainian-Canadian mother with such questions. Fascinated by these Ukrainian folk songs, although I did not understand the lyrics as I spoke English only, I was intrigued by why these songs evoked such strong emotions. Listening to these songs, I experienced this "tesknota" as I wondered why did these songs make me sad, especially given that I did not understand the words. The majority of these songs focused on stories of the heart and relationships, and my mother often struggled as she attempted to answer my persistent questions of "What does this song mean in English?" Quite often her response was simply, "I cannot sing this song in English—there are no words that share the same meaning." As a child, I would often puzzle over my mother's response, and wonder how could there be words in Ukrainian but no words in English? I would ask myself how could the words make sense in Ukrainian but not in English? I was even more puzzled by my change in emotional response to the translated song, as I asked myself, how could listening to the Ukrainian songs cause me to feel such strong emotions that gripped my heart, but when I heard the same words in English I did not experience the same emotional response? I thus learned quickly that you can understand a different language by feeling it with your heart and not just with your mind.

More than three decades later, such questions continue to fuel my interest in emotions and language, particularly the question of why does language or our mental script fail to express what we feel in our hearts? Why does the meaning of our inner dialogue often become distorted when we try to share the words with others? As the character Enoch in the chapter entitled "Loneliness" in Anderson's (1919) book Winesburg, Ohio states, "He knew what he wanted to say, but he knew also that he could never by any possibility not say it." (p. 153). Throughout most of my child and adult life, I remain fascinated and puzzled by the process of talking with ourselves in our minds and how our self-talk translates to our conversations with others. Also, how does our self-talk or private speech influence how we treat and care for ourselves and others? It is then of little "coincidence" that my program of teaching, learning, and research as a professor of education focuses on the role emotions and language play in children's self and social development.

Building on this life-long fascination with language, emotion, and self-concept, this book examines children's emotional lives at school, and provides an analysis of girls and boys perceived by their teachers to be socially withdrawn or shy. Drawing on a longitudinal study of elementary school girls and boys, it describes the emotional and social lives of six children in school. In the social and emotional world of school, the girls and boys share their experiences of self and emotional understandings and social relations through conversations as well as artwork. Emotional and social experiences seem to play different roles in girls' and boys' developing sense of self. It is my hope that this book makes a substantial contribution to our understanding of the complex emotional worlds that students and teachers create together. I hope it will encourage readers to learn more about the role that emotions play in children's school lives. In this book, I will explore the culture of emotion within the classroom—how do children's feelings affect how they work and play in school and treat others? How do their emotional worlds shape how they feel and think about themselves? To answer these questions, this book concentrates on the cultural and social factors that contribute to the shaping and the working of children's emotions within the classroom. This book emphasizes the role emotion and language play in self and social understanding and builds on the arguments of emotion researchers such as Susanne Denham, Judith Dunn, Paul Harris, Shinobu Kitayma, Michael Lewis, Hazel R. Markus, and Carol Saarni (among many others), who suggest that emotion, culture, and the self are intimately connected. Following White's (1994) claim that "at the core of most emotion words are social and moral entailments capable of sharing social realizes and of directly social behavior" (p. 217), this book emphasizes the role that language plays in children's emotional and social experiences within the classroom. I build on the notion that emotion is a scriptlike structure that functions as a mediator between the inside or private self and the outside or public self.

During my research conversations with children in their classrooms around issues of self-understanding and emotions, their stories often reminded me of my own school experiences. As I listened to their self-descriptions and their reasons for why they chose to describe themselves in such a way, many of their statements resonated within me. As the children shared their thoughts and feelings, I wondered how did their language and cultural background affect their self-cognitions and emotion? How did their emotional experiences affect their perceptions of their self-worth, their friendships and their academic competencies?

To address these questions surrounding children's emotional experiences within the elementary school classroom, this book emerged over the years from my teaching, learning, writing, research, and personal experiences. Throughout the past ten years, the questions and comments from my research participants, students, and colleagues have influenced my thinking around the topic of children's emotional worlds. Accordingly, I have incorporated these multiple voices throughout this book, as they have inspired me to think further on the role emotions play in children's lives within the classroom. In closing, I hope that this book inspires readers to appreciate the important role emotions play in learning, and to further their awareness of how our emotional experiences help to shape our identities and our social interactions in the classroom.

S. L. Bosacki

Introduction:
Schooling the Emotions:
A Psychocultural
Exploration

First keep peace with yourself, then you can also bring peace to others.

Thomas Kempis
(1379–1471, German monk, mystic, religious writer)

What is happening in the hearts and minds of children perceived as shy or socially withdrawn children within the classroom? To explore this question, this book focuses on both psychoeducational research and inclusive educational philosophies that investigate children's emotional experiences and self-knowledge within the classroom. To help excavate the landscape of children's emotional lives, drawing on a longitudinal study of Canadian middle school girls and boys, I describe the emotional and social experiences of six school-aged children. Within the learning context of the classroom, girls and boys share their experiences of self and emotional understandings and social relations through interviews and social cognitive tasks.

The chapters provide critical analysis, practical suggestions, and information for those who agree that emotions are paramount to children's development and well-being. This book examines how individual differences and classroom culture, including gender, social relations, and language may affect children's emotional experiences in school settings. Further, this book suggests ways in which educators can redesign and rethink an inclusive education that acknowledges these emotional experiences. This book aims to contribute to our understanding of the complex emotional worlds that students and teachers create together. As a lifelong learning, I hope that this book provides useful reading for anyone interested in learning more about the role emotions and self-knowledge play in children's learning.

This book draws on social cognitive and psychocultural theories to describe children's ability to understand human thoughts and feelings, and its relation to their self-conceptions, peer relations, and language competence within the gradeschool setting. Often referred to as Theory of Mind understanding (ToM), the ability to "read" others' mental states in the context of social action can also be referred to as psychological understanding (Bruner, 1996). This ability to read others' mental states enables children to understand multiple perspectives and to communicate with others (Astington, 2003; Nelson, Henseler, & Plesa, 2000; Watts, 1944).

Recent research in children's ToM shows that by age five, children begin to understand that people have desires that lead them to actions, and these actions are based on beliefs. Beyond the age of five, however, little is known about the links between this kind of psychological understanding and social experience. Given that children who possess high levels of psychological understanding are more likely to "think about their own and others' thinking" during the school day, such an ability has important educational implications (Wellman & Lagattuta, 2004).

For example, recent research shows that the ability to make a meaningful story out of people's thoughts and actions plays a role in self-regulated learning and language competence such as storytelling. Moreover, research has shown that the ability to "read others" or to make sense of the signs and symbols evident in human communication has an influence on children's self-conceptions and their social interactions. Thus, given that psychological explanations appear to play a key role in teaching and learning, further research is required, particularly on 8- to 13-year-old children within the elementary school context.

Accordingly, from a psychocultural approach to developmental research and education (Bruner, 1996; Dunn, 2005), in this book I build on my past and current research by investigating the social and emotional antecedents and consequences of psychological understanding in late childhood (Bosacki, 2003, 2005b; Bosacki & Moore, 2004). *How do children who are rated by their teachers as socially withdrawn or shy, use their psychological understanding skills to navigate their emotional and social relationships with themselves and their peers?* To address this question, I draw on cases from an ongoing longitudinal study to provide examples to discuss children's abilities to understand people's thoughts and feelings, and its relation to their self-concepts, peer relationships, and language competence within the school setting. Given that these skills prepare children for adaptive functioning in their personal and social worlds, I will also describe the role psychological understanding plays in school recess behavior.

Chapter 1 begins with a brief overview of the conceptual and theoretical background to explore social cognition in middle childhood, and why this may differ for children considered shy or socially withdrawn. Chapter 2 elaborates on this research and provides a critical review of the theoretical and empirical evidence. Chapter 3 illustrates the importance of children's emotional lives for their self-understanding and social relations by drawing on an ongoing longitudinal study on psychological understanding and social behavior. In particular, Chapter 3 describes the research context and design of the longitudinal study followed by Chapter 4 which describes the voices of 6 children who are participating in an ongoing longitudinal study. To illustrate the theoretical emphasis on the social context of emotional experience discussed in Chapters 1 and 2, Chapter 4 provides examples of what children discussed regarding issues of cultural, social, and self scripts. This chapter also discusses what the children did not talk about during the research interviews, or the "silences" in the conversations. Following a description of the children's voices, Chapters 5 describes the practical implications of the study's findings for theory, education, and future research. Finally, this book concludes with questions for educators and researchers to consider for future inquiry.

Thus, by providing both current research findings and practical applications, it is my hope that this book will be both inspirational in a theoretical and conceptual sense, and also practical (for both research and teaching purposes). More specifically, my goal for this book is to assist educators of all ages by providing them with ideas to integrate the concept of silence into their classroom, and to address issues of self-growth, especially the emotional and moral aspects. Although drawn from research with children aged six to ten years, this book describes issues of identity, emotionality, and communication, and thus, could be applicable to any age, thus, the audience could range from an early childhood educator to a university professor. Overall, this book addresses the paucity of research on children's concepts of self and silence within the grade school classroom and how this may be linked to self-growth and emotional and mental health. Socioemotional understanding and moral action will be emphasized and the voices of children labeled as shy or socially withdrawn will be discussed within the framework of current psychoeducational research.

This book builds on the existing body of work on emotions and education (e.g., Denham, 1998; Harris, 1989; Noddings, 2003, 2006; Saarni, 1999, etc.) by further exploring emotional understanding for self-knowledge and caring. That is—in this book I explore the question of how can we encourage children to develop the ability to be critical and reflective of themselves and others, but also caring and understanding? What kind of world are we going to live in if the main focus of education is to promote children's academic and behavioral school performance to the detriment of all other aspects of learning? How can we ignore the fact that how children think and care about themselves provides the foundation for all learning and development? More specifically, we need to explore carefully our definitions of "moral exemplars" in light of our cognitive, social, emotional, and moral expectations of children. For example, if as Gardner et al. (2001) suggest that schools and the adult workplaces should promote both excellence and ethical and moral competence, what happens when a child may excel academically and may behave as a moral "exemplar" but shows a lack of self-care and who may fail to believe that she or he is important or worthy? Thus, how can we ensure that a child considered to be moral exemplar is also an "emotional exemplar?"

Overall, this book explores how children's understanding of others' thoughts and emotions influence the way they think and feel about themselves, and how they interact with others. Based on the assumption that children's capacity to think about others and feel about themselves both influences and is influenced by their social interactions and peer relationships (Hinde, 1987; Mead, 1934; Wellman, 1990), the theoretically plausible correlates of psychological and emotional understanding include (a) self-perceptions and feelings, and (b) social interactions and peer relationships. Furthermore, given the claim that girls are socialized to understand others' minds (see Maccoby, 1998), it is expected that girls may outperform boys on psychological and emotion understanding tasks. Given that schools provide a data-rich environment in which to explore how children make sense of their social world, little is known about the role of social-cognitive and linguistic processes in middle childhood. Furthermore, the lack of attention to gender issues in the links between higher-order reasoning and social behavior advocates the need for further research (e.g., Goldberger, 1996; Hill & Lynch, 1983).

What use is such information? In general, we know very little about the extent to which children's emotion understanding carries over into the school context and whether it relates to school and personal success. Neither do we know the role of self-feelings and thoughts, nor the role of sociocultural influences such as gender, language, and social class. In addition to exploring psychological and emotion understanding, this book may also help educators to develop assessment and educational tools. More specifically, the last few chapters of the book focus on how various educational tools and strategies can be used within the teaching/learning context to explore the concept of psychological understanding through focusing on relationships within the classroom, critical enquiry and dialogue (Haynes, 2002; Wellman & Lagattuta, 2004). Thus, in both theoretical and practical ways, it is hoped that this book will be a valuable tool and resources for both researchers and educators.

As Silverstein and Perlick (1995) suggest, we need to examine what is the emotional and psychological cost of this academic competence? Consistent with Dunn (2006) who warns that the connections between emotional understanding and social and moral action are multifaceted and complex, as educators and researchers concerned with children's emotional health and well-being, we should question the assumption that children apply their emotional thinking equally to themselves and others, and what implications does this have for their social and moral behavior? Rather, research needs to question this assumption of overall competence and confidence, and explore why do some children achieve competence in various areas, but lack confidence in themselves? How do such children learn to acknowledge and celebrate their successes and develop more of an emotional presence or visibility in the classroom? In the end, I hope that my book helps readers to learn how important children's emotions are to their understandings of themselves and others. Above all, my goal is to encourage or inspire the reader to become excited about the topic of emotions, and hopefully motivated to continue to explore and learn about the role that emotions play in children's learning.

1

Meanings: Exploring the Emotional Landscape of Classroom

1.1. Introduction

Most recently, across educational and psychological research domains, there has been a rise in the interest of the emotional and social aspects of learning. This focus on the psychocultural or personal aspect of education (Bruner, 1996), includes the investigation of the concept of shyness within the educational milieu (Rubin, Burgess, & Coplan, 2002). Increasingly, recent research with young school children shows that shyness or social withdrawal may play a significant role in children's development of socioemotional and cognitive competence (Harrist, Zaia, Bates, Dodge, & Pettit, 1997; Rubin & Coplan, 2004; Wichmann, Coplan, & Daniels, 2004). Despite the theoretical and practical implications of investigating the inner and social world of the shy or socially withdrawn child, empirical support for the links between social withdrawal and socioemotional correlates in both girls and boys during middle childhood remains sparse and existing findings are inconsistent and variable (Chang, 2003; Prakash & Coplan, 2007; Rubin & Asendorpf, 1993).

The goal of my ongoing program of teaching, learning, and research is to gain a comprehensive picture of the development of children's psychological and emotional understandings in relation to self-concept, and social behavior. Specifically, in this book I will draw on examples of empirical research and my ongoing longitudinal research program to discuss individual and developmental differences in the ways that children understand thoughts and emotions in self and others, self-concept, language, and peer relationships. In addition to drawing on examples from my ongoing longitudinal research on the development of these relations in both experimental and naturalistic contexts, I will provide an overview of theoretical and empirical evidence, as well as educational implications.

The main development occurring after five years of age examined so far in the field of social cognition is children's ability to deal with embedded representations, such as, "She thinks that he thinks that …" (Lalonde & Chandler, 1995; Lewis & Carpendale, 2002; Perner & Wimmer, 1985; Shantz, 1983). This ability, also referred to as "Theory of Mind" (ToM) understanding, also includes the understanding and experiencing of complex emotions such as, "She feels that he is angry that Tom is jealous about their friendship," and this ability may also be connected to the increasing experience of complex or self-conscious emotions. For example, past research on social cognition shows that beyond the age of five, individual differences among children begin to increase in the following areas: (a) children's understanding of self-conscious or complex emotions such as pride and embarrassment ("I feel proud because I know that my mom thinks that I am smart"), (b) complex self-understandings of oneself as a psychological being with mental states and emotions, and personality traits (e.g., shy, friendly, quiet, helpful, kind, etc.), and (c) the ability to understand and engage in sociomoral, psychological, and emotional behaviors such as empathetic sensitivity or emotional aggression (e.g., exclude or ignore someone with the intention to damage the victim's sense of self.)

Relatedly, within the context of emotional competence or understanding, past researchers have also explored the notion of emotional intensity or sensitivity. Viewed by many researchers as an affective or emotional human characteristic (e.g., Baska, 1989; Clark, 1988; Lovecky, 1992, 2004), sensitivity is a complex process that focuses on both the personal and social with both emotional and cognitive components. Given that much has been written about the various cognitive and affective components of sensitivity, a comprehensive review is beyond the scope of this book (for a more detailed review see Mendaglio, 1995). With the focus of this book on children's emotional experiences, in Chapter 2, drawing on Dabrowski among others, I will discuss how sensitivity and intensity also play important roles in children's emotional worlds, and how the concept of sensitivity could be also incorporated into our vocabulary to describe children's emotional experiences within the classroom.

Although a majority of the research on children's emotional sensitivity and intensity deals with a select population often been labeled as academically talented or gifted (e.g., Cross, 2005; Davis & Rimm, 2004; Silverman, 1993a), such studies are relevant to all children as they help us to understand the complexities of emotional development. In particular, these studies may help to deepen our understanding of the antecedents of individual differences in children's developing sense of moral and emotional understandings which will be further elaborated in subsequent chapters. Thus, this book aims to help readers make meaning from these related, but different findings. I hypothesize that children's ability to interpret their inner worlds and the inner world of others is linked to their developing understandings of socioemotional and self-knowledge.

In sum, this book investigates links among socially withdrawn children's emotional understandings, self-concept, and peer relationships. Specifically, within the context of middle childhood, this book explores how (a) gender and language play a role in the link between children's understanding thoughts and emotions in others, (b) various aspects of children's self-understanding (graphical and verbal representation of the subjective and objective self) are related to emotional understanding, and (c) developmental patterns between cognitive and socioemotional competence for children rated as socially withdrawn by their teachers. Hopefully this book will encourage researchers to continue to investigate the developmental patterns that exist among children's socioemotional reasoning and social behavior. Also, to continue to strengthen partnerships with developmental and educational researchers and the elementary school context, perhaps this book could be used as a tool to promote collaborative work with researchers, educators and therapists, and school children in the future to develop curricula and teaching/learning tools that will promote the development of effective social relationships and emotional health through philosophical or open-ended enquiry and social dialogue.

1.2. Emotion and Social Communication during Middle Childhood

Over the past two decades educational research has come to view children as psychologists who depend upon a mentalistic construal of reality to make sense of their social worlds (Bruner, 1996; Flavell & Miller, 1998). This psychocultural approach to education provides a new framework in which to investigate connections between children's thought and action, including "theories of mind and literacies" (e.g., Homer & Nelson, 2005; Zelazo, Astington, & Olson, 1999) and the "self" (e.g., Harter, 1999). Despite the increasing evidence that suggests understanding of mind may grow from a foundation of understanding of emotions (Bartsch & Wellman, 1995), and mental state understanding develops in part through peer relationships (e.g., Astington & Jenkins, 1995; Dunn & Cutting, 1999; Spatz & Wright Cassidy, 1999), few studies have examined such a link in middle childhood (Banerjee & Watling, 2005; Yuill & Coultas, 2007).

As noted by Dunn, 2000), we still do not yet know how emotion understanding and theory of mind are linked beyond early childhood. Given the growing amount of existing literature (Filppova & Astington, 2008; Moore, 2006; Sullivan, Yuill, & Slade, 2007; Talwar, Murphy, & Lee, 2007), it can be expected that the social and emotional thought-action connection may also continue to develop throughout childhood and beyond.

Past research suggests that children's abilities to understand others are noticeably transformed when they become aware that human actions are ruled by mental states such as desires, beliefs, and intentions. Given that a key stage in this acquisition of ToM is the recognition that mental states involve representations of reality, and may thus be mistaken, this ability to recognize false belief is the most studied aspect of children's ToM development (Hughes et al., 2005; Wimmer & Perner, 1983). Research suggests that at around four years of age, children understand that people act on their representation of the world, even in situations where it misrepresents the real situation. That is, at this age children can represent and reason from people's first-order beliefs (one mental state): X believes p, or that X feels c. From as young as age five or six, children are able to represent and reason from second-order beliefs (two or more mental states): X believes that Y believes that p, or that X believes that p feels sad and angry (Sullivan et al., 1994). The development of this second-order understanding has received relatively little attention in the literature particularly during the middle and late childhood years. This is surprising, given that much of our social interaction depends on what people believe and feel about other people's beliefs and emotions (Astington, 1993; Dunn, 1988; Harris, 1988; Pons, Lawson, Harris, & de Rosnay, 2003). The importance of second-order reasoning has been shown in relation to children's ability to understand speech acts such as lies and jokes (Leekam, 1993) and in their ability to understand self-representational display rules (Banerjee & Yuill, 1999). This book will explore the possibility that perhaps such higher-order reasoning is also fundamental to children's understanding of simple and complex emotions, their self-concept, and social interactions.

Regarding the further development of higher-order mentalizing ability during childhood, growing evidence suggests that emotion understanding and experience also continues in complexity during this time, particularly regarding complex and ambiguous emotions (Pons, Lawson, Harris, & de Rosnay, 2003). In contrast to the simple or basic emotions (e.g., happy, sad), to understand complex emotions (e.g., pride, embarrassment), children must hold in mind two separate pieces of information, other people's and societal norms (Saarni, 1999). That is, children must imagine what others think of their behavior and self-evaluate against internalized behavioral standards.

Although complex emotion understanding hinges in part on cognitive abilities such as second-order reasoning and self-evaluation including self-conscious emotions, to date, no studies have systematically investigated the links among the three concepts in middle childhood. Despite the growing interest in the links between ToM and emotion understanding, the majority of these studies have focused on preschoolers, first-order ToM understanding, and basic emotions such as happy and sad (Cutting & Dunn, 1999; Hughes & Dunn, 1998). At the time of writing this book, few studies have investigated the links between second-order ToM, and the understanding of complex emotions (Carpendale & Shelton, 1999), and future researchers need to investigate the links between the understanding of complex emotions and higher-order or an interpretive ToM. Furthermore, future studies should also explore this relation longitudinally, including investigating gendered differences within the school context during middle and late childhood.

Children's ToM and Self-Concept

Prominent early (Cooley, 1902; Mead, 1934) and contemporary developmental theories (Cole, Jacquesz, & Maschman, 2001; Harter, 1999) suggest that children' sense of self-worth emerges from an internalization of the beliefs and emotions of significant others. Despite this theoretical connection between ToM understanding and self-perceptions (Wellman, 1990), few studies have investigated these areas of research (e.g., Banerjee & Henderson, 2001; Banerjee & Watling, 2005; Banerjee & Yuill, 1999; Boerger, 2000; Bosacki, 2000; Johnson, 1997). Furthermore, in relation to the connections to higher order ToM, at the time of writing this book, no studies have looked at various self-representations such as verbal and graphical, or other aspects of the self-system such as self-evaluation or self-agency (Bruner, 1996). Although the majority of research supports a positive link between psychological understanding and self-concept (Selman, 1980; Trudeau & Reich, 1995), some investigators claim that the later correlates of ToM and emotion understanding may not be uniformly positive (Bosacki, 2003; Dunn, 2000, 2005). Consistent with a growing body of theory and research suggesting that various psychological attributes and abilities have trade-offs for development (e.g., Boden & Barenbaum, 2007; Cross & Madson, 1997; Higgins, 1991; Rudolph, Caldwell, & Conley, 2005), there is some evidence to suggest that high levels of children's psychological understanding result in greater sensitivity to teacher criticism and lower self-esteem (Cutting & Dunn, 2002; Dunn, 1995; Veith, 1980). Similarly, in a recent study of children's need for approval and well-being, Rudolph et al. (2005) found that a heightened need for approval has both positive and negative implications for well-being. That is, compared to negative-approval-based self-appraisals, positive approval-based self-appraisals were associated with less emotional distress and more socially competent behavior.

In addition, studies have shown that children and adults with high levels of psychological understanding may suffer from diminished self-concept and emotional difficulties, given the time spent on self-reflection and imagining what others think of them (Hatcher & Hatcher, 1997). Similarly, in a sample of university students, Boden and Berenbaum (2007) found an association between emotional awareness and suspiciousness. Regarding children, given the finding that children who scored high on second-order ToM tasks were able to better understand self-presentation rules (Banerjee & Yuill, 1999), perhaps children who are adept at reading social cues are also skilled at pretending to be who they think people would like them to be. Interestingly, Burton and Mitchell (2003) failed to find a relation between children's understanding of self-knowledge and ToM ability. Thus, given such contradictory findings, investigations of the possible links between psychological understanding and self will help us to understand the complex connections between understanding oneself and others.

Psychological Understanding, Self, and Peer Relations

Although social interactions and the understanding of complex emotions require second-order reasoning, the majority of past research studies have investigated these three areas separately. Despite the increasing number of studies on ToM and children's peer relations and friendships, the majority focus on preschoolers (e.g., Astington & Jenkins, 1995; Dunn, 2004; Dunn & Hughes, 1998), with only a few studies focusing on older children (e.g., Bosacki & Astington, 1999; Watson et al., 1999). In general, results from past studies suggest that for young children, a sophisticated or proficient ToM ability is linked to greater social competence. That is, research suggests that children who are skilled at reading the thoughts and emotions of others also appear to be socially competent.

However, the picture becomes more complex once self-concept, gender, and language are considered, particularly within social relationships. A potentially rich context within which to investigate such connections is children's peer relations and play behavior during school recess. Play has been linked to language development and many areas of social-cognitive including ToM and self-concept (Hughes, 1999). In particular, past studies have shown that particular types of play in early childhood (e.g., pretend, cooperative) may be more linked to psychological understanding than others (e.g., Brown et al., 1996). This book will extend the exploration of children's emotion understanding, social behavior, and self-understanding into middle childhood.

In contrast to pro-social play behavior, aggression may be linked to psychological understanding such as relational aggression (when one tries to damage the self-esteem or feelings of others) (Pacquette & Underwood, 1999; Sutton, Smith, & Swettenham, 1999). In contrast to physical or overt aggression, little is known about children who exhibit behaviors of relational or psychological aggression such as telling lies about one's peers. Similarly, research on behavioral disorders has focused mainly on physically aggressive children as compared to children labeled as withdrawn or socially inhibited (Tremblay, 2000). In general, evidence suggests that physically aggressive children may have lower levels of psychological understanding than nonaggressive children (e.g., Hughes et al., 1998). Given the evidence that suggests a link between low self-worth and social inhibition (Rubin & Asendorf, 1993), surprisingly few studies have examined social-cognitive abilities in socially withdrawn children (Coplan & Armer, 2005; Harrist et al., 1997). Throughout this book, I will discuss the need for further research in this area, as further work is needed to explore (a) psychological and emotion understanding and psychological aggression and victimization in children, and (b) the mental and emotional worlds and social experiences of socially inhibited children. To help us unravel some of the complexities surrounding these connections, throughout the book, I will build on my past and current research findings on the linkages among social and self-understanding and social behavior by investigating these areas within the naturalistic context of the elementary school classroom.

Gender Issues

Despite recent investigations of gender differences in social-cognitive (Bussey & Bandura, 1999; Hughes & Dunn, 1998; Maccoby, 1998), results from such studies remain contradictory and inconclusive. Regarding mental state understanding, there is some evidence to suggest that girls and female adults possess higher levels of ToM and emotion understanding (e.g., Boden & Barenbaum, 2007; Bosacki & Astington, 1999; Cutting & Dunn, 1999), other studies showed boys to possess higher levels of emotion understanding than girls (Laible & Thompson, 1998), and still others have shown no gender differences (Astington & Jenkins, 1995; Racine, Carpendale, & Turnbull, 2007). Unlike the research on emotion and psychological understanding, the self-concept literature has shown that in general, girls report lower levels of perceived self-worth than boys (see Harter, 1999). Given the link between gender, understanding others, and self-worth (Finders, 1997; Hatcher et al., 1990; Veith, 1980), surprisingly little is known about these connections during middle childhood. Relatedly, some researchers suggest that gender differences need to be investigated in terms of interaction effects between biological sex and gender role (Geary, 1998). To support this view, results from my past research with preschoolers showed that parents' gender role perceptions of stereotypic feminine behavior were related to high levels of emotion understanding in both girls and boys (Bosacki & Moore, 2000). Such links remain to be examined in middle school–aged children in relation to emotion understanding and will be discussed in further detail in Chapter 2.

1.3. Sensitivity, Emotions, and Language

Social Withdrawal and Shyness: A Brief Overview

Given the link between emotionality and solitude, as noted previously (Bosacki, 2005b), some children may find solitude as a phenomenon that brings psychological safety and peacefulness. That is, such children may view emotionality and solitude as safe retreat from others' judging eyes for quiet reflection. In contrast, when children experience victimization either by psychological bullying or harassment, peer ostracism, or other intrinsic reasons, such as low self-esteem, feelings of worthlessness, hopelessness, and depression, some children may withdraw from the social group. Solitude and emotionality may raise feelings of social wariness, fear of rejection, victimization, and loneliness. To explore the negative correlates and consequences of silence and social withdrawal, in the past 20 years, a rapidly increasing literature has accumulated on the emotional experiences associated with social withdrawal or solitude during childhood (Danon-Foileau, 2001; Dunn, 2004; Erwin, 1993; Lane, 2007; Rubin, Burgess, & Coplan, 2002).

Although past researchers have used the terms *social withdrawal, isolation, shyness*, and *inhibition* interchangeably, social withdrawal refers to the consistent display of all forms of solitary behavior when encountering familiar and/or unfamiliar peers (Rubin et al., 2002). In general, social withdrawal occurs when children decide to consistently (across situations and time) isolate themselves from the peer group (involving familiar and/or unfamiliar peers). For some children, this social silence and withdrawal may carry social and psychological costs and benefits. That is, social withdrawal can either exacerbate or ameliorate positive mental health and interpersonal relationships.

Also embodied within the broad, multidimensional construct of social withdrawal is the more specific construct reticence. Reticence is a construct embodied within social withdrawal and should not be confused with the broader construct of social withdrawal, and it has been operationalized as expression of cautious, solitary behavior (Rubin et al., 2002) Some have claimed that it is a reflection of shyness in unfamiliar peer settings and social wariness among familiar peers (Coplan & Rubin, 1998; Rubin, 1982). Behavioral reticence stands in contrast with solitude that reflects social disinterest (e.g., solitary play in early childhood) or social immaturity (e.g., solitary-active play in early childhood). Solitary-active play comprises sensorimotor and/or dramatic activity acted out by oneself despite being in a social company such as biking, archery, solitary skipping, walking, running, hula-hooping, etc. Social withdrawal, is operationalized by all forms of solitude across contexts of familiarity and unfamiliarity; thus, reticence and solitary-passive and active play together comprise the "umbrella construct of social withdrawal."

Overall, early developmental theories and data suggest that peer interaction influences the development of social cognition, and ultimately the expression of competent social behavior. Peer interaction and dialogue also enable the adolescent to develop an understanding of the self in relation to others. Thus, children who refrain, for whatever reason, from engaging in social interaction and avoid the company of their peers may suffer some developmental cognitive, social, and emotional consequences (Rubin et al., 2002; Williams, 2001).

Past research reveals that the constellation of social withdrawal, social inadequacy, and peer rejection and neglect may be associated with internalizing difficulties such as low self-esteem, social anxiety, depression, and loneliness (e.g., Rubin & Burgess, 2001). Investigators have found that by middle childhood and early adolescence, children considered by others to be socially withdrawn and verbally reticent or perhaps labeled as "quiet" (i.e., children who are compared to others as less vocal in social situations) may also develop negative self-perceptions and experience various sociocommunicative and anxiety related difficulties such as selective mutism, and experiences feelings of anxiety, loneliness, and depressed mood (Bosacki, Pelletier, & Astington, 1997; McHolm, Cunningham, & Vanier, 2005; Rubin et al., 2002). Thus, given the possible negative psychological state of the socially withdrawn child, researchers need to explore how peer relationships and social dialogue can either exacerbate or ameliorate negative personal and social experiences.

For example, one of the most popular intervention for socially-withdrawn children is social skills training and it has had moderate effects on increasing the social interactions of mildly to moderately withdrawn adolescents (Sheridan, Kratochwill, & Elliott, 1990). However, many intervention programs are hampered by various conceptual and methodological difficulties. As many educators and cognitive therapists who work with children to help them modify their cognitions and behaviors have noted (e.g., Seligman, Meichenbach, Rubin, etc.), one problem that is specifically related to social skills training for socially withdrawn, shy, and/or silent children is that the cognitive changes may not necessarily lead to affective or behavioral change. That is, if social cognition and related behaviors are a process with multiple components (e.g., affective, behavioral, physical, etc.), change may not occur in all of the necessary components or stages of the process—such that the cognitive change may not be in parallel with the affective system, and/or the physical.

To help illustrate within the context of the grade school classroom, cognitively, by middle childhood, most children know what they should do in social situations, but they cannot or will not express their emotions and feelings through action. As some researchers and therapists suggest (e.g., Markway & Markway, 2005; Silverstein & Perlick, 1995), the action may be inhibited or prevented by children experiencing strong negative emotions such as anxiety, fear, embarrassment, and/or shame. For example, a ten-year-old girl may be able to score relatively high on a social understanding questionnaire that assesses social or interpersonal understanding such as ask what a girl should if she would like to make new friends and to meet new people when. However, in reality, the same child may not be able or willing to enact her personal theory of social interaction, for example, if she chooses to stand by herself in a corner of a room full of strangers. Such a behavioral response would be in direct contrast with the child's mental ability, and thus contradict some of her thoughts.

Overall, past research suggests that the social and emotional development of socially withdrawn, shy, and silent children may be challenged and perhaps in some way impeded (McHolm, Cunningham, & Vanier, 2005; Rubin et al., 2002). Thus, researchers need to be more active in exploring the reasons why some children choose to withdraw socially and remain silent. Such research may help to develop ameliorative, if not preventive, interventions for these children. Interestingly, at the time of writing this book, the majority of research and writing on social withdrawal in children has focused on the early childhood years, especially the transition from behavioral inhibition in toddlerhood to social reticence and withdrawal in middle childhood and beyond. Given these gaps in the developmental trajectories of social withdrawal, although past research suggests that social but not nonsocial toddler inhibition predicted shy, inhibited behavior at five years when children played with an unfamiliar peer. Thus, behaviorally inhibited toddlers may be at risk for being socially reticent as preschoolers. However, little is known how behavioral inhibition in toddlerhood affects social relations and self-concept in the middle childhood and adolescent years.

Another unknown piece of the social withdrawal puzzle is that children's shy/reticent behaviors in unfamiliar context are not strongly predictive of socially withdrawn behavior in any form in familiar contexts (Asendorf, 1990). Similarly, Asendorf (1994) has argued that the relation between children's social behaviors in familiar and unfamiliar novel settings is mediated by the quality of children's peer relationships and their internalized thoughts/perception, and or affects about these relationships, As Rubin et al. (2002) suggest, the underlying factors and correlates between the social cognitive, emotional, moral pieces of the child may help us to further understand their experience and behaviors. Although in the past five years in particular, many social cognitivists and developmentalists have started to investigate children's psychological understandings as they relate to self-concept and social relations, especially regarding social withdrawal within childhood (e.g., Banerjee & Henderson, 2001; Bosacki, 2005a; Kagan, 2005; Prakash & Coplan, 2007; Rubin et al., 2002; etc.), some of my previous and current research described in this book also focus on children's psychological and emotional understanding and social interaction, as one of the main goals of my research is to help understand the connections between children's emotional and cognitive development, self-concept, and social relations.

However, given the complexities of children's emotional experiences within the classroom, such research may be hampered by methodological challenges, especially given the ethical and moral issues surrounding emotional development and self-worth. To discuss such challenges, the following section outlines some methodological issues that researchers may experience when attempting to unravel some of the complexities of the causes, correlates, and consequences of exploring emotions and social cognition within the elementary school classroom.

Language, Self-Perceptions, and Gender in Shy Children's Socioemotional Competencies

A substantial part of children's emotion understanding is mediated through language processes in particular cultural settings such as parent-child conversations in the home, or peer-peer and teacher-child conversations in the school context (Kitayama, Markus, & Matsumoto, 1995; Lee, 2003). A psychocultural approach to emotion development assumes that the development of language and emotion concepts are interdependent, and have their origins in social interactions with more skilled partners (Gergen & Walhrus, 2001; Vygotsky, 1978). That is, cultural frames or culturally shared systems of meaning help to shape emotional experience and one's developing sense of self through the social interactions and communication with others (Behrens, 2004; Kitayama, Markus, & Kurokawa, 2000; Lutz, 1988).

Regarding the connections between emotional competence and language in middle childhood, many researchers (e.g., Harre, 1986; Russell, 1990; Saarni, 1999), have asserted that emotion words or labels play a large role in the development of the child's conceptualization of emotion. Thus, according to Kopp (1989), emotion language "provides children with an especially powerful tool for understanding emotions" (p. 349). Several recent studies have highlighted the importance of language abilities in children's understanding of emotions. For example, researchers have suggested that the links are complex, especially those concerning emotion understanding across gender and countries (Cutting & Dunn, 1999; Harris, 1989; Jenkins & Astington, 1996). More recently, Gergen and Walhrus (2001) have extended the notion that language and emotion are inextricably linked, by proposing that people should create the emotional forms or scripts that are essential to encourage people to take responsibility for their actions.

Furthermore, different aspects of language competence (e.g., receptive and expressive) may have differential effects on children depending on their cultural background and gender. In support of this view, Cutting and Dunn (1999) found that although the receptive and narrative aspects of language ability were linked to emotion understanding in young girls and boys, language competence and social cognitive abilities such as mental state understanding were associated only for boys. In contrast, for girls, associations were found between narrative ability and mental state understanding only. Thus, if we apply Astington and Jenkins' (1999) language-thought debate to socioemotional competence, and self-perception, shy children may acquire socioemotional and communicative competence and a positive sense of self within sociolinguistic classroom experiences (Menyuk & Menyuk, 1988).

Given the strong conceptual link between language, self, and emotion, it is surprising that relatively few researchers have examined the role that language competence plays in the development of socially withdrawn children's socioemotional competence. To control for all aspects of language ability in emotion understanding and expression, both expressive and receptive language ability should be assessed (e.g., Cutting & Dunn, 1999). However, some researchers, have assessed emotion understanding in the absence of any general language measure (e.g., Laible & Thompson, 1998). Consistent with past studies which often include standardized measures of language competence (vocabulary ability) (e.g., Cain & Staneck, 1999; Carroll & Steward, 1999; Dunn & Hughes, 1998), the present study investigated receptive, vocabulary ability. Despite the potential to shed light on socially withdrawn children's social and emotional worlds, few researchers have investigated socially withdrawn children's emotion understanding and self-perceptions from a psychocultural perspective (for exceptions see Capps et al., 1992; Harris, 1989; Russell & Paris, 1994). Given Maccoby's (1999) conceptualization of gender as a culture, a psycho-cultural approach to the study of socioemotional competence could help to examine the links among gender, shyness, language, and self-perceptions. Extant literature has focused on socioemotional competence among older children and adults; the results, in general, suggest that girls and women exhibit a higher level of socioemotional competence than do boys and men (Bybee, 1998; Markus & Kitayama, 1994).

Regarding gender differences, the few studies on children's socioemotional competence reveal contradictory findings. For example, compared to boys, girls have been found to exhibit a greater expression of pride (i.e., girls showed more positive expressions after success than boys did) (Stipek, Recchia, & McClintic, 1992), and to express greater emotional regulation and displays of shame and guilt (Kochanska, 1994). In contrast, some studies have not demonstrated to find gender differences among emotions of pride, shame, and guilt (Griffin, 1995; Kornilaki & Chlouverakis, 2004). Accordingly, given the complex gendered patterns of associations among socioemotional competence, self-perceptions, and language (Denham, 1998), more research is needed on individual differences on these variables among socially withdrawn or shy children.

Given the crucial role teachers play in both the gender role socialization and co-construction of children's social-cognitive and linguistic abilities (Cervantes & Callanan, 1998; Denham, 1998; Haden, Haine, & Fivush, 1997; Purkey, 2000), it is surprising that so few researchers have studied the links among teachers' perceptions of children's socioemotional competence, children's self-perceptions, and language ability. In general, the empirical evidence concerning gender-related differences in emotional competence remains inconsistent and fairly scarce. In brief, past research has found that girls outperform boys in emotion understanding tasks and receive higher emotional competence teacher ratings (Cutting & Dunn, 1999; Parent et al., 1999), as do middle-school children (Bybee, 1998) and adults (Brody & Hall, 1993). Although researchers have claimed that girls seem to internalize earlier and more completely the message that it matters how people feel, some studies have demonstrated either no gender differences exist in emotion competence (e.g., Banerjee & Yuill, 1999; Denham, Cook, & Zoller, 1992) or that school-aged boys outperform girls (Laible & Thompson, 1998; Whissell & Nicholson, 1991).

Regarding gender differences and social withdrawal, there is accumulating evidence to suggest that due to societal expectations, shyness may hold more negative psychological implications for boys than for girls (e.g., Rubin et al., 2002). These findings have been attributed in part to the notion that shyness appears to be less socially acceptable for boys than for girls (Sadker & Sadker, 1994). That is, given societal stereotypic gender-role expectations, some adults may perceive shyness as a more stereotypic "feminine" trait and thus some adults may be more likely to accept and reward shyness in girls as compared to boys. In contrast, for boys, some adults may perceive shyness as a personality weakness rather than a strength, and shyness may be more likely to be discouraged among boys as compared to girls.

For instance, parents tend to respond more negatively to shy/withdrawn behaviors in boys as compared to girls (e.g., Radke-Yarrow, Richters, & Wilson, 1988; Simpson & Stevenson-Hinde, 1985; Stevenson-Hinde, 1989). Across the lifespan, for boys as compared to girls, social withdrawal is more strongly associated with negative outcomes (Coplan et al., 2004; Morison & Masten 1991; Stevenson-Hinde & Glover, 1996). However, within Western society, regardless of gender, shy and socially withdrawn behaviors are considered to be socially deviant, where sociability is considered to be highly valued (Rubin, 1998).

However, the majority of researchers interested in exploring gender differences have either (1) investigated parent-child conversations regarding emotions, but not teachers' beliefs of students' emotional competence (Parent, Normandeau, Cossett-Richard, & Letarte, 1999; Racine, Carpendale, & Turnbull, 2007), or (2) investigated parents' beliefs and expectations of their children's emotional development, but not the connections to language ability and self-perceptions (Casey & Fuller, 1994; Hughes, Deater-Deckard, & Cutting, 1999), or (3) investigated self-perceptions, socioemotional competence and language abilities in normal children (i.e., not labeled as socially withdrawn) (Verschueren, Buyck, Moarcoen, 2001).

Recent findings from one of our past studies suggest that complex connections among receptive vocabulary ability, perceived self-worth, and teacher ratings of emotional competence may differ according to gender and shyness (Bosacki, 2005). Such findings support previous research (e.g., Cutting & Dunn, 1999; de Villiers, 1999; Jenkins & Astington, 1996) and theorists' claims that language and social interaction play significant roles in children' emotion understanding (e.g., Gergen & Walhrus, 2001; Harre, 1986; Vygotsky, 1978). However, gender analyses revealed that the relation between vocabulary ability and perceived self-worth remained significant for shy boys only. Thus, compared to girls, general vocabulary ability may play a larger role in boys' self-development.

However, although for girls overall, vocabulary ability was not found to be related to emotional competence among both shy girls and boys. Perhaps the lack of relation between vocabulary ability and emotional competence for shy girls and boys suggests that receptive vocabulary ability remains separate from emotion understanding and that other aspects of language ability, such as narrative ability may play a larger role. As Astington and Jenkins (1999) pointed out, we need to know what aspects of language play important roles in emotion understanding and self-perceptions, and how does this differ according to gender and shyness?

One of our current cross-sectional research studies explored the relations among socioemotional competence, self-perceptions, and receptive vocabulary ability among shy or socially withdrawn children. Regarding emotional understanding, our study built on Denham's (1998) conceptualization of emotional competence and examined one set of skills referred to as emotion understanding that consists of children's ability to use emotion words or labels, and children's understanding of their own and others' situational determinants of emotions or their causal theories. Although emotion labels directly refer to emotional experiences (e.g., she is happy), explanations link emotion words to causal information (e.g., she is happy because she has a present) and thus reflect how children interpret and make sense of emotional experiences.

Specifically, our first line of inquiry involved the exploration of shy and non-shy children's responses (i.e., general pattern of responses and gender-related differences) regarding: (1) self-perceptions, (2) teachers' perceptions of students' social and emotional competence, and (3) language competence as defined by receptive vocabulary ability. On the basis of past gender research (Maccoby, 1998; Pajares, Miller, & Johnson, 1999; Saarni, 1999), we expected gender-related differences to reflect stereotypic gender role expectations. That is, given that social reticence or passivity, emotion understanding and vocabulary ability are considered to be stereotypically feminine traits (Maccoby, 1998), girls were expected to receive significantly higher teacher ratings than boys on socioemotional competence and score higher than boys on the vocabulary task. Further, based on past research which suggests that in North American society, shy boys may be at a greater risk for socioemotional problems than shy girls (Coplan & Armer, 2005); in this particular study we explored the question of whether or not this gender difference would be accentuated among children rated as shy by their teachers? Similarly, we hypothesized that correlational patterns found among children' socioemotional competence: self-concept, and vocabulary ability would differ according to gender and shyness.

Regarding the first research question, the hypothesis that correlational patterns among the variables would differ according to gender and shyness was supported. That is, for shy boys only, perceived global self-worth was significantly positively associated with general vocabulary ability and negatively associated with emotional competence ratings. In contrast, for girls, significant positive relations were found between teacher ratings of emotional competence and perceived self-worth. Furthermore, the hypothesis that girls would score higher than boys on emotion and vocabulary tasks was partially supported. That is, both gender and shyness interacted together to influence girls and boys scores on vocabulary and emotional competence ratings. Although girls did not differ from boys in vocabulary ability, shy girls received higher emotional competence teacher ratings than shy boys. Overall, the findings present an intriguing picture of how gender, shyness, and language play an important role in children' s perceptions of self, and teacher ratings of social and emotional competencies.

Cultural Frameworks and Emotions

As mentioned by past theorists and researchers (e.g., Blos, 1979; Coopersmith, 1967; Harter, 1999), throughout childhood, the process of self-development requires that children reorganize and differentiate the self-concept based on their interactions with others. That is, given that the sense of self is derived from social experience (e.g., Berger & Luckmann, 1967), children's social experiences with their peers, family members, teachers, and others play a significant role in the development of their social cognitive and linguistic abilities including the development of a self-concept, self-regulation, cognitive flexibility, etc. (e.g., Jacques & Zelazo, 2005; Rosenberg, 1989; Selman, 1980, 2007; Sullivan, 1953). Accordingly, a psychocultural approach to emotional and self-understanding in childhood may assist in the investigation of the links between cognitive representations of self and other and their links to social communication (Bruner, 1996; Moore, 2006). That is, how children think and feel about, and make sense of social situations and themselves, may influence how they interact with others. Thus, by focusing on the cognitive and emotional elements of social understanding, social-cognitive theorists (including Theory of Mind researchers), suggest that higher-order mental states are necessary for effective social interaction (e.g., Astington, 2003; Banerjee & Watling, 2005, 2007; Cutting & Dunn, 2002; Dunn, 2005; Flavell & Miller, 1998; Happé, 1994; Harris, 1989; Mant & Perner, 1988; Perner, 1991; Selman, 2003; Wellman, 1990; Yuill & Coultas, 2007).

  Children's social experiences and sense of self emerge from, and are influenced throughout life by cultural frameworks or schemas (Markus & Kitayama, 1994). A cultural framework refers to an interpretive grid or meaning system, schema, or script (Bruner, 1990; Bruner & Kalmar, 1997; D'Andrade, Markus, & Kitaymaa, 1994; Shweder, 1993; Wierzbicka, 1994). It consists of a set of language and implicit social understandings or "vital understandings"as well as social representations and practices that reflect these understandings in daily life (Quinn &

Holland, 1987). Similar to Markus and Kitayama (1994), I will use the term cultural framework which refers the cultural group's ideas and ideals or its cultural "software" such as its values, attitudes, beliefs, and norms, and also its traditions and social practices including its behavioral rituals, languages, rules, legal practices, or its "cultural hardware." (Kitayama, 1994, p. 96).

The cultural frame consists of ways of being or a set of beliefs and affects about the self (see Markus & Kitayama, 1991 for further discussion). Consistent with Markus and Kitayma (1994), the view that the self functions as an integrative, interpretive, or orienting framework for individual behavior, suggests that divergent self-views reflect divergent emotional experiences. For example, whether one's identity is shaped by a EuropeanCanadian ontological tradition that promotes independence, or by an identity that promotes a collective one of interdependence, or a combination of both frames, has the potential to make a critical difference in how life is lived, what kinds of experiences will feel "good" and what social behavior will be coded as "positive" or "acceptable." And what kinds of experiences will produce "bad" feelings and will accompany "negative social behavior." Thus, a cultural framework includes a group's sense of and attitudes toward emotions. That is, what emotions or feelings are, why they are experiences, and what their significance is in social life, as well as the implicit answers to questions like when, where, and how does one feel.

A cultural framework also includes an understanding of what kinds of events and processes emotions are. For instance, emotions are considered to be individual products that are produced and experienced privately and corporeally, or are they considered to be communicative processes or interpersonal moods that define the relationships among two or more people. Further, Miller (2000) suggests that cultures help to create the understandings of emotion as well. According to psycholinguistic and anthropological evidence (Potter, 1988; Shweder, 1991) some cultures do not share the concept of emotion derived from psychological theory. In contrast to the psychological view of emotion, some cultures may link what might be considered to constitute emotional elicitors only to physical illness, making no distinction between thoughts, feelings, or objectifying emotions.

Lutz (1988) described an emotion concept as a conflux of cultural worldviews and scripts for social behavior and identity. Lutz suggested that to understand the meaning of an emotion is to be able to envisage and perhaps to find oneself able to participate in a complicated scene of life with actors communicating with one another. Thus, viewed that emotions are more than just biologically prewired internal processes or bodily states, the category of emotion can be constructed or assigned meaning in a variety of ways (Lutz & White, 1988). As such, the answer to the question "what is an emotion?" may depend upon on how a group thinks about the nature of its functional relationship with the cultural environment. This understanding, in turn will determine which aspect of the emotional experience or combination of aspects such as the subjective, the physiological, etc. will be emphasized and elaborated in experience as well as the role of these emotions in social behavior.

From the perspective of cross-cultural sociolinguistics, Wierzbicka's explores the relation between emotion and culture and the notion of universal emotions. Wierzbicka's (1999, 2006) proposes that, gleaned from linguistic and ethnographic studies of various languages and cultures, ten or so "emotional universals" exist. Such universals do not mean that there are no "universals of seeing" or that there are no "universals of feeling" but it suggests that in our search for these universals, we should carefully listen to how people and children in different cultures talk about what they see and how they feel (Fridlund, 1994 cited in Wierzbicka, 1999, p. 275; White, 1992). In contrast to some views among cognitive scientists belief that mental life is partly independent of particular languages (Fodor, 1975), Wierzbicka (1999) suggests that we should avoid analytical categories based on culture and not assume that they represent specific aspects of our own language. Thus, according to Wierzbicka (1994), emotion and culture are inextricably intertwined and that to investigate the role of emotion in cultural patterns and the role of culture on the shaping an conceptualization of emotions, we need to focus on all aspects of language (e.g., lexical, grammatical, and pragmatic).

Accordingly, an emotion is some blend of component processes that are organized by the nature of the functional relationships between the self and the cultural environment, then somewhat different sets of these aspects are highlighted and affect behavior differentially contingent upon the relevant cultural frame. This means that outer or external cultural frames are inscribed into the inner or internal emotional experience. In this way, emotion may serve as the most proximate or near-experience carrier of cultural imperatives or assumptions about what creates the self, others, and the connection between the two. Thus, ways of being and ways of thinking and feeling are interrelated and part and parcel of the ideas and practices of the dominant cultural frames.

Given such a complex myriad of emotions, thoughts, and behaviors, what implications does this have for children living within countries populated with individuals who share a variety of "dominant" cultural backgrounds? How does the language of the culture help to create the set of emotions, beliefs, and practices and how does this influence the self? For example, in a culturally diverse country such as Canada, its educational system promotes cultural competence within a "cultural and emotional mosaic," which "self" dominates for children who live within such a culturally, emotionally, and linguistically diverse environment? How can a child co-create with others a coherent and organized sense of self with(in) such a cultural and emotional kaleidoscope? Further, how coherent and "structurally" sound is an omnibus self and as Cederblom (1989) asks, is the concept of "self" representative of a set of beliefs, or a belief-forming process; or is it a combination of both? If the self is a dialogical or omnibus self it suggests that the self is a cultural-specific, multilayered, dynamic entity that reconceptualizes itself as a combination of cognitive, emotion, moral, and social experiences (Bruner, 1996; Cederblom, 1989; Markus & Wurf, 1987; Marsh & Shavelson, 1985), how do we ethically and systematically explore such an entity among children?

According to folk or commonsense psychology, social interaction is actually an interaction or meeting of minds that consists of mental states and emotions expressed through speech acts or acts of silence. That is, social interaction does not proceed directly via the interaction of these mental states but proceeds indirectly by way of language (Astington, 1993; Moore, 2006). This notion is expressed in various speech act theorists' claims that communication relies on both speaker and hearer taking account of each other's knowledge and intentions (Austin, 1962; Grice, 1968; Searle, 1969) and the corresponding definition of communicative competence as intention attribution (Levinson, 1995; Sperber & Wilson, 1986). Thus, experiences of silence can occur whether or not the speaker and listener acknowledge or understand each other. Similar to the notion of "speech acts," both the speaker and the listener may also create the meaning of the "silence acts" and the interpretation may be influenced by additional nonverbal communication (e.g., body language, posture, tone of voice, etc.).

Similar to this notion of social interaction as a meeting of minds, social interactions according to Selman (2003), from the intimate and personal to the public and political are central to the human experience and I would agree with Selman's (2003) position that social interaction involves the meeting of minds and hearts. As many researchers and practitioners have noted (Bruner, 1996; Coles, 1990, 1997; Kagan, 2005; Moore, 2006; Noddings, 2006, Wertsch, 1989), our development as social beings begins when we are infants with our families, and then continue in wider circles as we grow throughout life. Similar to "theory of mind" or social understanding (and also referred to as folk psychology, commonsense psychology), Selman (2003, p. 2) claims that the coordination of social perspectives—how children come to identify their own wants, needs, and feelings, and understand those of others, and act to manage differences and conflicts, as well as closeness, within relationships.

The focus on emotion attribution has not received as much attention as intention or knowledge attribution. Many theorists and researchers claim, that sociocommunicative acts rely on both speaker and hearer taking into account each other's knowledge and intentions, but also their emotional states (e.g., Bruner, 1996; Filoppova & Astington, in press; Morton & Trehub, 1991; Wierzbicka, 1999). Interestingly, although the period of middle childhood includes numerous developmental transitions regarding social relationships and emotional and cognitive developments, the investigation of children's emotional experiences during grade school remains limited. For example, children's peers and families become increasingly important as children learn to co-construct their self-concepts within the social realm. Children are also likely to experience the increasing set of rules and standards associated with elementary school participation, and increasing expectations from both teachers and parents regarding academic and personal competence (self and social).

Significant changes in children's social and personal lives during middle childhood are associated with changes in children's cognitive and emotion development during middle childhood. Beginning in young childhood and developing into middle childhood, some children are capable of abstract, recursive thought, and some children may begin to show an understanding of the more cognitively complex or self-conscious emotions, also referred to as the secondary, higher order, social, moral, or sociomoral emotions (Denham, 1998; Griffin, 1995; Piaget, 1963; Saarni, 1999; Thompson & Lagattuta, 2006). Although children experience these self-conscious emotions (e.g., pride, shame, embarrassment) during young childhood, recent research suggests that emotion understanding of such cognitively based emotions begins to emerge during the early grade school years (Lagattuta, 2007; Pons & Harris, 2005). Regarding information processing abilities, Case et al. (1996) have shown that by approximately age seven or eight, in varying levels of ability, children's increased processing abilities (i.e., central conceptual structures) allow them to integrate multiple perspectives and relate them to each other in a coherent fashion (Case et al., 1996; Miller & Aloise, 1989; Selman, 2003). Within the context of narrative thought, studies on narrative complexity and cognitive competence have shown that the structural complexity of children's narratives increases with age and that this increase may be attributed to information processing capacity (McKeough, 1992). The emotional experiences and associated competencies in middle childhood will be discussed further in Chapter 2 when I explain how children learn to make sense of such complex emotions within increasingly complex social contexts.

These changes in children's social lives and relationships coincide with significant advances in cognition that enable the development of more complex knowledge about the causes of self-conscious emotions. That is, although children begin to personally experience self-conscious emotions early in life, their conceptual knowledge about the determinants of these emotions relies on further development during middle to late childhood. Notably, starting around age seven, children become better able to self-reflect on the contents of their minds, and they become more accurate in judging when other people are thinking and what they are thinking about (Flavell, 2000). Between the ages of five and ten years children also become more skilled at considering multiple dimensions of a problem at the same time (see Case & Okamoto, 1996; Miller & Aloise, 1989; Piaget, 1981). These cognitive achievements are important because in order to assess self-conscious emotions accurately, the child has to be able to think about both the *outcome* of the person's behavior (was it positive or negative) and the person's *control* over that behavior (was it intentional, was it due to internal vs. external causes) at the same time (Weiner & Graham, 1985). As I discuss in further detail in Chapter 2, during middle childhood children increasingly understand how people's attributions are causally connected to their emotions, and they demonstrate advancing knowledge about the specific causes of pride, shame, and guilt.

Research demonstrates that children in the middle school grades (e.g., 10- to 11-year-olds), are capable of creating and understanding interpretive narratives (e.g., Fox, 1991; McKeough, Templeton, & Marini, 1995). To illustrate, Fox (1991) explored children's developing awareness of mind in children's narrative writing and found that the majority of 11-year-olds spontaneously wrote stories that focused on Bruner's landscape of consciousness in contrast to the landscape of action. That is, most of the 11-year-olds' narratives involved a self-reflective protagonist or several characters capable of thinking and feeling about themselves and others. Such narrative tasks may be a valuable tool to investigate the role emotion plays in children's cognitive ability to simultaneously represent and reflect upon the relation between two events. Given that such a cognitive capacity may underlie socioemotional reasoning skills (Bruner, 1986; Case et al., 1996), an increasing number of researchers suggest that narrative tasks may help us to understand how children make sense of, and feel about themselves and others (e.g., Astington, 1993; Hatcher et al., 1990; Tager-Flusberg, Sullivan, Barker, Harris, & Boshart, 1997).

Regarding language, mental states, emotions, and social interaction, various researchers have agreed that the understanding of mental states in others is reflected by the use of both metacognitive (e.g., believe, think, know) and metalinguistic verbs (e.g., assert, say, concede) (representing mental states and speech acts respectively) (e.g., Astington & Pelletier, 1996; Slomkowski & Dunn, 1996). The use of such mental-state verbs has implications for reflective interpersonal relations in that it represents one's own stance or position toward another person's mental states (Laing, 1961; Leech, 1980). For example, if Oscar states "Skye claims that she is tired," this statement implies that Skye believes it is true that she is tired, but the speaker (Oscar) may not share Skye's belief. Thus, the expression of mental states in speech acts facilitates interpersonal communication and provides the basis for the ability to "read each other."

In addition to metacognitive and metalinguistic words, mental state language also includes emotion and moral words. Although the process for emotional and moral language may be similar, there may be different dynamics occurring among emotional language, identity, and interpersonal communication (Wierzbicka, 1994). Viewing emotions as meaningful social processes, emotions connect individuals to their social words and thus are the key to social integration and regulation because they are the basis of the reinforcement and reproduction of behavior. As such, a group's dominant cultural tendencies or emphases intersects with identity formation. For instance, D'Andrade (1984) stated that the socialization process may help individuals to become more sensitive to the emotional worlds of others and achieve culturally prescribed goals and interact with others according to cultural-specific patterns of behavior. Individuals may view such culturally directed social behaviors to be motivationally satisfying. In contrast, social behaviors that are not followed according to cultural directives and culturally prescribed goals may help to produce negative emotions such as social anxiety and self-doubt.

Similar to the example I outlined above with metacognitive terms, the use of such emotion words have implications for interpersonal relations in that it represents one's own stance or position toward another person's emotional state and/or moral disposition, and this may also include a sense of identity and moral character (Laing, 1961; Leech, 1980). For example, if Kathleen states "Michael claims that he is angry," this statement implies that Michael believes it is true that he is angry, but the speaker (Kathleen) may not share Michael's belief or emotional state. Thus, the expression of mental states in speech acts facilitates interpersonal communication and provides the basis for the ability to read both the thoughts and emotional states of others.

The importance of speech acts for social communication also has implications for those individuals who choose to remain silent; silence is ambiguous in that the receiver of silence (or "silencee") can interpret the received silence in many ways. For example, if one is the recipient of another's silence, the silencee may believe that either the silence represents a lack of the speaker's willingness to share one's mental state with the other, or that the silence refers to the speaker's lack of mental state (i.e., speech = mental state, lack of speech = lack of mental state).

Although children's ability to relate to their peers may partly be influenced by their ability to understand mental states in others as expressed through their speech acts, peer relations are often excluded from studies that investigate psycholinguistic, pragmatic, and emotional issues. For example, although links between communicative ability and theory of mind have been studied with children and adults in terms of speech acts, such as the understanding of promising and irony (Astington, 1988; Filoppova & Astington, in press; Keenan, 1995; Winner, 1988; Winner & Leekam, 1991), within this age group (late childhood—early adolescence), related areas of social cognition (including self-concept and social competence) have yet to be approached from a ToM perspective. Furthermore, few studies investigate the role of silence in speech acts and how sociocultural factors may affect the situation. To address this gap in research, studies on children's understanding of mental states and their acquisition of mental-state vocabulary may assist in the investigation of how children (and eventually adolescents) come to understand intentional relations in the peer milieux, including the understanding of silence, feelings, intentions, and beliefs of others (Astington & Pelletier, 1996; de Villiers, 1995).

As mentioned briefly above, language also plays a role in how children make sense of emotions, particularly the complex social or moral emotions. Wierzbicka (1999) reminds us that to investigate the language and understanding of human emotion, we need to be cautious of how difficult it is to investigate the intertwined and interdependent concepts of a culture's emotional universe and emotional lexicon. Thus, researchers need to address the instrumental role that language plays in creating and maintaining the conceptualization and expression of emotions across cultures, and the implications this has for self and social understandings.

A related area of higher-order mentalizing that incorporates understanding the emotional lexicon is emotion understanding, particularly regarding the complex and self-conscious or social moral emotions. In contrast to the simple or basic emotions (e.g., happy, sad), to understand complex emotions (e.g., pride, embarrassment), children must hold in mind two separate pieces of information: other people's and societal norms (Saarni, 1999). That is, children must imagine what others think of their behavior and self-evaluate against internalized behavioral standards. Although complex emotion understanding hinges on cognitive abilities such as second-order reasoning and self-evaluation, to date no studies have investigated the links among the three concepts within the middle childhood years. Despite the growing interest in the links between ToM and emotion understanding, these studies have focused on preschoolers, first-order ToM understanding, and basic emotions such as happy and sad (Cutting & Dunn, 1999; Hughes & Dunn, 1998; Hughes, Deater-Deckard, & Cutting, 1999). Research on the links between second-order, or higher-level ToM, and the understanding of complex emotions has just begun (Banerjee & Watling, 2005; Carpendale & Shelton, 1999), and future researchers will need to continue to explore this relation longitudinally and include sociocultural factors (Banerjee & Watling, 2007).

As mentioned above, the literature suggests that a substantial part of children's emotion understanding is mediated through language processes—in particular, in cultural settings such as parent-child conversations in the home or in peer conversations during free play (Kitayama, Markus, & Matsumoto, 1995). A psychocultural approach to emotion development assumes that the development of language and emotion concepts are interdependent and have their origins in social interactions with more skilled partners (Rogoff, 1990, 2003; Vygotsky, 1978). Many researchers have asserted that emotion words or labels play a large role in the development of the child's conceptualization of emotion (e.g., Saarni, 1999; Wierzbicka, 1999). Thus, according to Kopp (1989), emotion language "provides children with an especially powerful tool for understanding emotions" (p. 349). Several recent studies have highlighted the importance of language abilities in children's understanding of emotions and have suggested that the links are complex, especially when investigating emotion understanding across different genders and countries (Cutting & Dunn, 1999; Harris, 1989; Jenkins & Astington, 1996).

Despite the potential to shed light on children's developing emotional worlds, few studies have investigated children's and adolescents' understanding of complex emotions from a psychocultural perspective (e.g., for exceptions, see Bybee, 1998; Capps et al., 1992; Harris, 1989). Given Maccoby's (1998) conceptualization of gender as a culture, a psychocultural approach to the study of self-conscious emotions could help to unpack the links among language, gender-role socialization, and emotion understanding. Extant literature has focused on emotional expression among older children and adults, with results in general suggesting that girls or women exhibit a higher level of self-conscious emotion understanding and experience than boys or men (see Bybee, 1998; Markus & Kitayama, 1994).

Given that many of our interpersonal interactions involve comprehending and responding to emotion, or discussing emotion-laden situations and issues, strong emotion is not a rarity. Oatley and Duncan (1994) conducted a diary study of emotional experiences among adults. On average, their research participants recorded one episode of emotion each day that was described as strong enough to consume thoughts to be accompanied by a perceptible bodily responses, and to simulate some urge to action. The importance and salience of emotional experiences, as a feature both of subjective consciousness and of interpersonal relationships, contrasts with the comparative rarity of emotion words in daily conversation. Even though emotional experience occurs frequently, and we give priority to reading others and managing our own emotions, emotion language is a very small proportion of natural speech (Wierzbicka, 1999). Past research suggests that in general, children do not usually use emotional labels with much frequency in regular day-to-day conversation (e.g., Denham, 1998).

Although we talk about emotion all the time, surprisingly, in natural conversation, reference to emotion is often made in oblique terms, and not often with specific labels for emotion. Emotional labels, by virtue of their rarity, are a powerful statement of value, and, it would seem, are seldom applied in a value-neutral way. The act of labeling emotion is an act of evaluating the content of experience or behavior on several dimensions: its authenticity, rationality, legitimacy, and hedonic tone. Naming an emotion conveys something about controllability and intensity. Few researchers have undertaken the task of collecting information about emotion talk in everyday conversation, as it could take hours of tape recording to yield a handful of emotional labels. Anderson and Leaper (1998) investigated conversations about people and emotion and found that undergraduate women and men talked about the same kinds of emotions and referred to specific emotions equally frequently. Given the low frequency of emotion words, such silences around emotion terms remains to be explored. For example, researchers need to explore why some adolescents choose to talk about particular emotions over others and how does this preference differ across gender, ethnicity, social class, and so forth.

Shields (2002) discusses how the completeness of conventional accounts of emotional socialization are now being questioned by social-constructivists or psychocultural views of development. In general, consistent with a psychocultural approach to development, social-constructivists claim that developmental progress is defined in terms of the child's approximation and variation on culturally agreed-upon norms of conduct. Developmental progress is defined in terms of a fixed, mature state. Regarding emotional socialization, family and peer groups cultivate a "nice girl" orientation in girls (quiet and compliant) that deletes anger from the normal emotional script and, in contrast, encourages the expression (and understanding) of happiness, shame, fear, and warmth or friendliness. Boys, however, are encouraged to express (and understand) emotions that reflect a sense of entitlement, anger, contempt, pride, and so on, while other emotional expressions are dampened.

Emotions also figure prominently in social experiences within the classroom, although this is seldom explicitly acknowledged. As many researchers have noted, emotions are significant because they help to regulate social behavior that is also governed, in part, by the cultural context. Commonly observed behaviors, whether it is grade school girls acting appropriately quietly and kindly or grade school boys acting loud and boisterous toward teachers, are not a result of a blind adherence to powerful norms or of a principled holding fast to a system of values and beliefs. As D'Andrade (1984) and others suggest, normative behavior typically feels "good" or "right."

Markus and Kitayama (1994) suggest that the connection between good feelings and normative behavior is intertwined with the developing sense of self. That is, Markus and Kitayama suggest that a cultural group's ways of feeling are shaped by the group's habitual and normative social behavior. In turn, these ways of feeling influence the nature of this social behavior. Thus, how adolescents experience silence implies affective reactions and also shows the variation in social behavior, which provides a window on the interdependence between emotion and culture. For example, some adolescents have learned that "good girls" are quiet and "bad girls" are loud; such a lesson may influence their social behavior and emotional states.

Thus, the connections between the social order and emotional responses has been of pervasive interest to many social scientists and educators as they explore how the self provides a meeting point as well as a framework for the relation between the individual and the social world. Each person is embedded within a variety of sociocultural contexts or cultures (e.g., country or region or origin, ethnicity, religion, gender, family, birth cohort, profession, etc.). Each of these cultural contexts makes some claim on the person or plays a role in that person's mental schema or script that involves a set of beliefs and practices that (i.e., a cultural schema or framework) about how to be a "good" person. A sense of the "good" is an integral part of one's sense of the self, and one's sense of self may help to shape what is "good" (e.g., of value, concern, appropriate, etc.) and what is not (Oyserman & Markus, 1993). The self, then, is an organized locus of the various, sometimes competing and contradicting, understandings of how to be a person. This self-concept functions as an individualized orienting, mediating, interpretive framework giving shape to what people notice and think about, how people make meaning from information, to what they are motivated to do, and to how they feel and their ways of feeling.

According to some theorists (e.g., Bruner, 1996; Neisser, 1988), a psychocultural approach to development suggests that the self is the entire person considered from particular points of view, and contingent upon different contexts; it is the ways in which the person is made meaningful or given significance. Thus, the concept of the self as the particularized locus of various sociocultural influences suggests that children maintain some kind of agency in their socialization (self-socialization). As Maccoby (1998) claims, this notion of self-socialization helps to explain why two children in similar sociocultural contexts (e.g., two 8-year-old girls in a third-grade classroom) are unlikely to experience emotion exactly the same way within a given set of social experiences.

Connecting the self-concept to moral behavior, many theories have proposed that moral internalization rests in part on the social-cognitive ability to recognize the self and differentiate the self from other (e.g., Zahn-Waxler & Robinson, 1995). Stipek et al. (1990) hypothesized that toddlers who have not achieved an understanding of themselves as entities with distinct characteristics will not recognize themselves as the targets of caregivers' emotions. Thus, according to Stipek et al. (1990), such children may not experience negative emotions such as remorse, shame, and guilt. If some children are capable of experiencing these negative emotions and developing related constructs, in contrast to "all-of-nothing" framework, the children may experience these emotions at various levels of intensity.

Generally, studies on moral development demonstrate connections between self-recognition and moral emotions and behaviors, and affirm the significance of social-cognitive developments in the second year of life that may underlie moral patterns. As Zahn-Waxler and Robinson (1995) note, the links between self-development and moral development, particularly empathic orientations remains complex, especially as this connection may become more complicated during middle childhood. Past research with younger children such as studies which found that self-awareness or self-consciousness may predict noncompliance or oppositional orientations during the second and third year of life may help researchers to unpack the complex conditions in middle childhood (e.g., Brownell & Gifford-Smith, 1992). Future research may build on these findings, and help to determine individual differences in whether growing self-awareness is more likely to culminate in empathic or noncompliant (oppositional) orientations in older school-aged children.

For example, if a grade school girl chooses to break her silence and "talk back" to the teacher, her sense of self will determine the nature of "good" feelings and of the social behavior that will promote and foster these good feelings. This means that emotional experiences are mediated in part by one's self-concept. It is the self-concept that acts as a selective filter or a personalized translator of the social context; what is experienced as happy or joyful (or sad or angry) depends upon the mediating self. Behaving in an ethical or moral manner (i.e., proper, right, or appropriate) according to one's group, feeling good, and being a person are all intimately connected. As I discuss in future chapters, this moral space may provide a compass for children who are searching for answers to questions about what is good/bad, what is worth doing and what is not, and what has meaning and importance in life.

1.4. Summary

Overall, empirical research on the development of emotions during middle childhood reveal insights into how children come to experience, identify, and understand emotions in self and others. Increasingly, evidence from numerous studies points to seven to eight years of age as a significant transition in children's developing emotional experiences and their self-concepts. During the grade school years, children become better able to simultaneously the mental states of others, and also become more sophisticated in their ability to conceptualize and evaluate their sense of self in light of others. Moreover, they increasingly reflect on their own emotions, evaluations, and beliefs as well as their thoughts about what others may be thinking about them. Changes in the social environment during middle childhood, particularly within the family and peer group may influence these cognitive processes. Thus, children's increased participation within the school context where their skills, characteristics, and behaviors are frequently compared to and evaluated by peers and other adults outside of the family may have an influence on how children learn to understand the emotional worlds of others and their sense of self. In the next chapter, I will elaborate on these key issues further elaborated within the context of the elementary school classroom.

2

Learning the Emotions: Developing Emotional Lives

2.1. Introduction

This chapter provides the theoretical and empirical background regarding the emotional and psychological roots of social withdrawal in middle childhood. Overviews of social-cognitive research and self-understanding will be outlined, as well as the main issues of language, sociocommunication, and schooling. Finally, issues of both the limitations and benefits of shyness are discussed in terms of the educational context.

2.2. Roots of Social Withdrawal in Middle Childhood

To understand the complexities of children's emotional worlds, we must also understand their inner worlds and how they interact with others in social situations. Accordingly, to help us understand some aspects of the child's emotional experiences within the context of the school classroom, the following sections briefly outline research on links among children's psychological understanding, self-concept, and social relations. Such research agendas, then, may provide a rich database for the exploration of how children make sense of emotions within the school world.

To study the role of peer relations in self and social cognitions, researchers need to continue to explore the relations between self-concept and social behavior. In brief, the majority of studies involving children and adolescents suggest that positive feelings of self-worth are related to positive social experiences and pro-social behavior (e.g., Boivin & Hymel, 1997; Patterson, Kupersmidt, & Griesler, 1990; Schaffer, 1996). More specifically, such studies have shown a positive relation between self-concept and social competence (e.g., Harter, 1999; Harter, Waters, Whitesell, & Kastelic, 1997), self-concept and peer acceptance (e.g., Jones & Gerig, 1994), and self-concept and attachment (e.g., Jacobsen, Edelstein, & Hofmann, 1995).

Although peer relations may play a large role in children's social-cognitive and affective development (e.g., Parkhurst & Asher, 1992; Sullivan, 1953; Wentzel & Asher, 1995), family members and classroom teachers influence of family, peers, and teachers had a cumulative effect on 10- to 13-year-olds' general and academic self-concept, with teacher support correlating the highest. In addition to teachers and peers, sociocultural factors such as family structure (i.e., birth order, number of siblings) (e.g., Peterson & Leigh, 1990; Sulloway, 1996), cultural background (e.g., Phinney, 1990; Ward, 2004), and media exposure (e.g., Wilgosh, 1994) have also been suggested to influence social-cognitive thought and behavior.

Psychological Understanding and School Experiences

Although mental state and emotion understanding would seem to be foundational to child's educational experiences, few researchers have studied the influence of psychological understanding on school success beyond the age of five or six (Astington & Pelletier, 1997; Bosacki et al., 1997). Regarding academic competence, associations have been found between ToM and the production of stories and general language ability (Astington & Jenkins, 1995; McKeough, 1992). As noted by Wellman and Lagattuta (2004), ToM has also been claimed to facilitate children's ability to self-monitor their cognitive process and engage in reflexive thinking (Astington & Pelletier, 1996). Taken together, these claims suggest that psychological understanding is linked to higher-order, metacognitive thought or more advance reasoning (Siegler, 1995). That is, children who possess high levels of psychological understanding or provide psychological explanations are more likely to "think about their own and others' thinking" and engage in philosophical enquiry and shared dialogue during the school day (Harter & Buddin, 1987; Haynes, 2002).

In contrast, results from research on ToM and school social experience have produced contradictory evidence. Some studies have shown that sophisticated ToM and emotion understandings have a positive influence on school experience (Brown et al., 1996), whereas others have found that such understandings do not guarantee an easier or more positive life at school (Cutting & Dunn, 2002). For example, research studies have found that children with more advanced social-cognitive abilities such as ToM understanding were more sensitive to teacher criticism (Cutting & Dunn, 2002; Dunn, 1995). Thus, given that teaching and learning is crucial to self- and emotion understanding (Bruner, 1996), the following section describes the work of researchers who are beginning to explore how emotional understanding and self-concept play a role in children's school experiences beyond the ages of five and six into middle childhood (Ladd, Buhs, & Troop, 2002).

Classroom Teachers and Children's Emotional Experiences

As children internalize parents' evaluative standards for themselves, they increasingly may experience self-conscious emotions such as guilt, pride, and shame, either on their own, or in situations where they are unsupervised and teacher and/or parental judgments are not immediately apparent. These internalized evaluations or judgments influence children's self-perceptions, and may help to explain why, over time, children come to perceive their characteristics and competencies in ways that are similar to how parents and teachers evaluate them (Marsh et al., 2002; Measelle et al., 1998). This illustrates the importance of providing a caring and nurturing learning environment given that in contexts where adult authority figures (e.g., parents, coaches, teachers, etc.) may be harshly critical, this process can contribute to excessive negative self-conscious emotions such as guilt or shame because some children may come to internalize these adult judgments and evaluations that are unreasonably negative. Given past research that suggests negative affect including negative self-judgments may have a deleterious effect on learning (Brunder, 1996; Dunn, 2005; Harter, 1999), it is imperative that adults who care for, and work with children should aim to provide a psychologically safe, and caring, learning community that will promote a sense of acceptance and connection, with authority figures providing positive and caring evaluative feedback in a mindful and caring way.

Teaching and Learning in Classroom Contexts

Discipline illustrates only one forum in which teacher evaluations of the child's conduct contribute to individual differences in children's proneness to experiencing guilt and shame. As Stipek (1995) has noted, young children's anticipation of parental reactions is one reason for their emotional responses to success or failure.

The expectant smile or the averted gaze of a young child in the parent's presence reflects the importance of the adult's response to his or her self-evaluation in achievement situations. Thus, parents who regularly applaud their child's accomplishments, and respond with disapproval when the child fails to meet expected standards, may contribute to the young child's emergence of feelings of pride, guilt, or shame. For example, Kelley, Brownell, and Campbell (2000) found that negative maternal evaluations of their toddler's behavior during a challenging task at 24 months predicted children's shame responses during subsequent achievement tasks at age three.

Such research on parenting and the emotional development of the young children is also applicable to the elementary school context. Parents and educators may also convey their expectations and evaluations of children's competencies in indirect ways as well. For example, Pomerantz (Pomerantz & Eaton, 2001) found that with increasing age, children more often view their parents' efforts to monitor, guide, and provide uninvited help with homework as an indication that their parents have a low evaluation of their competence. This is particularly true for children of low ability, suggesting that these children may be most prone to experience shame in these situations. More recently, however, Bhanot and Jovanovic (2005) found that girls, even those high in ability, were more likely than boys to interpret unsolicited parent or teacher intervention with their math homework as a sign that the adult believed them to be incompetent. Thus, ability perceptions as well as child gender may influence how children interpret and emotionally respond to adult assistance. More generally, then, in the same manner that discipline approaches contribute to children's comprehension of the associations between personal responsibility for misbehavior and feelings of guilt or rule compliance and feelings of pride, parental (and teacher) behaviors also contribute to children's experience as well as understanding of the reasons for feeling pride and shame in achievement situations.

Parental and teacher reactions to child success or failure may also shape children's developing theories about their own abilities within the classroom. There are individual differences in the kinds of self-directed thoughts children may have during challenging tasks. For example, Heyman, Dweck, and Cain (1992) found that four- and five-year-olds who attribute failure to internal, stable causes ("I am stupid, I can't do this") develop a more helpless response to criticism by others or to failure on a task compared to preschoolers who attribute failure to internal unstable causes ("I didn't try hard enough") or task difficulty ("that test was hard to do"). These response patterns, including the emotions that go with them (shame tends to be associated with stable and guilt with unstable attributions for failure

(Tangney, 1991), have significant consequences for learning in various contexts both at home and within the classroom. Helpless children tend to give up in the face of failure or criticism whereas mastery-oriented children persist.

To date, the majority of research findings on the link between children's social-cognitive and emotional abilities (particularly surrounding self-conscious emotions) remain sparse, contradictory, and inconclusive. Social-cognitive and social-emotional processes such as conceptual role-taking, empathetic sensitivity, and person perception have all been found to be related to both teacher and peer ratings of positive social behavior ratings and peer acceptance (e.g., Ford, 1982; Pellegrini, 1985, 2005). In contrast, some studies have failed to find a relation between various social-cognitive abilities and sociometric status. In particular, studies have shown that aspects of social reasoning such as referential communication and means-ends problem solving were not related to peer popularity among sixth-grade students (Matthews & Keating, 1995; Rubin, 1972). As Dodge and Feldman (1990) suggest, the lack of consistent findings concerning social-cognitive skills and peer ratings highlights the need for further study.

Despite the fact that a large amount of research exists on childhood social cognition, few studies investigate the connections among psychological understanding, self-concept, and social relations. As previous researchers have noted, this paucity of research could be due to the fact that the links between social thought, self-cognitions, and social behavior become increasingly complex as children reach middle childhood and early adolescence (Dodge & Feldman, 1990; see Thompson, 2006, for a review).

Although social interactions and the understanding of complex or self-conscious emotions require second-order reasoning, these areas have often been studied separately. Despite the increasing number of studies on ToM, emotion understanding, and social behavior in children, the majority focuses on preschoolers (e.g., Astington & Jenkins, 1995), with a few on older children (Bosacki & Astington, 1999; Watson et al., 1999). In general, results suggest that a sophisticated ToM is linked to greater social competence, and may also be connected to greater emotion understanding (e.g., Cutting & Dunn, 2002). However, the picture becomes more complex once self-concept, gender, and language are considered.

As an increasing number of researchers note (Paley, 1999, 2004; Pellegrini, 2005), a potentially rich context within which to investigate such connections is children's play behavior during school recess. Play has been linked to language development and many areas of social-cognitive, (Danon-Boileau, 2001; Jones & Cooper, 2006), including ToM and self-concept (Hughes, 1999). In particular, past studies have shown that particular types of play in early childhood (e.g., pretend, cooperative) may be more linked to psychological understanding than others (e.g., Brown et al., 1996). Future research needs to extend the exploration of play behavior and psychological understanding into middle childhood and adolescence.

In contrast to prosocial play behaviors, aggression may be linked to psychological understanding such as relational aggression (when one tries to damage the self-esteem or feelings of others) (e.g., Crick & Dodge, 1994; Pepler & Craig, 1995; Underwood, 2002). In contrast to physical or overt aggression, little is known about adolescents who exhibit behaviors of relational or psychological aggression such as telling lies about one's peers. Similarly, research on behavioral disorders has focused mainly on physically aggressive children and adolescents as compared to those labeled as withdrawn or socially inhibited (Tremblay, 2000). In general, evidence suggests that physically aggressive children may have lower levels of psychological understanding than nonaggressive children (e.g., Hughes et al., 1998).

Given the suggested link between low self-worth and social inhibition (Rubin & Asendorf, 1993), surprisingly few studies investigate social-cognitive abilities in socially withdrawn children, although over the past decade, the research has increased in this area (e.g., Banerjee & Henderson, 2001; Bosacki, Sargeson, Rose-Krasnor, Rubin, & Burgess, 2007; Prakash & Coplan, 2007; Rubin, Burgess, & Coplan, 2002). More research is needed to explore (a) psychological understanding and psychological aggression in children, and (b) the mental, social, and emotional worlds of socially inhibited children. To pursue this line of inquiry, I am currently working on a longitudinal research project involving Canadian grade school children that builds on my past and current research on ToM and social behavior by investigating social cognition, self-concept, and language within the school context (Akseer, Varnish, & Bosacki, 2007; Bosacki, 2007).

Given the previously mentioned link between social-emotional understanding and communicative competencies, children's emotional and social experiences within the classroom may be determined in part by their ability to understand mental states in others. Although the link between children's mental state understanding and school experiences remains to be studied from a psychocultural perspective, past studies on preschoolers and young school-aged children have shown positive links between the understanding of false beliefs and (1) positive teacher ratings of social-emotional skills (Lalonde & Chandler, 1995), (2) skilled aspects of pretend play, (Astington & Jenkins, 1995), and (3) peer ratings of likeability or popularity (Banerjee & Watling, 2005; Dockett, 1997). In addition to false-belief understanding, studies have also shown a positive relation between positive peer relations and emotional understanding/affective perspective-taking (Donelan-McCall & Dunn, 1996; Werner & Cassidy, 1997).

However, within the realm of ToM research, the individual difference, and links found among children's understanding of mental states, self-concept, and their social relations remain relatively undiscovered. The few studies that have investigated links among social cognition, self-concept, and social relations in adolescents have not worked within a psychocultural framework. That is, such studies have not incorporated the principles of "Theory of Mind" understanding or belief-desire reasoning into their research design or into the interpretation of their findings (e.g., Rubin, LeMare, & Lollis, 1990; Schultz & Selman, 1989). Thus, ToM research on children, particularly in middle childhood and early adolescence (e.g., approximately eight to nine years and beyond), needs to draw on the recent relevant studies on younger children that have examined mental-state understanding and social relations.

For example, past studies investigated the connections between school-aged children's personal and emotional school experiences and their mental-state understanding. Most recently, researchers have started to examine the personal school experience of young school-aged children and how this relates to their understanding of thoughts and emotions in others (Astington & Pelletier, 1996; Donelan-McCall & Dunn, 1996). In particular, Donelan-McCall and Dunn's study of six-year-olds' school experiences found positive links between emotional understanding and positive peer relations. Thus, such findings promote the need for further investigations of social understanding and social relations in adolescents within a school setting.

Furthermore, studies that have investigated the complex web of childhood social cognition and social behavior rarely examine how the self-concept may influence the relation between social and emotional reasoning and social behavior. The majority of research that investigates the various connections among three or more social-cognitive variables often assumes that self-perceptions may act as mediating variable. As many theorists note (e.g., Baron & Kenny, 1986), research needs to investigate the possibility that various aspects of the self-concept may act as either a mediator or a moderator.

To illustrate, Boivin and Hymel (1997) recently studied peer experiences and self-perceptions in preadolescents. Although Boivin and Hymel found that negative peer status and peer victimization mediated the relation between social behavior and self-perceptions, they did not test to see if these mediating variables also acted as a moderator. By using only a mediational model, Boivin and Hymel assumed that social behavior causes social preference or popularity. Alternatively, popularity could have acted as a moderator, either compensating or inhibiting the influence of social behavior on self-perceptions. As Baron and Kenny (1986) suggest, as opposed to using the terms *mediator* and *moderator* interchangeably, when studying the complex interrelations among three or more social-psychological variables, both mediational and moderation models need to be tested.

Within the complex world of a child's school life, a child's sense of self may have either multiple ways of influencing social behavior, and thus may serve as either mediator or moderators, or both, on the relation between social understanding and social relations. However, despite Baron and Kenny's (1986) claim, a recent study on preadolescents tested for the mediating and moderating influence of self-esteem, attributional style, and ethnicity on the relation of shyness and academic performance (Haines & Bartels, 1997). Results showed that self-esteem and a negative attributional style mediated the relation between shyness and academic performance. Future research needs to explore the mediating and moderating roles of children's voices and language abilities on their social-cognitive abilities and their emotional experiences within the classroom (Pinker, 2007).

Given the lack of empirical evidence for established links between children's perceived self-concept and the ability to reason about emotions, findings from past studies show that self-perceptions may have a negative influence on social behavior, irrespective of social-cognitive ability (Schultz & Selman, 1989). It could be suggested that self-perceptions and voice may have an inhibitory influence on the relation between interpersonal understanding and social relations. That is, there is evidence to suggest that irrespective of the ability to understand mental states in self and others, if a child holds a negative view or holds negative thoughts and feelings of the self, that child may interact with others in such a way to be perceived by peers and teachers as less socially competent.

2.3. Social-cognitive Psychology and Emotion: Is Emotional Competence Helpful or Hurtful?

*Sensitivity, Emotionality, and Overexcitability
in Childhood—An Overview*

As mentioned briefly in Chapter 1, within the framework of emotional development, the concept of sensitivity is discussed in the educational and psychological literature as multidimensional and complex. Viewed by many researchers as an affective or emotional human characteristic (e.g., Baska, 1989; Clark, 1988; Lovecky,

1992, etc.), sensitivity is a complex process that focuses on both the emotional and cognitive domains, and on self and others. Enhanced sensitivity and intensity are two of the characteristics that are often used to address exceptional emotionality of children, and although much has been written about the various cognitive and affective components of sensitivity, a comprehensive review is beyond the scope of this book (for a more detailed review see Mendaglio, 1995). Consistent with the theme of this book, the following selected theories focus on emotional development. Although the majority of the research on children's sensitivity and intensity deals with a select population often been labeled as academically talented or gifted (Silverman, 1993b), such studies are relevant to the general population as they help us to understand the complexities of emotional development. In particular, these studies may further our knowledge of the antecedents of individual differences in children's developing sense of moral and emotional understandings.

Kazimierz Dabrowski (1967, 1972), a Polish psychologist and psychiatrist, based his theory of emotional development (the Theory of Positive Disintegration) on the study of sensitive, creative, nonaggressive, and highly intelligent individuals. He found such individuals oppressed in societies oriented toward competition, power, status, and wealth. Dabrowski postulated that certain innate response patterns provide a foundation for the development of higher-order values in adult life. Through neurological examinations, Dabrowski (1972) stated that creatively gifted individuals had more pronounced responses to various types of stimuli. He labeled this phenomenon "*nadpobudliwosc*," ("superstimulatability") and it has been translated as "overexcitability." This powerful neural excitation comes in five varieties: psychomotor, sensual, emotional, imaginational, and intellectual. The overexcitabilities (OEs) may be thought of as an abundance of physical energy, heightened acuity of the senses, vivid imagination, intellectual curiosity and drive, and a deep capacity to care. Individuals may experience one or more of these OEs at varying degrees of intensity. Research shows that the greater the strength of the OEs, the greater the developmental potential for following an ethical, compassionate path (Piechowski, 1979). Numerous studies have shown the gifted to have stronger OEs than nonselected groups (see Nelson, 1996; Silverman, 1993b; for reviews).

Numerous authors' definitions of sensitivity and emotional intensity build on Dabrowski's (1967) theory of emotional development. For instance, Clark (1988) refers to two types of sensitivities: unusual sensitivity to the feelings and expectations of others; and, sensitivity to inconsistency between ideals and behavior. In this latter usage, Clark refers to being aware of inconsistencies or contradictions within self as well as others.

Consistent with Clark (1988), both Piechowski (1997; 2006) and Silverman (1993a) draw on Dabrowski's *Theory of Positive Disintegration* (Dabrowski & Piechowki, 1977) to discuss the emotional aspects of giftedness. In Dabrowki's theory, OE is a central concept. The idea of OE is analogous to the notion of intensity. Piechowski (1997), along with Clark (1988) who speaks of affective characteristics, distinguishes between emotional intensity and emotional sensitivity. In general, Piechowski believes that intensity refers to the depth of experience of emotions. For Piechowski, emotional sensitivity has several facets: sensitivity to feelings of others, to feeling in self, and sensitivity to injustice. Thus, we have a tendency to be sensitive to both personal and social issues.

Consistent with the multidimensional aspect of sensitivity, Baska (1989) also describes two types of sensitivity: (1) direct or aesthetic sensitivity, and (2) indirect or emotional intensity. Aesthetic sensitivity refers to a manifestation of the children's appreciation for complexity with particular reference to works of art. For example, a child described as sensitive in this aspect would be capable of interpreting complex works of art. The second type of sensitivity includes a combination of both intensity and sensitivity. According to Baska (1989), gifted children are sensitive to language expression and use and exhibit sophisticated awareness of subtleties in interpersonal communication.

Whereas Baska (1989) defines sensitivity as one aspect of the larger concept of emotional intensity, Lovecky (1992) includes intensity in her description of sensitivity. In her view, sensitivity is one of the five traits associated with gifted individuals. For Lovecky (1992, p. 21), the trait of sensitivity is characterized by a "depth of feeling that results in a sense of identification with others (people, animals, nature, the universe)." Passion, compassion, and empathy are associated with sensitivity, with passion being the central aspects of sensitivity. Passion is depth of feeling which results in a rich complex, intense, emotional life for these persons.

Lovecky (2004) also claims that children who are sensitive and compassionate are also empathic, and defines compassion as referring to a sense of caring for others. This caring for others may be motivated by aiming to reduce the pain of others, which in turn may facilitate commitment to social causes. Given that empathy refers to the person actually experiencing the feelings of another, and knowing or inferring those feelings, difficulties may arise out of this ability. For instance, such empathizing may lead the gifted person to believe that the other's feelings are actually one's own.

The inclusion of empathy in a discussion of sensitivity seems very appropriate. However, it also adds a whole new dimension, and an in-depth discussion of this complex construct is beyond the scope of this book. Within the context of emotionality and sensitivity, the use of empathy comes from the variety of definitions researchers use. Lovecky emphasizes the experiencing of another's emotions as empathy. For others (Roeper, 1982; Silverman, 1993b) the use of the term includes some form of altruistic behavior.

Roeper (1982) uses empathy to refer to the gifted individual's heightened sensitivity to the emotions of other and a sense of compassion. Roeper (1982) believes that some gifted individuals are very empathic and that such persons demonstrate emotional giftedness. According to Roeper, her definition of gifted is the following: Giftedness is a greater awareness, and a greater ability to understand and transform perceptions into intellectual and emotional experiences (Roeper, 1982, p. 21). Sensitivity, perfectionism, intensity and introversion are all aspects of emotional OE: "Emotional ties and attachments, concern for others (empathy), sensitivity in relationships"; "self-evaluation and self-judgment, feelings of inadequacy and inferiority"; "intensity of feeling: e.g., extremes of emotion, complex emotions and feelings"; and "inhibition (timidity, shyness)" (Piechowski, 1979, adapted in Silverman, 1993b, p. 14). Therefore, according to Dabrowski's theory, some gifted children who exhibit high degrees of sensitivity are endowed with high emotional OE. Perfectionism begins as a facet of emotional OE, but can evolve into the drive for self-perfection propelling the individual toward higher level of development (Silverman, 1989). Intensity, while a strong indicator of emotional OE, has at times been used synonymously with all the OEs.

Introversion, often perceived negatively in our extroverted society, is actually a developmentally positive trait since it indicates the capacity to inhibit aggression. Dabrowski (1979) described overexcitable people as: "delicate, gentle, sensitive, empathic, nonaggressive, industrious, wise though unsophisticated, never brutal, often inhibited, likely to withdraw into themselves rather than retaliate, having deep feelings, idealistic" (pp. 87–90). He felt that, because of their sensitivity and integrity, these individuals are capable of bringing humanity to a higher set of values, but that they are at great risk of being destroyed by society because of their inherent differences.

The values Dabrowski (1979/1994) considered indispensable to harmonious living include: an empathic attitude toward others; tolerance (not aggression); responsibility for others and for self; a just attitude (treating everybody by the same standards); helping each other; giving thought to the harmed and humiliated, to invalids, to the sick, to the ineffectual and those devastated by their own loneliness; truthfulness; authenticity; and just social care. However, according to Dabrowski, those who have such values are often pushed aside in an insensitive society, and treated as if they were maladjusted. Dabrowski considered the so-called neurotics with high ideals "a mine of social treasure. If their emotionality, talents, interests, and sensitivity were discovered at an early age, society and science would profit" (pp. 87–88).

Overall, despite the multiple definitions, common themes suggest that the core of sensitivity is an awareness or perceptiveness applied to both self (personal) and other (social), and include both emotional and cognitive content. To address the multifaceted perspective of sensitivity, building on the past definitions, Mendaglio (1995) defines sensitivity as an awareness to one of more of the following: thoughts, feelings, and behavior of self or others. In particular, the four components of sensitivity include intrapersonal cognitive (e.g., self-awareness), intrapersonal affective (e.g., emotional experience), interpersonal cognitive (e.g., perspective-taking) and affective (e.g., empathy).

According to Mendaglio (1995), cognitive sensitivity consists of perceptiveness. For example, gifted children tune into the nuances of interpersonal communication. They can detect and respond to the subtleties of nonverbal cues such as eye contact or vocal qualities. Although all children engage in this perceptiveness especially when engaged in communication with significant adults, the gifted child detects more of these cues than non-gifted. This heightened awareness of another person's verbal and nonverbal behavior can lead to some interpersonal complications as some children may be capable of reading mixed or contradicting nonverbal and verbal messages. One illustration of this is a situation where gifted children are asked to comply with a parent's or teacher's request. A gifted child may detect nonverbal signs of emotionality in the adult's nonverbal behavior, such as changes in vocal qualities or facial expression. Rather than responding to the verbal part of the adult's communication, the child reacts to the emotional tone that he/she identifies in the adult. In some cases, the gifted child may take issue with the "how" of the request rather than the "what." It is not uncommon for such scenarios to result in the child's responding with: "you have no right to talk to me that way!" In addition to not complying to the request, a gifted child often comments on the manner in which another person has communicated to the child.

In other situations such perceptiveness leads to expressions of concern. For example, a child may ask a peer, "What's wrong?" with appropriate vocal qualities when she/he notices nonverbal signs associated with negative emotions or stress. This ability to read others' emotions well may influence their relationships with others, as others may not wish to have their true emotions read, especially if they are attempting to mask unhappiness or anxiety with a false smile or positive expressions.

In the affective domain, sensitivity consists of the child's experiencing of emotions in self and others. When parents and teachers refer to sensitivity in descriptions of gifted children, it is the affective domain to which they refer. In this sense, gifted children are usually easily moved emotionally. As with the cognitive aspects of sensitivity, the affective facet is also double edged. In the positive sense, a gifted child may be awestruck by daily experiences or appreciate aesthetic objects such as paintings. On the negative side, he/she may be easily offended or hurt by remarks of others. In some cases, the child may be so sensitive to criticism that we witness an overreaction to neutral statements made to them. For example, a parent makes a statement that she has noticed that the child has not done his/her homework. Parents are often surprised at the intensity of the child's emotional reaction to statements which contain no explicit criticism or demands. Affective sensitivity also includes heightened awareness of the emotions in others. Some of these children are so adept at this that they actually experience the emotions of others. With this comes a concern for others. This empathic connection with others may extend well beyond a child's immediate family and environment. It can extend to feelings of concern, sadness, and frustration elicited by awareness of issues characterized by injustice around the globe.

Mendaglio believes that this awareness has the potential to promote a greater understanding and/or increased emotional responsiveness to the feelings of self and others, and a person's experiences of sensitivity may not be expressed to others. That is, although a child may claim that she or he is sensitive, that child may not appear to exhibit any behavioral signs of sensitivity to others such as empathy.

Social-Cognitive Psychology and Emotion: Psychocultural Implications

In all of the above sections, difference or diversity may play a role in how a child experiences emotionality in the classroom. The extent to which emotional competence can help or hinder a child's psychological growth may be in part influenced by whether or not the child is a girl or boy, from a different culture, speak a different language, differs in physical developments, etc. Given that an extensive review of issues of diversity are beyond the scope of this book, the reader needs to be aware that all issues discussed in this book are influenced by cultural, historical, social, and psychological factors. It is my hope that I provide somewhat a brief snapshot to encourage readers to continue to question the influence of these factors in development. Future research will have many opportunities to explore such issues in emotionality in middle childhood.

To highlight how one particular factor may influence emotionality in the classroom, I have chosen to focus on issues of gender and self-development. In particular, our current research project explores how the self-structure and emotional worlds may be shaped by culture as it is by gender, or rather, how each culture shapes both genders to be recognizable to each other in their difference.

Emotionality and Sensitivity: Gender Issues

Although the foundations of "I" are created in infancy through the interactions of the child and the care-giver (Mahler, Pine, & Bergman, 1975), in technologically advanced Western countries, children approaching early adolescence may experience a second individuation (Blos, 1968) when one must reestablish a sense of autonomy or distinctiveness from others. Cognitively, children in later childhood become increasingly capable of this intrapsychic restructuring by developing abstract conceptual abilities such as self-reflection, social awareness, and perspective coordination (Selman, 2003). However, given the multidimensional nature of the self, one's cognitive sense of the self may not develop in tandem with other aspects of the self such as the emotional, social, and spiritual. This lack of synchronicity in the rates of various dimensions of development may create inner tensions or self-conflict which in turn may lead to self-concept and interpersonal problems, often accompanied by negative emotions such as anxiety and nervousness, and feelings of inferiority and self-doubt (Dabrowski, 1964; Silverman, 1993a).

In addition to this self-restructuring, a process known as gender intensification occurs during preadolescence, when societal expectations of traditional gender-roles and their accompanying behaviors become emphasized (Hill & Lynch, 1983). During middle childhood, as children approach the boundary of adolescence, they may become aware of the conflicting societal messages that encourage traditional feminine behaviors such as passiveness, nurturance, and intimacy in girls, while at the same time encourage traditional masculine behaviors such as aggressiveness, egoism, and autonomy in boys. During middle childhood and early adolescence, children's cultural competence or their awareness and understanding of how cultural values play a role in their self and social development continues. For example, regarding the role society plays in the co-creation of gendered stereotypes, as children approach adolescence, some may begin to become aware of how modern Western industrialized society values the male-dominated "world of the mind" over the female-dominated "world of the body" while simultaneously suggesting that to be a competent woman in today's society, young girls must both achieve professionally and socially (Silverstein & Perlick, 1995). Thus, girls and boys who possess the cognitive capacity to become aware of the complexity and ambiguity of modern reality may also lose a sense of security and certainty, possibly resulting in feelings of self-doubt, low self-worth, and negative self-evaluations.

Similar to Erikson's psychosocial approach to identity formation where society plays an important role in assisting to shape the adolescent role, Dabrowski (1964) claims that self-development during middle childhood and adolescence is due to the combined factors of both internal and societal conflict. Corresponding to Blos' (1967) notion of early adolescence as a second individuation, Dabrowksi states that it is this period of "disintegration" or re-organizing and re-creating of the self-structure which provides the ground for the birth and development of a more sophisticated sense of self. In particular, Dabrowski's emphasis on the emotional effects of this disintegration process holds special relevance to self-concept development in middle childhood. Dabrowski claims that feelings of anxiety, nervousness, inferiority, shame, and guilt are an integral part of the disintegration process and may be experienced to a greater extent by children who appear more "sensitive" or "overexcitable."

In relation to girls and boys in middle childhood, it is those who are the most sensitive to these internal and societal conflicts who may suffer the greatest emotional difficulties. Thus, the extent to which a girl learns to resolve her inner conflict and eventually achieve self-actualization is partially dependent upon her ability to transcend cultural ideals and eventually fuse her vision of her "ideal" self (what she ought to be) with her "real" self (what she is in reality) (Dabrowski, 1964; Maslow, 1971). Building on the notions of gender intensification and identity formation, Perlick and Silverstein (1995) attempt to explain self-concept problems in girls especially during late childhood and early adolescence through their theory of gender ambivalence. From a psycho-cultural perspective, Perlick and Silverstein suggest that the gender-bias of modern Western industrialized societies creates an identity conflict in preadolescent girls between their gender identity and stereotypic gender-role expectations. For example, a nine-year-old girl who has stereotypic, traditional masculine personality traits (i.e., independence, analytical thinking style) may develop ambivalence toward her gender identity when she deduces that she is a member of a devalued social category based on her realization that society values traditional masculine traits over feminine ones. This sense of ambivalence may lead to a negative evaluation of the self and feelings of low self-worth, which in turn may give rise to psychological and emotional difficulties such as depression, disordered eating, and anxiety problems.

Previous empirical research and theoretical models suggest that female adolescents' self-perceptions are more likely than those of males to be influenced by their social relationships, given the high value that they place on close relationships (Harter, 1999; Maccoby, 1998). In addition, Hankin and Abramson (2001) posited that female adolescents may be more vulnerable to depression than males because they experience more negative interpersonal events, and tend to ruminate and make pessimistic attributions, including self-blame, about these peer relationship difficulties. Such findings suggest that negative peer experiences may be especially detrimental to the self-esteem of female adolescents, which may have implications for the development of internalizing difficulties. Accordingly, although these research findings focus on adolescence, it may have implications for younger children as peer relations become increasingly important during the middle childhood and early adolescent years. Thus, peer relationship difficulties may begin to have a more detrimental impact on females' self-esteem than that of males, and may mediate the link between peer relationships and internalizing difficulties more strongly during the middle childhood and early adolescent years. When one considers the immense complexity of children's mental and social worlds, many theorists agree that no single theory will adequately explain the puzzle of the psychosocial problems experienced by girls and boys during middle childhood. Psychocultural theory incorporates the dynamic interplay between biological, socio-cultural, and as Dabrowski (1964) called "the third factor" or all aspects of the self-system including self-awareness, self-control, and self-criticism and reflection. Similar to Levitt and Selman's (1996) psychosocial notion of personal meaning, Dabrowski's third factor acts as a lens through which individuals select and confirm/disconfirm certain dynamics of internal experiences and certain influences of external environments. It is this personal lens that theorists and educators must focus on to begin to understand the connection between children's identity formation and emotional development during middle childhood.

In contrast to the amount of research on socioemotional competence, self-perceptions, and language abilities of aggressive children (e.g., Crick & Dodge, 1994), surprisingly little research exists on the social-cognitive abilities of socially withdrawn or shy children (Rubin, Burgess, & Coplan, 2002). To date there remains little research on the gender-related differences among shy children's socioemotional and language competencies, and self-perceptions (Ruble & Martin, 1998; Wichmann, Coplan, & Daniels, 2004). Thus, to explore the emotional landscape of children's social worlds within the school context (Denham et al., 2003), an investigation of socioemotional competencies in school-aged girls may help to illustrate the gendered relations among emotional competence, self-perceptions, and language.

Past research findings suggest sophisticated, or advanced emotional competence may have both intrapersonal and interpersonal costs and benefits (Cutting & Dunn, 1999; Sutton, Smith, & Swettenham, 1999). For example, regarding interpersonal implications, children with a highly advance emotional understanding ability may also use this ability to harm others such as excluding certain peers from a group by developing friendship with someone else (Sutton et al., 1999). As researchers remind us (Denham, 2003; Dunn, 1988, 2005), a child's ability to understand someone's emotional state does not tell us how that child may behave in a relationship with that person. Another explanation for the contradictory teacher ratings about shy girls' social and aggressive behaviors is perhaps that due to the subtle nature of relational aggression (e.g., smiling at someone while writing her/him a hate letter?), teachers reported contradictory behavior exhibited by girls in the classroom (Crick et al., 2001). Thus, the subtle and contradictory aggressive behavior exhibited by shy girls may lead to conflicting teacher ratings and require further research.

Although the associations between social cognitions and aggression in childhood are well established (e.g., Crick & Dodge, 1994), the social cognitions, particularly the emotional competence of socially withdrawn children remain under-explored. Various conceptual mechanisms may underlie this association between social cognitions and social withdrawal. For example, global biases and deficits in socio-cognitive processing may contribute generally towards social maladjustment. It is also possible that socioemotional deficits or biases may be differentially associated with withdrawn and aggressive behaviors.

For example, some researchers suggest that socially withdrawn children do not have deficits in processing but differ in their ability to act upon their prosocial cognitions due to poor emotional regulation and social inhibition (Rubin et al., 2002). That is, withdrawn children may process social situations similarly to their more sociable peers, but lack the ability to sufficiently regulate their emotions in the face of arousing social situations. Thus, as Wichmann, Coplan, and Daniels (2004) suggest, socially withdrawn children may evidence a performance rather than a competence deficit. In light of previous literature which shows socially withdrawn children to be more depressed, anxious, and hold more negative self-perceptions than their non-withdrawn agemates, the present study explored the connections between self-perceptions, socioemotional competencies, and receptive vocabulary ability. Perhaps such negative self-perceptions or lack of self-worth and confidence may underlie deficits in effective social performance.

2.4. Hurtful Emotional Competence: Intrapersonal and Interpersonal

Emotionality, Social Withdrawal, and Shyness

Regarding the possible psychological costs of varying levels of emotional competence, gender may influence the interplay between emotional competencies and social interaction. Given the growing literature that suggests that being shy is more problematic for boys than girls (see Rubin & Coplan, 2004 for a recent review), interactions between gender and teachers' attitudes and responses to shy behaviors are complex and findings are inconclusive. For example, although some studies show that being shy is more problematic for boys than girls, some studies show that teachers' attitudes and responses do not differ for hypothetical shy boys vs. girls. More specifically, a recent study found no indication that teachers tolerated shy behaviors more in girls, or that they perceived a greater cost for this behavior for boys (Arbeau & Coplan, 2007). Arbeau and Coplan (2007) found no indication that teachers tolerated shy behaviors more in girls, or that they perceived a greater cost for this behavior for boys. They also found that teachers ascribed the most serious social costs to the behaviors of both the hypothetical shy and aggressive children. Arbeau and Coplan's (2007) recent finding builds on past research that found teachers believed that shyness and other socially immature behaviors were more costly to the child than aggression and socially defiant behaviors (Cunningham & Sugawara, 1988). Thus, given the increased research attention that shyness has received over the last 20 years (Lane, 2007; Rubin & Coplan, 2004; Zimbardo & Radl, 1981), the present findings could also reflect teachers' increasing awareness of shyness as being problematic for both girls and boys, and help to explain recent results indicating that teachers respond to shy behaviors with increased concern and attention (Arbeau & Coplan).

In contrast, preliminary results from one of our recent studies partially supports research that suggests shy boys might have greater psychological costs due to cultural stigmas attached to stereotypic gender-role expectations and behavior (Coplan & Armer, 2005). In addition, we have preliminary evidence to suggest that emotional competence may also have some psychological costs for shy girls (Bosacki, 2005a). Thus, the present findings add to the growing body of empirical evidence regarding gender differences in the experiences of shyness, self-perceptions, and socioemotional competence in middle childhood.

Our research findings also support the association between language abilities and social withdrawal as we found language differences across shy and non-shy girls and boys. In particular, the finding that shy girls scored the lowest on the receptive language task whereas shy boys scored the highest supports past research which shows that some socially withdrawn children may experience restrictions in their verbal communication (Danon-Boileau, 2001; Dunn, 2004; McHolm, Cunningham, & Vanier, 2005; Schneider, 1999). For example, regarding the anxiety-based condition of selective mutism where children do not speak in certain social situations (Vecchio & Kearney, 2005), research suggests that this condition seems to occur about one and half to two times more often in girls than in boys (McHolm et al., 2005). In contrast to past research that suggests that compared to girls, for boys social withdrawal may hold stronger negative implications for psychological adjustment (e.g., Morison & Masten, 1991; Rubin, Chen, & Hymel, 1993), our findings showed that shy boys scored the highest on the self-perceptions, and the highest on the language measure, but received the lowest emotional competence teacher ratings. Further, teachers rated shy boys as the most aggressive group, and according to the self-socialization theory (Maccoby, 1998), these teacher perceptions may also influence the boys' self-perceptions and possible aggressive behaviors.

Regarding the role teachers play in children's emotional experiences in the classroom, Arbeau and Coplan (2007) found that teachers reported differences in how they would *respond* to the behaviors of hypothetical shy vs. unsociable children in their classrooms. For example, as compared to the unsociable children, teachers reported that they would be more likely to directly intervene and promote social skill acquisition in the shy children, as well as to monitor the situation. Promoting social skills for shy children would seem like a particularly appropriate response, given previous evidence that showed shy children do not often demonstrate socially competent behaviors (e.g., Bohlin, Hagekull, & Andersson, 2005). In contrast, a lesser tendency to intervene with unsociable children may reflect teachers' beliefs and attitudes that unsociable children generally possess adequate social skills to interact socially in a competent manner when they choose to (Coplan et al., 2004).

To further understand the finding as to why shy girls and boys received low sociability ratings from the teachers, research on emotional intensity and sensitivity among gifted children may help us to understand the social emotional correlates of social withdrawal. As Mendaglio (1995) discusses, giftedness involves four psychological concepts of self-awareness, perspective taking, emotional experience, and empathy—although a person's experience of sensitivity is not necessarily expressed directly to others. Similarly, literature involving sensitivity, emotional intensity, and cognitive ability may shed some light on the question of why shy boys scored the highest on vocabulary ability, researchers need to further explore the complex connections which exist between language ability, socioemotional competence and social communicative acts (Edmunds & Edmunds, 2005; McHolm et al., 2005; Miller, 1997).

Moral Sensitivity and Sensitive Children

Researchers of the psychological development of gifted children have noted the moral sensitivity of gifted children who arc considered to be sensitive (Silverman, 1993a).

According to Silverman's clinical reports, many parents have reported that their gifted children seemed to have an innate sense of right and wrong and has documented multiple cases of gifted children conserving resources, fighting injustice, befriending and protecting handicapped children, responding to others' emotional needs, becoming terribly upset if a classmate is humiliated, becoming vegetarian in meat-eating families, crying at the violence in cartoons, being perplexed at why their classmates push in line, refusing to fight back when attacked because they considered all forms of violence—including self-defense—morally wrong, and writing poems of anguish at the cruelty in the world. Researchers have also found that the higher the child's Intelligence Quotient (IQ), the earlier moral concerns develop and the more profound effect they have on the child. But interestingly, many claim that it usually takes maturity before the child can translate moral sensitivity into consistent moral action.

Thus, this ability to become aware of other's evaluations and social standards and conventions may be heightened among children who are more sensitive to such social cues. Similarly, the ability to understand and experience the self-conscious emotions such as pride, shame, guilt, and embarrassment have developmental origins around the second birthday is further supported by evidence that the third foundation of self-conscious emotions—accepting others' standards for oneself—also begins to emerge at this time. Toward the end of the second year, toddlers become *personally sensitive* to normative standards and expectations for achievement and behavior.

For example, Kagan (1981, 2005) reports that during this age, children become visibly concerned when standards of wholeness and intactness have been violated, such as when they notice broken toys, missing puzzle pieces, misplaced objects, torn book pages, etc. (Lamb, 1993). Kagan claims that this phenomenon could be viewed as an emerging moral sense because each event violated the implicit norms or standards that are typically enforced by caregivers (teachers, family members, etc.) through sanctions on damaged or broken objects. Similarly, Kochanska, Casey, and Fukumoto (1995) assert that early responses to incompleteness, mishaps, or damage may reflect an emerging system of internal standards about right and wrong. Such an ability may lead to social and emotional consequences for children labeled as gifted and who may be sensitive to such self-conscious emotions (Thompson & Lagattuta, 2006).

The early leaders in the field recognized the moral component of giftedness. Lewis Terman (1925) studied the emotional stability, social adjustment, and moral character of the gifted because he recognized that all of these facets of development are interwoven with advanced cognition. The importance of understanding the complex inner lives, early ethical concerns, and heightened awareness of the world of the gifted population, was apparent to Leta Hollingworth (1942) as well. Many subsequent researchers have found evidence of advanced moral reasoning in this (e.g., Gross, 1993; Roeper, 1988; Simmons & Zumpf, 1986; Vare, 1979, etc.).

Gender, Emotionality, and Social Cognition in Middle Childhood

As I mentioned in Chapter 1, and briefly earlier in this chapter regarding gender differences in shy children, although there is a large body of research on gender differences in moral or self-conscious emotions and behaviors, research on moral emotions in middle childhood remains relatively sparse. Given the importance of the moral emotions in middle childhood, in this chapter I will focus on outlining some of the past literature regarding gender differences found in moral emotion understanding and related behaviors. In general, as outlined by Zahn-Waxler and Robinson (1995), there appears to be deeply ingrained cultural expectations for mature or sophisticated interpersonal behavior in young girls. Overall, research has found that girls seem to internalize earlier and more completely the message that it is wrong to hurt others, and more generally, that it matters how people feel. For example, in longitudinal research, parental efforts to inhibit aggression at age five are linked with heightened empathy levels in adulthood but only for girls, and that females are judged more harshly than males for failure to engage in the same altruistic act (Barnett, McMinimy, Flouer, & Masbad, 1987; Koestner, Franz, & Weinberger, 1990). More recently, Rudolph et al.'s (2005) study on the need for approval, self-appraisals, and psychological well-being found girls were more susceptible than boys to the emotional costs of negative self-appraisals, and these costs were not counterbalanced by greater protection by positive self-appraisals.

Furthermore, evidence for an association between self-conscious emotions and theory of mind development builds on research by Cutting and Dunn (2002). As I discuss further in Chapter 3, Cutting and Dunn investigated whether having an earlier, more sophisticated understanding of mind might lead to greater sensitivity to criticism. That is, the more a child knew about what others might be thinking and believing, the more cognizant she or he might also be that she or he could be the subject of negative evaluation. Their findings showed that three- and four-year-olds who demonstrated advanced false belief understanding were more likely as kindergarteners to lower their evaluation of a "student" puppet's performance after it received negative remarks by the "teacher" puppet compared to kindergarteners with low false belief understanding in preschool.

Similarly, Dunn (1995) found that children's ability to pass a false belief task at 40 months predicted greater sensitivity to teacher criticism of their own work. Relatedly, children impaired in theory of mind understanding, perhaps those diagnosed with developmental challenges such as autism may demonstrate more limited knowledge about self-conscious emotions (Heerey, Keltner, & Capps, 2003). Thus, as I have noted previously (e.g., Bosacki, 2000, 2005), development in children's theory of mind understanding may influence the emergence of a "looking glass self" (Cooley, 1902), or knowledge about the self that incorporates other's evaluations. This could result in increased vulnerability to feelings of shame, guilt, and embarrassment when standards are not met, and this could occur more frequently in children labeled as sensitive, or socially withdrawn.

Gender is considered an integral factor in all aspects of human development, affecting both our mind and body. As Shields (2002) notes, new models of gender question the notion that gender is attained as a secure status throughout life, and agrees with Maccoby (1998) in that gender is considered more of a "culture" than a fixed trait. That is, gender is now viewed by some theorists as a fluid construct, one that must be negotiated in social relationships and challenged by changing social, cultural, and historical contexts (Shields, 2002).

As noted by Halpern (1992) and Miller and Scholnick (2000), most studies on social cognition and language have not specifically aimed to investigate gender-related differences and/or patterns. As I discussed in Chapter 1, a psychocultural approach to ToM may provide a valuable form of inquiry to investigate the role gender plays in children's emotional and social-cognitive development (Astington, 1996; Astington & Olson, 1995; Lamb, 2001; Lillard, 1997; Yuill, 1993). This approach to ToM asserts the notion that an individual's ability to understand mental states in others is largely relativistic and socially constructed. Consistent with this view, transcultural research has shown that the development of social-cognitive abilities, including ToM, may be dependent upon one's social and cultural experiences (McCormick, 1994; Vinden & Astington, 2000).

A psychocultural approach to development suggests that individual differences in the ability to understand mental states in others may indicate that this ability is acquired in different ways for women and men. The process of learning to understand self and other within a social context may be contingent not on whether a child is female or male but on the way in which a child's gender interacts with her or his environment. Thus, if a child is viewed as a "cultural invention" (Kessen, cited in Cahan, 1997, p. 205), gender helps to create a separate culture for that particular child. This conception of gender as a social category or particular culture suggests that acknowledging the contribution of cultural milieu to a ToM may prove to be a fruitful avenue for future research on development of gender-role conception and behavior (Maccoby, 1998; Nelson, Henseler, & Plesa, 2000).

A social-constructivist enquiry into the associations between children's minds and their emotional experiences, and the social implications regarding social inter-actions would enable researchers to view gender in context (e.g., Shields, 2002), as it operates within the social and emotional worlds of the grade school classroom. In opposition to the more traditional sex-differences model (i.e., gender differences not mentioned a priori, only posthoc statistical tests to indicate differences), such a gendered approach to research is in line with Hill and Lynch's (1983) gender inten-sification hypothesis. This hypothesis claims that during preadolescence, gender differences increase among girls and boys due to the increased pressure to conform to traditional gender-role stereotypes. For example, research has shown that during preadolescence, traditional gender-role behavior, and ascription (i.e., femininity = sociality, submissiveness; masculinity = autonomy, aggression) become intensified (Hill & Lynch, 1983; Tavris, 1992).

In accordance with research that shows a link between traditional female ste-reotypic behavior and depression among women (McGrath, Keita, Strickland, & Russo, 1990), intensification of gender identity among preadolescent girls may strengthen behavioral tendencies hypothesized to hold special relevance for vulner-ability to depression, such as interpersonal sensitivity, an eagerness to please, and an increased concern for others (Zahn-Waxler & Robinson, 1995). Thus, preado-lescent girls who appear to be relatively competent in the ability to understand and be sensitive to the needs of others may be at risk for developing future self-concept disorders such as depression (Silverstein & Perlick, 1995).

In support of the gender-intensification hypothesis (Hill & Lynch, 1983), many gender-related differences gleaned from research on social behavior and social cognition in late childhood and early adolescence are usually consistent with traditional gender-role stereotypes. Concerning social behavior, a majority of research findings show that girls are rated as more socially competent and popular by both their peers and teachers than are boys (e.g., see Maccoby, 1998). Similarly, research on teacher perceptions shows that girls are perceived by their teachers to be more compliant and prosocial than boys (e.g., Harter, 1996). However, com-pared to adolescence, during middle childhood, gender-related findings regarding psychosocial and sociocommunicative development are conflicting and incon-clusive (Peterson, Sarigiani, & Kennedy, 1991; Steinhausen & Juzi, 1996). In contrast, boys have been found to display more externalizing behaviors such as aggressive, antisocial behaviors (Underwood, 2002). Given the conflicting find-ings, as researchers suggest, researchers, practitioners, and all adults working with school-age children need to be sensitive to gender differences when interpreting children's social interactions and self-perceptions (Maccoby, 1998; Rinaldi & Heath, 2006).

According to teacher expectancy research (e.g., Jones & Gerig, 1994), perceptions and labels of teachers may play a role in how adolescents experience silence and interact within the classroom, particularly if an adolescent is labeled as "quiet, shy," or "delinquent, troubled." Reflecting a self-fulfilling prophesy, this label may become integrated into the adolescent's identity. That is, once a teacher labels a student as quiet and shy, that child may become to believe that she or he is quiet and shy, which in turn may cause the child to exhibit quiet and shy behaviors. To validate the teacher's label, the child may choose to speak less or to avoid and withdraw from conversation (either intentionally or unintentionally). Such behaviors may thus perpetuate the teacher's original label of quiet and shy.

Furthermore, the majority studies on teacher expectancies have shown that teachers' expectations of their students and subsequent student-teacher interactions have an effect on student behavior and self-concept (e.g., Jones & Gerig, 1994). Given the crucial role teachers and peers play in both the gender-role socialization and co-construction of social-cognitive and linguistic abilities of adolescents (Denham, 1998), it is surprising that few researchers have studied how the links between teachers' and peers' perceptions of other students' social and academic behavior, and the students' self-perceptions may shape children's emotional experiences in the classroom.

Regarding social-cognitive abilities, research shows that boys score higher than girls on nonsocial spatial perspective-taking tasks (Coie & Dorval, 1973), whereas girls score higher than boys on social perspective-taking and empathy tasks (Jahnke & Blanchard-Fields, 1993; King, Akiyama, & Elling, 1996; Zahn-Waxler & Robinson, 1995). Likewise, Offer, Ostrov, Howard, and Atkinson (1988) reported that across ten countries, girls were more likely than boys to express a desire to help a friend when possible and thus gave evidence of a "more sociable and empathic stance" than did boys (p. 70). Gender-related differences have also been found in the social-cognitive area of person perception. In general, girls have been shown to emphasize such categories as interpersonal skills, psychological traits, and social relationships (e.g., Honess, 1981). In contrast, boys have been found to emphasize such categories as physical aggression, interests, and academic ability (Peevers & Secord, 1973).

Surprisingly, although social-cognitive researchers investigate social-cognitive abilities like the ones mentioned above, the exploration of gender-related differences among ToM abilities has just begun. Of the few ToM studies that actually do test for gender effects, most report nonsignificant results (e.g., Jenkins & Astington, 1996). In contrast, some recent ToM studies have found evidence to support gender-related findings gleaned from the more general social-cognitive research area. More specifically, results obtained on young children show that girls score significantly higher on ToM types of tasks as compared to boys. For example, regarding preschool children, Cuttting and Dunn (1999) investigated theory of mind and emotion understanding in preschoolers. Cutting and Dunn found that compared to boys, girls referred to mental-state verbs more frequently and their choice of emotion words was more sophisticated or developmentally advanced.

Although the research base in this area is thin, there is some correlational evidence that shows gender differences in the development of psychological under-standing of self and others during middle to late childhood. In particular, Hatcher et al. (1990) found that among 13-year-old girls, abstract reasoning was related to the understanding of others but not oneself, whereas the reverse was found for boys, abstract reasoning was positively related to self-understanding but not to the understanding of others. The authors claim that this finding suggests that girls may be more likely to understand others than to understand themselves. This focus on caring for others may be based on the tendency of some modern Western cultures to label interpersonal understanding and empathetic sensitivity as "natural" personality traits for females. The implications of these findings for language abilities and emotional experiences are interesting, given that at times silence or no-verbal speech could provide some time for reflection and deepening one's self-awareness.

Given Hatcher et al.'s findings, perhaps for girls, increased amounts of silence or quiet solitude may promote the understanding of other's inner lives as com-pared to furthering one's private world. In contrast, perhaps for boys, quiet times may promote the development of self-awareness and self-knowledge. Given the expanding focus on gender and education to include gender-role perceptions and orientations (Noddings, 1984, 2006; Weaver-Hightower, 2003), researchers will need to continue to explore the gendered implications language holds for children's emotional understanding.

Likewise, implicitly supportive evidence derived from investigations that sug-gest that a heightened awareness and understanding of the mental states and feelings of others may have negative consequences for later psychoemotional func-tioning, which may differ according to gender (Boden & Berenbaum, 2007). For example, research with young adults have found that females have higher levels of emotional awareness than males (Boden & Berenbaum, 2007; Parker, Taylor, & Bagby, 2003). For example, longitudinal studies investigating gender differences in developmental models of depression have found that as young girls, depressed adolescent females were more concerned with maintaining interpersonal relationships, more able to recognize the feelings of others, and more likely to include moral issues in their play patterns than boys (Block, Gjerde, & Block, 1991; Gjerde & Block, 1991).

Further supportive evidence derives from the literature on the socialization of empathy and guilt, which suggests that high levels of empathy and guilt may serve as precursors for later depression in women (Bybee, 1998; Zahn-Waxler et al., 1991; Zahn-Waxler & Robinson, 1995). Similarly, in a study of 115 preadolescent girls and boys (8- to 12-years-old), Fraser and Strayer (1997) found that the most robust correlation between sensitivity and shame existed among the older girls (11- to 12-year-olds). Hence, such studies may suggest that a high level of interpersonal sensitivity including the ability to be aware of, and concerned with the psychological and emotional needs of others, may have negative implications for children's psychological and emotional development, especially if such high sensitivity leads to the possible detriment to their own psychological and emotional needs (Park & Park, 1997; Silverstein & Perlick, 1995).

In sum, what do the past gendered findings on social cognition among children and adolescents tell us about their emotional experiences in the classroom? Based on the findings described above, compared to boys, adolescent females may be more likely to engage in solitary, social-relational activities that may affect their emotional experiences in the classroom. Compared to adolescent males, adolescent females may also be more likely to engage in thinking about the inner worlds of others rather than their own (Hatcher et al., 1990). Drawing on this research, given that the emotional health of the child is developing during middle childhood, researchers need to explore the implications of the gendered connections between children's emotional experiences and their psychological development and functioning for the grade school classroom.

Accordingly, connections between works on feminist epistemologies and psychoeducational research provide a valuable starting point for investigating the roles in which emotions may play in the children's understanding of self and other, and how this may influence their emotional experiences and social interactions within the classroom (e.g., Belenky et al., 1986; Brown & Gilligan, 1993; Debold, Tolman, & Brown, 1996; Pope 2001). Definitions and assessments of the processes that enable children and adolescents to understand social situations may offer some insight on gender-related research findings. Such a research agenda may help to illustrate the wealth of findings from social-emotional studies that show around the age of 11, some girls (in contrast to boys) experience a significant decrease in positive feelings and thoughts of self-worth (e.g., Harter, 1999), an increase in self-consciousness (e.g., Simmons, Rosenberg, & Rosenberg, 1973), and an increasingly negative sense of self-worth despite high academic achievement, particularly among "gifted girls" (e.g., Silverstein & Perlick, 1995; Winner, 2000). Research on emotions understanding and its links to self-concept and social relations may help to further examine the question of why girls may be more at risk than boys to lose their sense of self or "inner voice" during early adolescence (Brown & Gilligan, 1992; Harter, 1999). Finally, we as educators aim to understand gendered emotional experiences within the classroom, research programs and educational applications that explore gender in complex and interrelated ways, by looking beyond issues of gender inequity to examining problematic definitions of femininity and masculinity (Bussey & Bandura, 2004; Hammack, 2005; Weaver-Hightower, 2003).

The cognitive-developmental framework conceptualizes children's developing relations to their own emotional understanding and experience in terms of the goal of emotional self-regulation. That is, the endpoint of development is identified with the capacity for successful control or containment of emotion through self-understanding and the capacity for behavioral self-restraint. Hall (1986) stresses the significant role language plays in the child's successful development of self-control. Advocating that the child be encouraged to use words to "master strong emotions," Hall infers a progression from directly acting on the impulses generated by strong feelings of self-control through clarifying, tolerating, and containing feelings through language. Although Hall's writing is based on work with pre-schoolers, the underlying concepts of his theory can be applied to all ages, and may be especially relevant to middle childhood and early adolescence, given that middle childhood is a sensitive time for identity development. Of particular relevance to middle childhood may be the strong psychocultural gender-typed messages received by our youth regarding which emotions to display and/or experience based on gender.

For example, as Maccoby (1988) suggests, across various cultures, girls are still expected to comply, smile, and not show anger, whereas boys are expected to not be caring, and to be free to express anger and pride. Overall, stereotypic societal messages concerning gender-roles continue to be created and perpetuated by modern society.

Doing emotion the "right" way, which is often a gendered way, serves as verification of the authenticity of the self. Not "I feel, therefore I am," but "I feel as I believe I ought to, therefore I am the person I believe I am." Gender may be marked by any of the other major categories of social identity such as age, class, or racial ethnicity, as well as other distinctive features such as attractiveness, status, developmental exceptionalities, and so forth. Overall, the combination of gender and emotion is a potent identifier, and when we talk about the multiple components of an individual's identity, gender is always implicated.

Despite recent investigations of gender differences in social-cognitive (Hughes & Dunn, 1998; Maccoby, 1998), results from such studies remain contradictory and inconclusive. Regarding mental-state understanding, as outlined earlier in this chapter, some studies have shown girls to possess higher levels of ToM and emotion understanding (e.g., Bosacki, 2003; Bosacki & Astington, 1999; Cutting & Dunn, 1999). In contrast, other studies have found either that boys possess higher levels of emotion understanding than girls (Laible & Thompson, 1998) or no gender differences (Astington & Jenkins, 1995). Unlike the research on psychological understanding, the self-concept literature has shown that in general, girls report lower levels of self-worth than boys (see Harter, 1999). Given the link between gender, understanding others, and self-worth (Finders, 1997; Hatcher et al., 1990; Veith, 1980), surprisingly little is known about these connections during middle childhood and early adolescence. Relatedly, some researchers suggest that gender differences need to be investigated in terms of interaction effects between biological sex and gender role (Geary, 1998). To support this view, results from my postdoctoral work with preschoolers showed parents' gender-role perceptions of stereotypic feminine behavior were related to high levels of emotion understanding in both girls and boys (Bosacki & Moore, 2004). Furthermore, a strong positive association was found between receptive language ability and emotional understanding for boys only.

Such links remain to be examined in middle school–aged children and adolescents in relation to psychological understanding and language. For example, regarding children in middle childhood, why do girls talk more about emotions than boys and how does this preference relate to the preschool findings? Is there a reason why boys are more "silent" about emotions in their conversations? Does a reliance on language competence influence the ability to develop and express emotion language? Or do adolescents feel silenced by their peers, teachers, and parents? In any case, although research on boys has increased during the past decade (Weaver-Hightower, 2003), further research is needed on the gendered emotional life and the sociocultural context of literacy among adolescents.

Given the lack of research on this area, the few studies on self-conscious, social emotions in children reveal contradictory findings. For example, compared to boys, girls have been found to exhibit a greater expression of pride (i.e., girls showed more positive expressions after success than boys) (Stipek, Recchia, & McClintic,

1992), and express greater emotional regulation and displays of shame and guilt (Kochanska, 1994). In contrast, some studies have failed to find such gender differences regarding emotions of pride, shame, and guilt (Griffin, 1995). Accordingly, given the complex interrelations among emotion expression, emotion regulation, and emotion understanding (Denham, 1998; Fridja, 1986), more research is needed regarding how children experience emotions in schools, especially given their ability to understand self-conscious emotions and how such understandings may be connected to children's language development and self-concept within the classroom.

Given that according to some developmentalists (Denham, 1999; Harris, 1989; Harris et al., 1987; Saarni, 1999), cultural influence and emotion understanding are inseparable, how might emotion scripts merge with gender-role socialization? Given that the specific focus on the nature of the self is an extension of the ideas of many emotion theorists (e.g., see Frijda, 1986), emotions arise when events are relevant to the individual's concerns. Lutz (1988) contends that emotions reflect commitment to viewing the world in a particular way and refers to "what is culturally defined and experienced as intensely meaningful" (p. 8). These concerns and commitments converge in a view of self that structures ongoing experiences and the very nature of emotional experience.

According to the self-socialization hypothesis (Maccoby, 1998), during the preschool years, gender differences begin to increase among girls and boys due to parental pressure to conform to traditional gender-role stereotypes. For example, as mentioned earlier, research has shown that traditional gender-role behavior and ascription (i.e., femininity = sociality, submissiveness; masculinity = autonomy, aggression) categorize the ability to be empathetic and emotionally expressive as a feminine characteristic (Harter, 1999; Tavris, 1992). Maccoby contends that children self-socialize their behavior by means of having their actual thoughts and emotion scripts socialized or shaped by their parent's expectations.

Following this gender-role development during the early years, as mentioned earlier, according to the gender intensification process (Hill & Lynch, 1983), the next pivotal transition time occurs during late childhood and early adolescence (approximately 8 to 12 years of age). According to the gender intensification process, preadolescents may become exposed to the increase in societal expectations to follow stereotypic notions of femininity and masculinity. Given Maccoby's (1988) claim that children self-socialize their actions in part by means of having their emotion and mental scripts socialized or shaped by their parent's expectations, peers and teachers may also help to shape children's ability to develop a sense of self and to help them create multiple roles for themselves within different contexts.

Gender differences in self-conception, emotional understanding, and social behavior, then, may reflect differences in children's stereotypic gender-role ascriptions such as femininity and masculinity in contrast to differences in biological sex (Harter et al., 1998). That is, guided by their own self-scripts that have been co-constructed through social interactions with their parents and others (e.g., siblings, peers, teachers), children's self-perceived emotional competencies and social behavior may reflect gender-role stereotypes, resulting in observable gender differences. Thus, the process of learning to understand one's emotional world within a social context may be contingent upon the way in which a child's gendered self-conception or identity interacts with her/his environment, in contrast to a child's biological sex (Maccoby, 1998). That is, the types of "audiences" children choose to "present" to, or perform for, may influence how they see themselves and behave (e.g., Brody, 2001; Harre, 1986). Therefore, parents and teachers who endorse stereotypic gender-role expectations may have an indirect influence on the development of a child's social-cognitive abilities, including her or his emotion understanding.

As Bruner (1996) suggests, "School judges the child's performance, and the child responds by evaluating herself in turn" (p. 37). That is, how does a child learn to incorporate the judgment of "other" (school) into the development of a sense of self-worth and self-judgment—and what implication does this have for emotional experiences in the classroom (personal and social)? Moreover, how does a child develop the motivation or ability to self-reflect including both praise and criticism, and how is self-criticism and self-imposed standards such as perfectionism related to children's emotional experiences within the classroom?

Similar to describing adolescents' experiences of silence (Bosacki, 2005), we can also draw on Goffman's (1959) metaphor of theatrical performance as a framework for exploring the children's emotional experiences within the classroom, as self-presentation differs according to the particular "audience" that the self performs to, or the particular context within which the performance occurs. Within the context of the school experiences of the grade school child, given that the self is co-constructed with others (Bruner, 1996), researchers and educators need to ask to what extent does the child's onstage character, or the self that they present or express to others (presenting self) connect with the backstage character (or the authentic self)? Also, in what way does the child choose to represent her or his inner, emotional world on stage? That is, to what kind of audience will children choose to share (or not share) their thoughts and emotions using speech, movement, dance, song, etc.? Also, what kinds of audiences may create fear or a sense of being judged by others in children? How can some audiences lead some children to feel vulnerable or exposed so that they may inhibit or decide to not perform in front of others, and thus may choose to remain silent or to withdraw backstage? In contrast, what kind of audience creates an atmosphere of psychological acceptance and safety that allows children to learn how to express their "authentic selves?"

As discussed earlier in this chapter, given the crucial role parents and teachers play in both the gender-role socialization and co-construction of children's linguistic and social-cognitive and emotional abilities (Denham, 1998; Haden et al., 1997), surprisingly few researchers have studied the links between adults' and peers' perceptions of gender role and children's emotion understanding and language ability. Regarding parents' and teachers' socialization of children's emotion understanding, the majority of studies have either (1) investigated parent-child conversations and not parental beliefs or (2) have studied parent's beliefs and expectations of their children's emotional development but not of gender-role behavior (Hughes, Deater-Deckard, & Cutting, 1999).

Although the majority of past research has shown that parents' beliefs and expectations about children's emotional development are in part gender specific (Brody & Hall, 1993), findings on parents-child emotion talk are mixed. Some researchers have shown that mothers tend to talk more about emotions with young girls and focus more on emotion labels, and that both mothers and fathers reminisce more about emotions with daughters than with sons, and girls tend to include more emotion in their reminiscing than do boys (Fivush & Haden, 2005). Whereas for boys, research suggests that parents tend to focus more on the causes or explanations of emotions, and talk about emotions less overall (Fivush, 1989, 2000). In contrast, others have found no differences (Denham, Cook, & Zoller, 1992).

For example, in a study of narrative structure in parent-child reminiscing (Haden et al., 1997), 40-month-old girls were found to produce more emotion words than boys, despite the fact that no gender differences were found in general vocabulary ability, and that fathers and mothers did not differ in how they structured past narratives. Current research investigates the possibility that gender-related differences in parent-child reminiscing may lead girls to have a more embellished and nuanced subjective perspective on the past and on themselves than do boys (Fivush & Haden, 2005). Thus, researchers continue to explore the role child-parent talk, especially joint parent-child reminiscing, plays in shaping children's ability to co-construct a subjective sense of self or a subjective perspective on their personal past based on how they thought, felt, and reacted to past life events (Fivush, 2000, 2004).

2.5. Summary

Despite the increasing research interest in children's emotional lives, in general, the empirical evidence concerning gender-related differences in children's emotional worlds remains inconsistent and fairly scarce (especially concerning children's understanding of complex emotions). In brief, past research has found females to outperform males in emotion understanding tasks in young children (Cutting & Dunn, 1999; Parent et al., 1999), middle school–aged children and adolescents (Bybee, 1998), and adults (Brody & Hall, 1993). Although researchers suggest that girls seem to internalize earlier and more comprehensively, the message that our emotions play important roles in our social and personal lives, some studies have found either no gender differences in emotion understanding (Banerjee & Yuill, 1999), or that school-aged boys outperform girls (Laible & Thompson, 1998). In sum, findings from emotion understanding and gender in younger children can help to inform researchers' explorations of children's emotional experiences within the classroom.

3

Research Context and Methodology: Where and How?

3.1. Introduction and Tradition of Inquiry

Given the need to investigate the rich and complex emotional lives of children within the classroom, I chose a mixed method approach which would help me to develop "a complex" picture of social phenomenon such as the emotional worlds (Green & Carfacelli, 1997, [p. 7] cited in Creswell, 2005, [p. 510]). This research design is a procedure for collecting, analyzing, and "mixing" both quantitative and qualitative data and according to Brewer and Hunter (1989), it is a "legitimate inquiry approach." (p. 28). As the following section describes, I collected both qualitative and quantitative data simultaneously to provide a more comprehensive picture of children's emotional experiences within the classroom. The following sections describe the details of the research including the research sites, participants, and data collection sources.

3.2. The Present Study: Design and Procedure

Surprisingly little research exists on school-aged children regarding gender-related linkages among children's drawings of play, and their understandings of self and other (Willats, 2005). As noted above, given this gap in the literature, the present study focused on the role that gender plays in children's drawings of self and play and self-perceptions. To explore the emotional landscape of children's personal worlds within the school context (Denham et al., 2003), an investigation of emotional competencies in school-aged girls and boys may help to illustrate the gendered relations among play, meaning making, and self-perceptions.

Although the associations between social cognitions and social behavior in childhood are well established (e.g., Denham, 1998), children's emotion understanding and its intrapersonal correlates remain under-explored. Various conceptual mechanisms may underlie this association between social cognitions and self-perceptions. For example, it may be possible that socioemotional deficits or biases may be differentially associated with low levels of self-esteem. Regarding socioemotional understanding, the present study examined one set of skills referred to as emotion understanding that consists of children's ability to use emotion words or labels (Denham, 1998; Saarni, 1999), and children's understanding of their own and others' situational determinants of emotions or their causal theories. Socioemotional competencies exhibited through socially competent behaviors were also examined as reported by the teachers.

Following ethical clearance from the university and school board, written permission was obtained from the participating schools including the principals, teachers, and the participants' parents/guardians. Only those children who received written parental permission and who also provided verbal assent participated in the study. As part of larger, multidimensional study, the present research focused on some tasks that were administered during the first school visit. More specifically, this present study consisted of a group, in-class session in which children were group administered within the classroom a pencil-and-paper self-report questionnaire regarding self-perceptions, gender-role perceptions, and the self-and-play drawing task. Participating classroom teachers completed teacher rating forms of children's socioemotional competencies. All tasks were administered within the regular classroom during the school day by experienced researchers, myself included. In collaboration with the participating school principal and classroom teachers, our research team aimed to incorporate the research into the everyday routine of the classroom activities. As suggested by Richer (1990), this "natural" incorporation was aimed to minimize the anxiety sometimes associated with the administration of projective instrument (see Rabin, 1986). Consistent with conducting respectful research (Tilley, 1998), throughout the research process, children were reminded that their responses would remain confidential, and that they had the opportunity to ask questions or stop at any time during the research process.

3.3. Research Sites

I chose to conduct this research in two schools that shared a similar geographical location within Canada, but compared to one another, differed in the school population. Although overall, both schools were mainly English-speaking, and of Euro-Canadian heritage with varied socioeconomic status, compared to School 1, School 2 had a larger student population with the majority of the student population speaking English as their first language. Collecting data at two separate sites enabled me to see that children had similar concerns about their emotional lives at school that transcended the differences in the student population.

3.4. Participants

Taken from a larger longitudinal study that included 91 children (52 females, M = 6y, 4m; 39 males, M = 6y; 3m) and their teachers (N = 20,18 females) (see Bosacki, 2005a, for further details), the research discussed in this book focuses on the emotional lives of six children (3 girls, 3 boys) during the years 2003–2007, following the children from Grades 1 and 2 (ages six to seven years), through to Grades 4 and 5 (ages nine—to ten years). From the larger sample, these six children (3 girls, 3 boys) were chosen based on their total teacher rating score social competence as reflecting the highest socially withdrawn or shy score.

Participants engaged in the research tasks twice each year, once during autumn followed by a visit in late winter, early spring. Upon receiving ethics clearance from the university ethics review committee and the school board authorities, children were recruited from the two schools as described above. Only those children who received written informed consent from their parents and who also provided verbal assent participated in the study.

3.5. Procedures and Data Sources

My interest was solely with children's emotional and mental worlds, that is, my research question aimed to explore how children constructed meaning of their world, and what language they used to create and describe their worlds. My decision to use an interpretive research design was based in part on Alder and Moulton's (1998) claim that an interpretive research design is used when "research takes place in a natural setting and researchers want to know about meaning-making and the points of views and particular people in particular settings," (p. 17). This research explored the children's perspectives and emotions as they negotiated the psychological, social, and emotional terrain of childhood within the elementary school. As outlined in the sections below, this research involved various data-collection activities including children's drawings, interviews including story-based tasks, paper and pencil self-report questionnaires, and teacher ratings. This book will focus on the six children only, and the findings are focused on the interviews and tasks concerning emotions and self-understanding only. For further details regarding the larger sample see Bosacki, Varnish, and Akseer (2006).

Research Activities (Data Sources)

Overview of Drawing and Story-telling Interview Method

Children's drawing, mental state understanding, and language

According to Willats (2005), if we as researchers and educators are to make sense of child art and children's drawings, we have to understand what these rules are and the cognitive and emotional processes underlying how children learn to draw. Research on the development of child's drawing, language, and self has been filled with contradictions and inconsistencies, particularly the assumption that children draw what they know, and that adults draw what they see (e.g., Piaget, 1963). However, as Willats (2005) points out, this statement is not that clear and simple. That is, children learn to draw in similar ways to how they learn a language, by acquiring increasingly complex and effective drawing rules. Children use rules creatively, making infinite use of finite means. Learning to draw is like learning a language, and thus, one of the major cognitive achievements of the childhood involves children learn to draw.

For example, past research shows that in the early childhood years, from about the ages of two to six or seven, children reveal these emotions with respect to artistic activities, play, and explorations of nature. For example, according to Willats (2005), children go through a period from about five to seven years of age, when their drawings are fresh, lively, and well organized. As mentioned by Willats (2005), some adult artists have claimed to capture the art "attitude" of the young child (see Willats 2005 for a detailed description of past research on children's drawings).

After the age of approximately seven years, research shows that children are better able to handle academic work, but they still think most enthusiastically when they are engaged in concrete or collaborative projects. As Dewey (1966) notes, children learn by doing, and later elementary and middle school children work and enjoy creative projects and activities such as building things, drawing, role playing, gardening, and so on.

According to some cognitive developmentalists who explore cognition and drawing, drawing and intention are related (e.g., Bloom, 2004; Gardner, 1985, 1991). We draw with an idea of an audience, or with the idea of being aware of what other people might think about, or how they will judge our drawings. Therefore, we should expect perhaps negative relations between socioemotional understanding and related mental-state-understanding variables. That is, this would perhaps explain why some children with autism spectrum disorder draw exceptionally well, however, they often score relatively lower on emotional and mental-state-understanding tasks as compared to normally developing children (e.g., Frith, 1989). This could also explain in part why most children are more likely to draw more freely and spontaneously during young childhood. However, according to many developmentalists and researchers (e.g., Gardner, 1991; Malchiodi, 1990), this ability may decrease once they reach the ages of eight—to ten and beyond (Malchiodi, 1998).

As mentioned in chapter 2, Cutting and Dunn (2002) found that children who were more likely to understand the mental states and emotions of others, were also more likely to understand, and be sensitive to teacher criticism. Thus, perhaps children who are not aware of others' imagined mental worlds are less likely to imagine any negative feedback and/or judgments, and thus may have fewer psychological barriers as they draw. Furthermore, they may also be less likely to engage in self-criticism and be more accepting of the work that they produce, which is also something that we explored in our study. As I explain later on in the chapter, six months after they produced their drawings, we interviewed children and showed them their drawings and asked them if they were happy or satisfied with their drawings, and if they had a chance to change their drawings – would they change it – in what way would they change it, and why.

Building on the work of Cutting and Dunn (2002), perhaps children who are more aware of other's mental states may be more likely to state that they are not happy with their drawings, and if given the opportunity, they would in some way change their drawing. As a researcher, I was interested in exploring how our social awareness or our understanding of other people's emotional experiences may either help or hinder how we think and feel about ourselves. I will discuss this issue in Chapter 4 when I discuss some current research findings.

Children's drawings and understanding mental states: Gendered relations

Given that gender values and beliefs of adults, peers, and mass media influence children's sense of gender-roles, and that their gender-related beliefs may be reflected in their drawings and descriptions, little research has explored the gendered nature of children's drawings (Anning & Ring, 2004). The few existing studies show that children's spontaneous drawings (ages three to ten years) reveal that boys' drawings tend to reveal concerns for actions of violence and destruction, machinery and sports contests, whereas girls depicted more tranquil scenes of family life, landscapes, and children at play. Research findings suggest that boys are more likely to depict exploits, conflict and displays of power and motion, whereas girls are more likely to draw happy girls and small animals, and draw smaller, more controlled diagrams, particularly regarding emotional content (Burkitt, Barrett, & Davis, 2003; Dyson, 2000; Thomas & Silk, 1990).

Gardner's (1982) work with children and art activity revealed that girls are more likely than boys to excel in mixed media, symbolic play, narrations and three-dimensional forms, whereas boys are more likely to excel with clay or single-medium tasks. Gardner also found that boys are more likely than girls to represent a certain character or superhero such as Batman, whereas girls are more likely to represent themes of fairy tales including animals such as princesses on horses (Golomb, 1990). Overall, the few studies on gender-related differences in drawings suggests that girls and boys produce different kinds of drawings, particularly in the areas of size and content of drawings (e.g., Burkitt et al., 2003; Goldberg, 1997; Koppitz, 1969).

In addition to studies that investigated children's spontaneous drawings and other art products, some studies have focused specifically on self-portraits, including the context of play. For example, Malchiodi's (1990) work with youth and their self-portraits showed that males were more likely to draw themselves in action, and to depict motion, whereas adolescent females were more likely to portray either their heads or full-body portraits. Similarly, Richer's (1990) study on both Canadian and Polish children's drawings of themselves playing, showed that across both cultures, girls were more likely than boys to draw their faces, and often showing expressions of happy emotions, whereas boys were less likely to draw the face, preferring to depict action or motion pictures.

Despite the recent interest in children's drawings, the majority of researchers interested in exploring gender differences in children's drawings have only (1) investigated children's drawings of self, but not within the context of play (Gardner, 1982; Golomb, 1990; Malchiodi, 1990; Silver, 1997), or (2) investigated teachers' beliefs and expectations of their children's emotional development, but not the connections to drawing and stories of self and play or (3) investigated the connections between children's drawings of self and play, but without focusing on the middle childhood years and without focusing on the connections between their self-perceived competencies or teacher-rated social competencies (Richer, 1990). Overall, to date, there remains a gap in the literature concerning research on the gendered relations between children's sense of self and play through self-stories and drawings, and whether these abilities are connected to their socioemotional competencies.

During the following story-telling semi-structured interviews, although the interviews were semi-structured and provided some guidance to the field of inquiry (Fontana & Frey, 1994), I attempted to incorporate some aspects of van Manen's (1990) suggestion to maintain a certain openness that helped me to choose directions and explore techniques, procedures, and sources that emerged throughout the research process. This allowed me to be flexible in the sense that although the interviews provided some structure to the conversations, I was still able to follow some topics or directions that emerged from the interviews that asked to be explored (from the participants' understanding). This semi-interpretivist approach helped me to both provide some structure to the conversations, but also allowed a varying degree of flexibility in the sense that the interviewees were able to partially guide the line of questioning. Thus, given that interpretive theory views schools as places where meaning is constructed through the social interaction of peoples (Bennett & LeCompte, 1990), I viewed all of the research activities as necessary pieces of the research puzzle, as all components allowed me the opportunity to become involved in the participants' daily lives at school and to document their actions within a social context.

Children's Drawings. Given the lack of data on children's perceptions of emotions, play, and self-assessment through drawings in the classroom context, we choose to incorporate a task which asked the children to draw a picture of themselves playing. To provide pictorial, nonverbal data on the children's conceptions of self and play, each child was provided with an 8" × 11" blank piece of paper, with a box of eight crayons and was asked to draw a colored picture of themselves playing, and then to provide a written brief narrative description. Following Richer (1990), to allow for maximum spontaneity and originality, the verbal instructions were brief, "Draw a picture of yourself playing and when you are finished, draw a circle around yourself. When you are finished, write a short story describing your picture." This task assesses a child's subjective self-view and adds to the verbal self-understanding interview and questionnaire in that it provided pictorial data.

Self-Narrative Task. Based on Engel's (1999) work on children's autobiographies, in this task, about five to six months after the original drawing activity took place, we showed the child her/his self-portrait and accompanying story from the previous fall session, and asked her/him to either explain the picture, or if they would like, to change their picture or story and explain the changes. Some questions focused on the inclusion/omission of verbal content in the drawings, and we asked the children to explain their reasoning for their drawing decisions.

Emotion Understanding Puppet-Interview. To assess emotion understanding (i.e., understanding of emotion labels and emotional explanations, or the ability to explain why people experience emotions), four brief vignettes that consisted of stereotypical emotion-eliciting social situations were created. We borrowed from (1) theoretical works that claim that verbal report is a credible index of preschoolers' emotion experience (Denham, 1998), and (2) studies that have explored emotion understanding in young children through the use of puppet-interviews (Cassidy, Ross, Butkovsky, & Braungart, 1992; Dunn & Hughes, 1998). This task was designed to assess children's ability to discern meaning from stories about emotion labels and the determinants of emotional situations (see Bosacki & Moore, 2004 for details and story protocol). The puppet task or interview involved two stories for simple or basic emotions (happiness, sadness) and two stories for complex or self-conscious emotions (pride, embarrassment). These emotions were chosen based on their use in past research (Capps et al., 1992; Seider et al., 1988) and on the fact that the two sets of emotions are matched for valence but are cognitively differentiated (happy-proud; sad-embarrassed). As a result, we could examine empirically the assumption that children's emotion understanding becomes more differentiated.

Before each puppet task began, the researcher introduced the child to the puppet as the researcher's friend who is interested in learning about how girls and boys feel. The researcher then explained that the puppet would be reading the story and asking the questions. Once the child was given the opportunity to ask any questions, the puppet would read each story which consisted of stereotypical scenario (e.g., dropped an ice-cream cone for sadness). Following each story, the children were asked three questions (a mixture of forced choice and open-ended). The first question assessed children's emotion-labeling ability or their knowledge of emotion words (How do you think Millie (cat puppet) feels?) If children did not respond, they were asked to make a choice between the two emotions at the appropriate complexity level (e.g., simple emotions: Does Grover feel happy or sad?, complex emotions: Does Grover feel proud or embarrassed?) The order of the forced choice was counterbalanced across stories. Following emotion labeling, two open-ended questions assessed children's understanding of what would cause such an emotion in themselves, followed by what would cause such an emotion in those of their peers (What kind of things make you feel happy? Pretend that you saw your friend looking happy, why do you think s/he would look happy?). Based on past research in both social and emotional understanding (e.g., Capps et al., 1992; Dunn, Maguire, & Brown, 1995), stories were presented in a fixed order (simple before complex), with the order of emotions counterbalanced for each level of complexity (happy/sad for simple; proud/embarrassed for complex). Question order was also fixed across all stories, emotion labeling first, followed by self and peer explanation, with self explanations always appearing before peer.

Conceptions of self. To assess the relations between language and the self-system, children were asked questions about their sense of self and their perceptions and attitudes toward their emotional experiences within the classroom. Children were asked to describe two aspects of the self, self-agency or the subjective aspect of self, and self-evaluation or the objective aspect of self (Bruner, 1996; Damon & Hart, 1988). Building on the research of Damon and Hart (1988), Harter (1999), and others, to assess the subjective self, questions from past research and my past work with preschoolers and preadolescents (see Bosacki & Moore, 2005; Lagattuta, Nucci, & Bosacki, 2007), the questions explored how children make sense of their self-continuity, agency, and distinctiveness or uniqueness. All interviews were audiotaped and then transcribed for data analysis.

Ambiguous Social Narrative Task. Adapted from my past research (Bosacki, 1998; Bosacki & Astington, 1999; see Bosacki, 2005b for further details regarding the stories), children listened to two short stories that described an ambiguous social situation within the school peer context with three peers of the same sex in each story (female story/male story). For example, one scenario describes a social situation where two girls who are friends see a new girl in the school play yard and decide to approach her:

> Nancy and Margie are watching the children in the playground. Without saying a word, Nancy nudges Margie and looks across the playground at the new girl swinging on the swingset. Then Nancy looks back at Margie and smiles. Margie nods, and the two of them start off toward the girl at the swingset. The new girl sees the strange girl walk towards her. She'd seen them nudging and smiling at each other. Although they are in her class, she has never spoken to them before. The new girl wonders what they could want.
>
> —Bosacki, 2005b, p. 177

In the scenario with the boys, two boys who are on a soccer team need to choose one more player to join the team and they see one another boy who has not yet been chosen for the team sports:

> Kenny and Mark are co-captains of the soccer team. They have one person left to choose for the team. Without saying a word, Mark winks at Kenny and looks at Tom who is one of the last children left to be chosen. Mark looks back at Kenny and smiles. Kenny nods and chooses Tom to be on their team. Tom sees Mark and Kenny winking and smiling at each other. Tom, who is usually one of the last to be picked for team sports, wonders why Kenny wants him to be on his team.
>
> —Bosacki, 2005b, p. 175

Both stories do not include any verbal dialogue, nonverbal communication only, and both deal with a situation where two peers who are already friends need to decide whether or not to include a third person. During the interview, children listen to the researcher read ambiguous scenarios and enact the story through the use of dolls. Following the story, children were asked to share their thoughts with the researcher regarding their thoughts as to what they think is happening in the story and to predict what will happen next. All interviews were audiotaped and then later transcribed for analysis as I describe further in Chapter 4.

Social and Self-Communication. In addition, adapted from my recent work on classroom silence (Bosacki, 2005b), some children were also asked their interpretations of, and preferences for silences within a social setting. To explore children's thoughts on communicating with others as they approach preadolescence (ages nine to ten years), we asked children to think about their role in the process of talking and listening within different contexts such as friends and family. Similar to the other social narrative tasks, the children were individually interviewed and the conversations were audiotaped for later transcription and analysis. We asked the children the following questions:

> Would you call yourself or think of yourself as more of a "talker" or a "listener?" (with friends/family) Why?
>
> Are listening and talking the same thing? If not, how are they different?
> 1. When you are talking with someone, how do you know that s/he is listening to you?
> 2. What evidence would make you think that s/he are listening to you? For example, what are the clues or signs that help you think that s/he ids listening to you?
> 3. How do you feel when you think that s/he is listening to you? What are you thinking?
> 4. How do you think s/he feels when she/he listens to you? What do you think s/he is thinking?

Questions 1–4 were repeated for someone *not* listening (e.g., When you are talking with someone, how do you know that s/he is *not* listening to you?)

Vocabulary Ability

To assess children's receptive vocabulary ability, children were administered the Peabody Picture Vocabulary Test (PPVT-III; Dunn & Dunn, 1997). This test requires children to point to one of four drawings that correctly illustrate vocabulary items spoken by the researcher. High correlations have been found to exist between the PPVT-III and verbal components of standardized intelligence tests. The PPVT-III is frequently used in developmental and educational research.

Socioemotional Maturity (Teacher Ratings)

Due to the limited research found on the links between teachers' perceptions of children's social and emotional behaviors, For the purpose of this study, I created a teacher rating scale of emotional maturity of school-aged children, based on Denham's (1998) characterization of emotional competence (Children's Emotional Competence Scale for Teachers—CECS-T). In particular, teachers completed a 12-item rating scale of children's behavior within the classroom (e.g., "this child understands others' emotional states such as knowing that the teacher's smile as she comes in to the classroom means that she is feeling happy"; Cronbach's alpha = 0.88) (see Bosacki, 2005a for further details).

3.6. Summary of Data Collection and Data Analysis

Consistent with Malchiodi's (1998) description of taking a phenomenological approach to exploring children's drawings in particular, I looked at children's drawings with an emphasis on an openness to a variety of meanings, the context in which they were created, and the artist's way of viewing the world. It is a way of understanding children's expressive work from many perspectives, allowing the viewer to acknowledge the images and construct meanings from more than one vantage point and to develop a more integral view of children's art expressions. Thus, similar to Malchiodi (1998)'s phenomenological approach, I aimed to take a stance of "not knowing" and viewed my role as a researcher as a co-creator rather than an expert researcher/advisor. Thus, throughout the entire research process, the children are viewed as the expert, and I serve as the guiding co-creator.

As Malchidoi (1998) explains, viewing the child participant as an expert on her or his experiences, I was able to approach the research with an openness to new information and discoveries. Although art expressions may share some commonalities in form, content, and style, taking a stance of not knowing allowed the child's experiences of creating and making art expressions to be respected as an individual and to have a variety of meanings. A phenomenological approach also provided me with the opportunity to acknowledge different aspects of growth that are linked to art expression, including cognitive abilities, emotional development, interpersonal skills, and developmental maturity and thus, this multiplicity of meaning provided me with material for developing my relationship with the participants as a researcher, as well as provided me with the opportunity to truly understand all levels of meaning and to allow for the possibility of "multimeaning."

To explore individual differences, building on previous research (e.g., Richer, 1990), the content of the drawings and stories were analyzed qualitatively for themes such as type of play (physical = 1/non-physical activities = 2, competitive = 1 autotelic or solitary = 2, cooperative = 3), setting (1 = classroom, 2 = home, 3 = playground/outdoors), number of characters, verbal content (1 = no verbal content, 2 = voice bubbles), emotional facial expressions of characters in the drawings (1 = sad, 2 = neutral or no expression, 3 = happy, 4 [playmates' expressions only, e.g., one happy, one sad friend, and external objects {1 = natural, e.g., sun/grass, 2 = cats/dogs 3 = play materials, e.g., ball/skipping rope} = building/house/school/pool, 5 = no external objects). In addition to the macrolevel codes of physical/non-physical, specific activities depicted in the drawings were also noted including activities such as skipping, playing ball, and playing with pets. The number of characters portrayed in the drawings were also recorded. All drawings ($N = 88$) were coded by an independent second rater. Kappas for the various categories of codes ranged from 0.80 to 1.00, suggesting relatively high inter-rater reliability.

Coding of Emotion Understanding Puppet Interview. Based on interview transcripts, a coding scheme was developed to obtain a total emotion understanding score. The questions for each story were grouped into four categories that represented the four emotions (happy, sad, proud, and embarrassed). Responses were coded according to conceptual sophistication, agency, and theme. The level of emotion understanding was coded according to the conceptual complexity of the responses. Thus, the coding of the responses reflected the child's ability to understand emotional-psychological worlds, moving from the simple, obvious ("surface") characteristics to the integration of multiple and paradoxical perspectives. Based on past research (Capps et al., 1992; Carroll & Steward, 1984; Denham, 1998; Hughes & Dunn, 1998; Russell & Paris, 1994), responses for each emotion were coded according to their accurateness (emotional labeling) and their level of conceptual sophistication (understanding of emotional situations, or of what causes emotions for both self and peers). Responses for emotion labeling were coded on a 4-point scale: 0 = no response, don't know, refusal; 1 = correct valence but incorrect forced choice (e.g., for the happy story, a response to "How does Grover feel?," a spontaneous response of "good" followed by choosing the forced choice option of "sad"); 2 = correct valence and correct forced choice (e.g., for the proud story, a response to "How does Grover feel?" spontaneous response of "happy" followed by choosing the forced choice option of "proud"); 3 = correct spontaneous response (i.e., no prompts required).

Responses to the emotion explanation were scored on a 3-point scale for both self and peers. 0 = no response, don't know, refusal. 1 = appropriate and plausible response but a general, broad explanation that includes one word or a simple clause such as "presents" for happy, or reference to a broad type of experience such as "I'm proud when I do something good." 2 = relevant appropriate response that includes appropriate sentence responses referring to specific instances such an identified time and place such as "I'm happy when I draw with my mom," or that include detail to suggest that she or he had a particular experience in mind such as "I'm proud when I wash dishes by myself." Each question received one score that corresponded to the highest complexity level achieved.

Inter-rater reliability analysis on 38% of the transcripts for the complexity level showed an average Cohen's kappa of 0.92 across the four emotions. Cronbach's alpha for the 12-item aggregate score (three items per emotion: emotion label, emotion situation knowledge for self and peer) was 0.78. For each emotion, scores were summed to result in the maximum total score of 7. Scores were also summed across emotions for a total emotion labeling and explanation score for both the simple and complex emotions (ranges 0–6; 0–8), an overall total emotion labeling score (range 0–12), and a total emotion explanation score (range 0–16). Aggregate scores were also created by summing across the emotion label and self and other complexity questions, to result in a total "self" score (range 0–20) and a total "other" score (range 0–20). Following the previous past research, an aggregate score of total emotion understanding (label + explanation) was derived from the sum of the four stories (range 0–28). Thus, a high score represented a more sophisticated level of emotion understanding.

Taken together, these research activities (interviewing, self-report questionnaires, paper and pencil tasks, drawings, observations) at the two school sites provided multiple meanings about girls' and boys' emotional experiences within the school context. As a researcher and educator, I conceptualized the participants' behavior as an expression of social contexts (the school context) (Reinharz, 1992). As an interviewer, I aimed to listen to, and learn from their voices, and I could explore what I observed of their actions. Most importantly, I aimed to understand the experiences of the children from their own points of view (Reinharz, 1992).

3.7. Methodological and Ethical Concerns and Cautions

As discussed in Chapters 1 and 2, the concept of children's emotions within the classroom is complex, ambiguous, and cuts across numerous academic disciplines, including psychology, education, sociology, anthropology, psycholinguistics, among many others. Given this complexity, a psychocultural approach may provide the researcher and educator with a lens complex enough to explore children's experiences of emotions within the school. Consistent with Fiske et al. (1998), I share their contention that "a premise underlying this work is that in order to participate in any social world, people must incorporate cultural models, meanings, and practices into their basis psychological processes" (pp. 915–916). Given that the premises of cultural psychology imply commitment to contextualism as a general explanatory framework (i.e., human behavior, including children's emotional experiences, can only be understood in the context of its own unique historical moment, as Harkness (2002) suggests, a transcultural explanatory framework may help researchers and educators to make sense of children's emotional experiences across various linguistic and cognitive abilities, socioeconomic, and ethnic/racial backgrounds.

Despite the importance of emotional experiences to both psychology and education, research on the connections between emotionality and psychological development (especially self-development) remain sparse. To date, the majority of the studies have focused primarily on cognitive development, but research on children's emotional experiences within the classroom entails observation of culturally structured practices and social interactions as they relate to school experiences. For research methodology that resembles traditional fine-grained ethnographic observation and interviewing, a major challenge has been to establish a way to cross-validate the observations and testimonials of children's experiences in social contexts. As Dockett and Perry (2007) suggest, researchers working with children should aim to present children's views as clearly and authentically as possible. Accordingly, the present study aimed to make sense of what children told us, and to explain how their views contributed to our understanding of children's emotional experiences in the classroom.

Criteria for Exploring Emotion Understanding in School-Aged Children

Regarding assessment issues, researchers need to develop standard criteria for reliably and validly measuring the emotional experiences of children, particularly the self-conscious emotions in grade school-aged children. That is, when is it valid to identify the gaze aversion of a seven- or eight-year-old in response to causing harm to another person, or her or his smile following success on a task, to be indicative of the experience of self-conscious emotions? How do we know that it is not simply feeling sad instead of ashamed or feeling happy instead of proud, or that the child's behavior reflects an anticipated teacher or parental response rather than an internal self-conscious emotion? There are, in short, alternative explanations for these behavioral responses besides that they reflect the experience of self-conscious emotions. Moreover, different criteria have been developed and used for identifying displays of pride, guilt, shame, and embarrassment. Similar methodological issues plague research with older adolescents and adults (i.e., determining the specific facial and postural behaviors for self-conscious emotions), however, language measures such as self-reports and interviews can be included to verify or confirm their emotional experiences.

Thus, researchers need to explicitly outline the specific criteria used to identify displays of self-conscious emotions in children to allow for valid cross-case analysis. Promising data in this direction is recent research demonstrating that adults (Tracy & Robins, 2004b) as well as children four years and older (Tracy et al., 2005) can reliably identify displays of pride (expanded posture, slightly tilted head, small smile) and distinguish it from other positive emotions including happiness. As evidence accumulates for identifiable display markers of self-conscious emotions, researchers will be better equipped to apply standardized criteria for measuring children's self-conscious emotion experiences and self-understanding within the school context.

However, in contrast to standardized performance-based procedures, many developmentalists seek further evidence from research methods such as in-depth interviews and naturalistic observation. Regarding research ethics, to address the truthfulness of data, the exercise of individual perceptions in a social context is often distributed among the participants in a seamless fashion, and thus difficult to separate into individual thoughts (Super & Harkness, 1997). Past research suggests that to explore sensitive issues such as emotionality, respectful research practices must be one of the researcher's main priorities, and young people's verbal skills need to be valued (e.g., Dockett & Perry, 2007; Hay & Nye, 1998; Nesbitt, 1998). As noted above, consistent with conducting respectful research with children in the classroom, careful measures were taken to remind the child participants that their responses were confidential, and that at anytime during the research process they had the right to refuse to take part or withdraw from any aspect of the study.

More broadly, interpretivist research approaches such as ethnographic research, implications of reflexivity in interpretation are also paramount. An empathetic and sensitive rapport, one that facilitates conversation about emotional and sensitive issues, is necessary to develop a reciprocal relationship between researchers and participants. As many interpretivist researchers suggest (e.g., Lather, 1986, 1991), to explore areas of great personal relevance and sensitivity such as emotional experiences, we need to conduct respectful research in that we actively respect what we do not know or understand, regarding our own views and the views of our participants. Thus, the need for researchers to maintain integrity through conducting ethical and respectful research remains paramount (Creswell, 2005; McGinn & Bosacki, 2004; Richer, 1990).

Regarding the self-script or role of the researcher, as Reinharz (1997) notes, what researchers bring to the research activity plays a role in how we interact with the participants and make sense of the research findings. For example, according to Reinharz, we bring various attributes to the research context such as gender, age, citizenship, ethnic origin, occupation, and family roles which may help to shape or obstruct the relationships that the researcher can form and hence the knowledge that can be obtained. Thus, these selves influence the researcher's ability to engage in the research. Thus, what the researcher brings to, and becomes in the research context is a necessary aspect to the research process. Given my brought self as a female, Polish Ukrainian researcher and educator, I needed to be aware of my selves, and how this affected my interaction with the children, and how my selves influenced my interpretations of the findings. In addition to brought selves, there are research-based selves or roles that emerge from the research activity or technique such as interviewing, observation, or survey administration. Given the multi-methodological design of the particular research study discussed in this book, my role as a researcher included an interviewer, observer, and self-report administrator.

Finally, Reinharz (1997) also suggests that situationally created selves may emerge from the research process which could be a combination of brought and research-based selves, or may emerge from the research context. Regarding my experiences within the schools, I found that during the process of the research, the interactions and experiences have enabled me to create a hybrid role which fused my researcher-based self with my brought selves.

Overall, my role or self-script within the research influenced my interactions and interpretations of the research findings, and consistent with the literature on reflexivity and the issues surrounding the insider/outsider dilemmas of the researcher, interpretivist researchers such as ethnographers are responsible for addressing their subjectivity and personal biases in their own research. Thus, throughout the research process, I remained cautious in the sense that I would need to "bracket my assumptions" or, as Peshkin (1988) claims, tame my subjectivity in an attempt to represent and interpret children's emotional experiences and self-stories within the classroom. As Nesbitt (2001) warns, ethnographic sensitivity entails an attentive listening not only during interviews but also when reviewing the audio recording and transcripts. Similarly, the notion of respectful research needs to be applied to those situations in which researchers ask participants to disclose personal and private information (Tilley, 1998). Such respect is necessary for exploring children's perceptions and experiences of emotional experiences.

3.8. Summary

Given the complex issue of emotionality in the classroom, particularly during middle childhood, the decision to employ a mixed-methodology aimed to provide a further understanding of children's emotional experiences within the grade school classroom, particularly those children rated as socially withdrawn or shy. As discussed, above, the various scripts or roles of the researcher also help to guide the representation of the children's experiences. Thus, guided by my self-scripts as a researcher and educator, the following chapter outlines how the collected data were analyzed and presented.

The Shadows Speak: Words from Wise Children

4.1. Introduction and Summary of Data Analysis

To further our understanding of children rated as socially withdrawn or shy within the grade school classroom and their emotional and social experiences, the following chapter provides a cross-case analysis of the six participants chosen from the larger study. Given the various data sources, to provide a profile or case of each child, various pieces of data were chosen to best represent that particular child's responses. When I include excerpts from the participants' interviews, the quotes are representative of the interviews in general. That is, as I read and re-read through the data, I aimed to select the most representative quotations from the participants.

In particular, the experiences captured in the sections below are rooted in the participating children's voices and actions across the years of the study (2003–2007; children ranged from approximately six to ten years of age). The six children (three girls, "L," "M," "T," and three boys "G," "Q," "W") speak on the following issues: Cultural and Self Scripts (Self, School, Family, and World Connections, Social Scripts (Friends), and Children's Drawings (Self and Play). I will also summarize what the children did not say in the conversations, Silences among the Shadows and discuss how can we explain these silences?) Finally, I will outline the key lessons learned by analyzing the children's voices across the various cases.

4.2. Self and Cultural Scripts (Self, School, Family, and World Connections)

As I discussed in previous chapters, given that divergent views of the self often serve as are critical underpinnings of emotional experience, these ways of being are significant elements of the cultural frame (Bartlett, 1932), and form the framework for individual experiences of emotions and social behaviors. If the self functions as an interpretive, integrative, or orienting framework for individual behaviors, then whether one has a self that is shaped by a Canadian identity for example has the potential to make a difference in how emotional life is lived and what kinds of experiences will feel good and what social behaviors will be coded as positive or negative.

Given Markus and Kitayma's (1994) claim that an emotion is some amalgam of component processes that are organized by the nature of the relationship between the self and the cultural environments, then different sets of components may be highlighted and they are, in turn, combined in different ways depending upon the pertinent cultural frame within they are allowed to function. Outer or external cultural frames are inscribed into the inner or internal emotional experience.

Thus, to explore how children's self views may influence emotional experiences and where they see themselves fitting within the larger cultural framework consisting of relationships with their school, family, and peers, we were interested in exploring children's thoughts and feelings about themselves in a semi-structured interview which assessed their sense of self-continuity, self-agency, and self-distinctiveness. Children's responses to each section of the interview will be described in the following sections, followed by a description of what was missing from the conversations, or where the gaps were.

To assess self-continuity, or the extent to which they think aspects of themselves remain constant or stay the same, children were asked "If you can change from year to year, how do you still know it's you," followed by questions such as, "What stays the same, if you had a different name, how would you know it's still you?"

Children's Voices

The majority of children across all ages referred to their name as a distinct self-labeling concept that helped them to remember who they are and this remained constant across their ages (from six until eight years). To further examine their sense of self-continuity, children were then asked, "If everyone called you a different name, would you still know it's you, and how would you know this, what would be some clues that would help you know who you are?"

All children across all age, the majority of children claimed that they would still know who they are, despite the fact that everyone would call them different names. For example, a six-year-old boy (Q, February, 2004) stated that "Hum, because you know inside yourself that its still you," and that he would know he is the same person because his hair and eyes would remain the same. Similarly, a six-year-old girl (L, February, 2004) stated that "my eyes" would stay the same, and "If I didn't dye my hair my hair would stay the same … my clothes. That's about it."

Some children also mentioned activities or preferences as continuing self-defining characteristics such as "Because I would like the same things … like game cube and playing hide and go seek or you could play tag and would still like tag." (six-year-old boy, W, March, 2004). Others stated events such as, "'Cause its my birthday." (six-year-old girl, M, February, 2004).

Further, some children discussed the fact that they would know who they were based on information from their parents as evidenced in this six-year-old boy's response: "I would know because I will know and because my mom will tell me that I am the same person that I am now but bigger. And that would be awesome because I can go different places by myself." (G, February, 2004). As the children were asked these questions one and two years later, the responses became increasingly reflective of mental states and psychological references such as responses would include things like, "my attitude … not hitting" (seven-year-old boy, Q, February, 2005), or in response to the question, "If you had a different name, would you know it's you, "I would just know," and a seven-year-old girl's response, "Because you still probably talk the same, and if you're shy you're still shy, and you probably know a lot of people. (L, February, 2005), or as this seven-year-old girl states (M, February, 2005), "Yeah, because my eyes haven't changed, my personality hasn't changed." However, some seven-year-olds believed that they would be a different person as this seven-year-old boy replies, "No, because it's not my name." R: "So you'd think you were a different person? "Yeah."(W, February, 2005).

Eight-Year-Olds

As children increased with age, most of the eight-year-olds began to expand on some of their personal interests and characteristics such as, "I love to golf, I love to play music" and (Q, January, 2006), "Me, My accent, My language. My birthday," (G, January, 2006) and the response to the question, "If you had a different name, how would you know you're the same person?" some children included family members and animal companions in their self-definitions such as the following eight-year-old boy's response, "I don't know how to answer, cause I'd still live in the same family with my mom and dad, and I would still know me and my dog because whenever I'm home he barks for me to come play with him." (W, January, 2006). Similarly, this eight-year-old boy commented on how his preferences and activities would remain the same, "I'd eat the same food, play the same games. I'd have the same voice, the same friends." (G, January, 2006).

For the eight-year-old girls, their responses also illustrated that they thought they would be the same person as this eight-year-old girl replied (L, January, 2006), "Yes, I'd still be the same but my name would be different, and I'd always want to play outside, and my birthday would still be August 9. I'd have the same face, it doesn't matter about my size, it only matters who I am."

To assess self-agency, or their perceptions of their role in helping to developing their sense of self, they were asked, "How did you get to be the kind of person you are/the way you are? Who helped you learn to be the kind of person you are?" This question aimed to explore children's perceptions of what/who determines the formation of self and if they think that they are in control of their destiny.

Children's Voices

Across all years, children often mentioned that they became who they are because of family and/or a religious deity such as "God." For example, some responses included, "My mom made me," (six-year-old boy, Q, February, 2004), "my mom taught me how to do stuff and my dad taught me too, and my teacher," (six-year-old girl, L, February, 2004), "I just became this way, from my mom and dad teaching me." (eight-year-old boy, G, January, 2006), (or "God make me the kind of person that I am today" (six-year-old boy, G, February, 2004). Some children included references to both their parents and their peers such as the following eight-year-old girl, "My mom and dad taught me to be a nice person and shouldn't be mean … my friend X helps me out, she does nice things and it teaches me to do those things. Also my mom and dad encourage me to do a nice thing each day" (L, January, 2006).

In contrast, some children stated that they would play an active role in their self-development such as the following six-year-old boy (W, March, 2004), "By thinking the way I would like to be and then by doing it … So like being … like … happy …", or "Because I am me." (six-year-old girl, M, February, 2004), or, "if it's raining I'd pick up a book": (eight-year-old boy, February, 2006),

Finally, to assess self-distinctiveness, or to what extent, and how do children perceive themselves as being different or special from others, they were asked,

"What makes you different from everybody else in the world; and how are you different from other children in your class, what makes you special compared to other children in your class?"

Children's Voices

Interestingly, children provided different characteristics or aspects of the self to distinguish themselves as different from everybody in the world as compared to being different from other children in their class. For example, regarding how children viewed themselves as different from everyone in the world, children were more likely to respond with "I don't know," or to provide characteristics that distinguished themselves from everyone else in the world often involved characteristics relating to physical appearance such as, "That you have a different voice and look different … by having different eyes and a different um face and stuff" (six-year-old boy, W, March, 2004). And, "Some people don't have brown eyes some don't have hair and some don't have the same clothes. Some don't have their ears pierced" (six-year-old girl, L, February, 2004).

Similar to the questions regarding self-agency, some children also responded with references to God such as "God makes us different" (six-year-old girl, L, February, 2004), and "God, my mom and dad" (eight-year-old girl, M, January, 2004).

In contrast, to distinguish themselves as different from others in the classroom, children often responded with physical characteristics such as the following response from a six-year-old boy, "our skin colour, some kids in our class, one kid has brown skin" (Q, February, 2004), "My face" (seven-year-old girl, T, February, 2005), or abilities regarding academics such as "I am smarter than other children in the class" (six-year-old boy, G, February, 2004), and the following response from a seven-year-old girl, "I'm different because once in a while I can't do the math questions, and then I quit but my other friends try to help me and I'm just like "stop bothering me" (L, February, 2005). Some children also mentioned activities in general such as the following seven-year-old boy, "I have different talents and I like different things, I have a different name" (W, February, 2005).

In addition to being asked to think how they see themselves as "different" from others in the classroom, children were also asked how they thought they were "special" compared to their classmates. Children's responses often included descriptions of particular activities or abilities that involved aspects of learning and teaching. For example, when asked what makes him special compared to others in the class, a six-year-old boy (G) referred to his identity as a pet-owner by stating, "Special because my mom buys another dog I would be special to him and he would be special to me … and if we get a new girl dog then she could teach me and she would have puppies" (February, 2004). One six-year-old boy (Q) stated that he was special from others in his class because, "That I can do stuff that I don't know I can do" (February, 2004). Other responses also included self-evaluative statements such as, "that I do my best and be good. … I don't hurt anyone" (six-year-old boy, W, February, 2004). Some children responded with the statement that there are no particular distinguishing characteristics such as a six-year-old girl's response (L, February, 2004), "We are all different."

Children's perceptions of how they were special from their classmates remained similar across the years, such that some children continued to respond with "I don't know" or "I can't think of anything" (seven-year-old girl, T, February, 2005). Other responses continued to focus on family identity such as, "Because I have a baby brother, and I'm a big brother" (seven-year-old boy, Q, February, 2005), or references to God such as "God made me special"(eight-year-old girl, M, January, 2006). Responses continued to include references to academic skills such as "I'm a good reader," (eight-year-old boy, Q, January, 2006), and/or emotional characteristics and/or abilities such as the following response from a seven-year-old girl who mentioned how she relates to a classmate distinguishes her as special compared to her classmates, "X, when he feels sad I try to cheer him up because he's kind of different from the rest of us," and I say "it's ok X, I have a few sad things that happened to me"(L, February, 2005), and the following seven-year-old boy's response, "I'm a bit older, I'm turning eight. I'm a good friend" (Q, January, 2006), and "I can do sports that none of the other kids know how to do like figure skating, hockey, or be good at defense. I'm an artist and I can make crafts really well, I can paint, I can colour in the lines really neat. At home my brother and sister sometimes tackle me and I let them 'cause we play on the floor" (eight-year-old girl, L, January, 2006).

Summary of Self-Understanding Interview

Overall, across the years, the six children remained mainly consistent in their perceptions regarding how they viewed themselves, and the data supports the previous literature I discussed in Chapters 1 and 2 regarding children's developing sense of selves during the middle childhood years, basically moving from physical/behavioral descriptions to more mental/psychological traits (e.g., Damon & Hart, 1988; Harter, 1999). Regarding the self-continuity, for all ages, the majority of the children stated that they would still know who they were it they had a different name, although the justifications became increasingly psychological as the children increased with age. The majority of children also discussed the permanency of physical characteristics as opposed to the personality/psychological traits, although more children mentioned psychological characteristics in the later years.

Regarding self-agency, or who plays an active role in the children's developing sense of self, the family played an important role. The common themes across all years involved the influence of relationships with others, especially the family throughout the years. Although peers were mentioned somewhat in the later years, the majority of responses concerning the self-agency involved family members especially the parents and siblings, and also animal companions, suggesting that relationships with family members, friends, and animal companions played the most important roles in their developing sense of self.

Regarding self-distinctiveness, overall the responses differed regarding whether or not children thoughts of themselves as different or special. Although children referred to their role in the family as an aspect of what distinguishes them as both different and special compared to others, children were more likely to refer to physical characteristics and behavioral abilities to distinguish themselves as different from others. In contrast, regarding what makes them special, more children referred to abilities that they perceived as unique or including a self-evaluative component such as I am a "good reader" or a "good friend."

In addition to the role the family plays in self-understanding, participants across all ages and genders, children discussed the role of a religious or spiritual Deity or presence such as God. This resesrch finding supports the suggestion that future research needs to explore children's perceptions of self and others from a psychocultural perspective within a variety of educational contexts including schools grounded in various faiths (e.g., Ream & Savin-Williams, 2004; Sweet, 1997). Such future research would be especially valuable within the North American context given our increasingly multicultural, multifaith, and multilingual society (Gollnick & Chin, 2002).

Regarding educational contexts in particular, educators agree that religion may act as a developmental asset, both in the lives of individuals and in their communities (Bosacki, 2005c; Trulear, 2000). That is, various factors that relate to religiosity in children may help to promote healthy emotional development that assist children to create a healthy and positive sense of self and other. Such factors including religious involvement, such as attending religious services (e.g., Church), service to others, placing high value on honesty, caring, integrity have found to have a significant positive influence on children's lives, and may help to protect them from developing negative self-perceptions and a low sense of self-worth which in turn may lead to engaging in self-harming and unhealthy behaviors and choices (Lantieri, 2001).

Silences in Self-Understanding

Compared to family, the children's peers were not mentioned in their self-under-standing. That is, their descriptions of their self-views and feelings did not include any references to their peers. Similarly, their description of their self-views, and so on, did not include a discussion of school activities or their teachers. Finally, children's descriptions of their self-views did not include references to popular media (tv/film/Internet personalities).

Regarding the aspect of self-distinctiveness, the majority of responses described physical differences and cognitive abilities in the early years, although as children's ages increased, the seven- and eight-year-olds were more likely to discuss psychological and emotional traits, especially connected to which aspects of the self helped them to feel special compared to others.

4.3. Social Scripts (Friends)

Across the socially ambiguous stories and the emotion understanding interviews, all six children discussed the importance of friends. Children were most likely to discuss their peer relationships within the context of self-conscious emotions including pride and embarrassment. Outlined below are examples of children's responses to the emotion understanding interviews.

Emotional Understanding

Children participated in semi-structured, emotion understanding interviews which were presented in the forms of stories (see Chapter 3 for further details). Two of the emotions were considered the simple or basic emotions (happy, sad), and two of the emotions represented the complex or social/moral, self-conscious emotions (proud, embarrassed). Across all ages, all children understood the concept of the basic emotions (happy and sad) as reflected in the children's voices described below.

Children's Voices: Happiness (Boys)

Regarding the question of what makes them happy, many six- to eight-year-old boys mentioned material objects and events such as, "When I get lots of toys and candy" (six-year-old boy, G, February, 2004), "When I get something new" (six-year-old boy,

Q, February, 2004), "When I get new toys and things" (six-year-old boy, W, March, 2004), "To play with friends and read books" (seven-year-old boy, Q, February, 2005), "Getting new toys, something at Christmas" (seven-year-old boy, G, February, 2005), "Included in stuff" (seven-year-old boy, W, February, 2005). "When I get new toys, when I get an allowance" (eight-year-old boy, G, January, 2006), "Reading, tv, and some other things …" (eight-year-old boy, Q, January, 2006), "When I get new toys, and when I get new things" (eight-year-old boy, W, February, 2006).

Children's Voices: Happiness (Girls)

Regarding the question of what makes them happy, the majority of six- to eight-year-old girls mentioned a combination of both material possessions and social events such as receiving gifts and playing with a friend such as described in the following statements: "When my friends invite me over" (six-year-old girl, L, February, 2004), "When I get presents on my birthday too" (six-year-old girl, M, February, 2004), "When my friends come over" (six-year-old girl, T, February, 2004). "When my friends put funny shows on, when my dad comes home and starts tickling me" (seven-year-old girl, L, February, 2005), "When it's my birthday and I get presents" (seven-year-old girl, T, February, 2005), "Playing with my friends. Getting surprises from my mom and dad" (seven-year-old girl, M, February, 2005), "When I give stuff and I receive stuff, and when my friends help me out" (eight-year-old girl, L, January, 2006), "When my friends come over" (eight-year-old girl, T, January, 2006), "When I get a surprise from my mom and dad, when my sister plays with me" (eight-year-old girl, M, January, 2006).

Children's Voices: Sadness (Boys)

Regarding the question of what makes them sad, most children responded with issues surrounding loss and/or injury such as the following response from this six-year-old boy G, "When my dog eats my candy" (Researcher, "Is there anything else that makes you sad?"), he continued with an experience that made him sad such as, "If I fell down" (G, February, 2004). Most boys provided similar responses such as, "If something breaks" (six-year-old boy, Q, February, 2004), and also references to social exclusion and/or negative social interactions with peers and siblings such as "When I don't get to play with anybody" (six-year-old boy, W, February, 2004), "Being punched, called names" (seven-year-old boy, Q, February, 2005), "When my sister steals my candies" (seven-year-old boy, G, February, 2005). "When I get left out of stuff" (seven-year-old boy, W, February, 2005). "When someone yells at me for no reason" (eight-year-old boy, G, January, 2006), "I drop something and it falls into a puddle" (eight-year-old boy, Q, January, 2006), "When I don't get to play with anybody" (eight-year-old boy, W, February, 2006).

Children's Voices: Sadness (Girls)

Similar to boys, the majority of six to eight-year-old girls discussed issues of loss, exclusion, and/or injury when discussing examples of sadness. The following statements below illustrate their thoughts:

"When someone hurts my feelings when someone doesn't let me play in a game, or hits me and it hurts" (six-year-old girl, L, February, 2004), "When I have nobody to play with" (six-year-old girl, M, February, 2004), "If ice-cream fell" (six-year-old girls, T, February, 2004). "When people hurt me, and my brother pulls my hair" (seven-year-old girl, L, February, 2005), "when I get into trouble for something I didn't do" (seven-year-old girl, T, February, 2005), "When my mom has to leave for work. When my friends don't want to play with me" (seven-year-old girl, M, February, 2005), "When my brother/sisters pull my hair, when I have do chores, instead of playing outside" (eight-year-old girl, L, January, 2006), "If ice-cream falls" (eight-year-old girl, T, January, 2006), "When my sister hurts me" (eight-year-old girl, M, January, 2006).

Complex or the Social-Moral, or Self-Conscious Emotions

Given the more complex, and self-reflective skills necessary to understand the self-conscious or complex emotions, we were interested to investigate whether or not stories regarding pride and embarrassment elicited any different responses as compared to happy/sad. Although a few children provided appropriate responses in the first year of the study, or when they were six years old, once the children were in the third grade and the majority were eight years old, all children provided appropriate responses as to what makes them embarrassed or proud, with the majority of children providing examples of social events or personal accomplishments. Children's responses are described in the sections below.

Children's Voices: Pride

For both girls and boys, stories of pride involved personal accomplishments, often connected with academic achievements or accomplishing a new task reflecting personal growth. Compared to boys, only one eight-year-old girl mentioned the importance of an audience as outlined below.

Children's Voices: Pride (Boys)

"When I learn how to spell words" (six-year-old, G, February, 2004), or "When I first zip up my coat" (six-year-old boy, Q, February, 2004), "When I get A's on my report card" (six-year-old boy, W, March, 2004), "When I save a dog or cat from a tree" (seven-year-old boy, Q, February, 2005), "Getting a cat" (seven-year-old boy, G, February, 2005), "Get to do things that I should do" (seven-year-old boy, W, February, 2005). "When I get new toys" (eight-year-old boy, G, January, 2006), "If I get a goal in hockey, if I do something I haven't done before" (eight-year-old boy, Q, January, 2006), "When I get A's on my report card" (eight-year-old boy, W, February, 2006).

Children's Voices: Pride (Girls)

"If I help someone on the computer and get a badge or a metal" (six-year-old girl, L, February, 2004), When I can read a book all by myself (six-year-old girl, M, February, 2004), "I don't know" (six-year-old girl, T, February, 2004). "When I was figure skating contest because everyone heard, I received a ribbon for a prize" (seven-year-old girl, L, February, 2005), "When I finish my work in school" (seven-year-old girl, T, February, 2005), "When I figured out a big word by myself" (seven-year-old girl, M, February, 2005). "When my nana and popa come to my game, when the teacher picks me to read in front of the class" (eight-year-old girl, L, January, 2006), "I don't know" (eight-year-old girl, T, January, 2006), "When I do great work in class" (eight-year-old girl, M, January, 2006).

Children's Voices: Embarrassment

In contrast to pride, both girls and boys across the ages mentioned the importance of audience in their explanations of what kinds of things make them embarrassed. The audiences included both peers and siblings in the audience that may lead children to feel embarrassed. Examples from the children's voices are listed below.

Children's Voices: Embarrassment (Boys)

"When my sister makes a noise and everyone laughs" (six-year-old boy, G, February, 2004), or "If I spilled milk like Grover (six-year-old boy, W, March,

2004), "When my sister said something about me that was gross" (seven-year-old boy, Q, February, 2005), "Making a mistake, but you can learn from mistakes" (seven-year-old boy, G, February, 2005). "Spilt milk" (seven-year-old boy, W, February, 2005), "Nothing really" (eight-year-old boy, G, January, 2006), "If I fall down in front of somebody, if my friend doesn't know something in a speech we did together" (eight-year-old, Q, January, 2006), "If I spilled milk like Grover" (eight-year-old boy, W, February, 2006).

Children's Voices: Embarrassment (Girls)

"If I tripped and everyone laughed at me or if I did something wrong and everyone laughed" (six-year-old girl, L, February, 2004). No response (M, February, 2004), "I don't know" (six-year-old girl, T, February, 2004). "When everyone hears something or sees something I didn't mean to do" (seven-year-old girl, L, February, 2004), "When I do something and everyone laughs (seven-year-old girl, T, February, 2005), "If I spilled milk in front of someone else" (seven-year-old girl, M, February, 2005). "If I miss school, if I try to make things and it doesn't come right in front of my friends" (eight-year-old girl, L, January, 2006), "I don't know" (eight-year-old girl, T, January, 2006), "When I have to talk in front of the class" (eight-year-old girl, M, January, 2006).

Regarding Table 4.1, children's emotional competencies varied from year to year, with the eight-year-olds scoring the highest in emotional understanding scores, and all six children scored above the mean score of the larger sample (see Bosacki, 2005). This finding is consistent with past research that shows in general, a positive association exists between age and emotional development (Denham, 1998). Regarding gender differences in the particular cases above, girls and boys did not differ in emotional understanding scores than the boys, although overall, this contrasts regarding findings found from the larger study (see Bosacki, 2005), as well as previous research suggesting that girls receive higher ratings in emotional understanding as compared to boys (e.g., Denham, 1998; Maccoby, 1998, etc.). In the larger study, only the eight-year-old girls' emotional understanding scores differed significantly compared to boys.

Regarding Table 4.2, the teachers' ratings of the children's emotional competencies varied from year to year, although the girls in general received higher ratings than the boys regarding emotional understanding which supports findings found from the larger study (see Bosacki, 2005), as well as previous research suggesting that girls receive higher ratings in emotional understanding as compared to boys (e.g., Denham, 1998; Maccoby, 1998, etc.). However, in

Table 4.1 Children's Total Emotional Understanding Scores

Participant Scores	6 years (Year 1)	7 years (Year 2)	8 years (Year 3)
Girls			
(*n* = 3)	*M* = 21.33	*M* = 21.33	*M* = 27.00
	SD = 5.03	*SD* = 5.03	*SD* = 1.41
Boys			
(*n* = 3)	*M* = 20.00	*M* = 18.50	*M* = 23.00
	SD = 3.60	*SD* = 3.53	*SD* = 4.24

Note. Range of Children's Emotional Competence Teacher (CEST, Denham, 1998; rating scores = 0–28 with 28 representing high emotional understanding. Year 1 (*M* = 22.16, *SD* = 3.64), Year 2 (*M* = 19.14, *SD* = .33), Year 3 (*M* = 19.87, *SD* = 5.37).

Table 4.2 Teacher Ratings of Children's Emotional Understanding Scores

Participant Scores	6 years (Year 1)	7 years (Year 2)	8 years (Year 3)
Girls			
(*n* = 3)	*M* = 41.67	*M* = 39.00	*M* = 42.00
	SD = 1.53	*SD* = 7.00	*SD* = 0.00
Boys			
(*n* = 3)	*M* = 29.67	*M* = 31.33	*M* = 32.00
	SD = 4.93	*SD* = 4.16	*SD* = 6.08

Note. Range of Children's Emotional Competence Teacher (CEST, Denham, 1998; rating scores = 0–50 with 50 representing high emotional understanding. Year 1 (*M* = 35.86, *SD* = 7.21), Year 2 (*M* = 31.70, *SD* = 15. 05), Year 3 (*M* = 37.29, *SD* = 8.57).

the larger study, in contrast to the children's emotional understanding scores, the teacher ratings showed that teachers rated girls as higher in emotion understanding across all three years, with significant differences in the six and eight-year-olds.

Regarding the associations between teacher ratings and children's emotional understanding scores, findings from the larger study showed that aside from the six-year-olds, for the seven- and eight-year-olds significant positive correlations were found between the teachers' ratings and the children' emotional understanding scores (r (88) = .21, p = .04; r (88) = .27, p = .05; respectively). That is, high teacher ratings were associated with high emotion understanding scores in children, Also, regarding gender, significant gender differences were found for the six- and eight-year-olds, with teachers consistently rating girls as higher on emotion understanding. Interestingly, only the eight-year-old girls scored significantly higher than the boys on emotion understanding, whereas the gender differences in the teacher ratings were found for the six- and eight-year-olds.

Children's Emotion Understanding (Simple/Complex): Summary

Given White's (1994) claim that that the core of most emotions words are social and moral entailments capable of creating social realities and of influencing social behavior. In the emotion tasks, children were asked to articulate their personal emotional meaning of the words in that the meanings of emotion and the emotions of meaning are not easily separated. The realms of cognition and emotion exist in mutual contingent interaction and that all emotions entail some element of interpretation or appraisal, just as according to Ochs & Schieffelin (1984) all language in use is emotionally valenced. Thus, to translate or interpret the children's representation of their emotional terms, I have relied on their words alone as a way of examining the significance of emotion within broader cultural models of the person, action, and social life. What I have outlined below are key themes that emerged form the children's conversations regarding emotions, and also, what the children chose not to discuss.

Regarding the simple emotions such as happiness and sadness, across all ages and both genders, children were more likely to mention material and/or physical objects regarding happiness such as gifts and toys, whereas for sadness, children were more likely to mention social events and relationships such as feeling left out, no one to play with, and so on. Compared to the simple or basic emotions of happiness and sadness, children's stories related to the complex or secondary emotions of pride and embarrassment involved the importance of audience, although this was found for embarrassment only.

Regarding emotions of happy/sad and proud/embarrassed—discuss importance of "audience" for definitions of embarrassment, but not necessary for pride. For example, across the ages, most children defined embarrassment as when they do something such as fall in front of their friends—and their friends laugh at them. For pride, most children provided examples of individual or personal success such as learning a new skill, or achieving good grades in school, reading a challenging book. According to Harris (1989), the ability to experience the complex emotions such as pride and embarrassment requires the child to imagine the emotional reaction of the other. This imaginative anticipation leads to feelings of pride as in children imagine what their parents will say once they win an award at school. According to Harris (1989), the ability to understand these emotions requires the ability to imagine the circumstances under which the emotions will be aroused in another person or "I can imagine how Debbie will feel when she imagines how her dad will feel."

Receptive Language and Emotion Understanding (Teacher Ratings and Children's Scores)

Regarding Table 4.3, the children's scores on the receptive vocabulary task varied from year to year, and demonstrate no significant gender differences which support findings found from the larger study (see Bosacki, 2005), where results showed that girls' and boys' emotional understanding receptive language scores did not significantly differ across the 3 years. Also for the larger sample, significant correlations were found between the total language scores and children's emotion understanding scores for six-year-old girls' only.

As discussed in Chapter 2, language skills including both expressive and receptive language have been found to have an influence on children's emotional understanding (Harris, 1989), especially socially withdrawn children (Coplan & Armer, 2005). Although this present research investigated receptive language ability only, across the three years, for the larger study, no associations were found between children's receptive language scores (PPVT scores) and their total emotion understanding scores. However, a positive correlation was found

Table 4.3 Children's PPVT Scores (Receptive Language Ability)

Participant Scores	6 years (Year 1)	7 years (Year 2)	8 years (Year 3)
Girls			
(*n* = 3)	*M* = 85.33	*M* = 106.67	*M* = 97.50
	SD = 8.14	*SD* = 16.80	*SD* = 10.60
Boys			
(*n* = 3)	*M* = 103.33	*M* = 109.67	*M* = 104.00
	SD = 18.92	*SD* = 2.52	*SD* = 8.49

Note. Range of Peabody Picture Vocabulary Test (PPVT, Dunn & Dunn, 1997; scores = 66–145 with high scores representing high receptive vocabulary ability. Year 1 (*M* = 102.91, *SD* = 14.53), Year 2 (*M* = 112.10, *SD* = 13.56), Year 3 (*M* = 120.06, *SD* = 13.42).

between teacher ratings of children's emotion understanding scores and children's receptive language ability for seven-year-olds only. That is, for seven-year-olds only, as teacher ratings of children' emotional understanding increased, so did children's receptive language scores. Given the possible role that language ability may play in the social and emotional development of girls and boys in the middle school years (Denham, 1998), Coplan and Armer (2005) suggest that future research needs to explore the role language abilities (receptive and expressive) play in socially withdrawn children's emotional development within the classroom in further detail. As mentioned in Chapter 2, given that language may provide a vehicle through which the theories of self, others' minds, and feelings are created (e.g., Bruner & Kalmar, 1997), previous research suggests that language ability may help children to create self-scripts or schemas. Thus, researchers need to draw from psycho-linguistic and cross-cultural literature (e.g., Salovey & Sluyter, 1997; Vinden, 1999) and begin to integrate language tasks (both receptive and expressive) into socioemotional and self-concept research with children. Implications for theory, education, and research regarding the promotion of children's language and socioemotional competence are further discussed in the following chapter.

Social Ambiguity (Social Stories)

Socially Ambiguous Stories (Nancy/Margie and Kenny/Tom Stories) (see Bosacki, 2005 further details concerning the stories and interview questions)

As mentioned in Chapter 3, to assess children's understanding of the social messages within school situations, particularly regarding the more ambiguous or nonverbal and indirect messages, children listened to two brief stories describing socially ambiguous situations (one story included all males, one story included all females), and then children were asked various questions regarding their perceptions of the story such as if the children would do something good or bad as they approached the child who needs a friend. To reflect children's understandings of socially ambiguous events, described below are selected responses to the interview questions: *Nancy/Margie Story—New Girl:* As described in Chapter 3, the interviews began with the Researcher reading the stories to the children, in which the children would help the Researcher to act out the ambiguous scenarios through the use of dolls. Following the story, children were asked to share their thoughts with the Researcher regarding their thoughts as to what they think would happen next.

Regarding the Nancy/Margie story, the majority of children suggested that the two girls (Nancy and Margie) should play with the new girl (swinging by her self in the playground). For example, a six-year-old girl said (L), "They probably look back and see someone new and they let her come and play with them and they become best friends" or "They will ask her to play" (six-year-old boy, G), or the new girl acts such as the following response from a six-year-old boy, "She walks over to them and asks them if she may play" (Q), or "They will want to play with her" (W, six-year-old boy).

Regarding the Kenny/Mark story, similar to the Nancy/Margie story, the majority of the children suggested that Kenny and Mark should choose Tom to be on their soccer team. Responses included "I think Tom would come and they would pick him" (L, six-year-old girl, March, 2004), and "They choose him first." (Q, eight-year-old boy). For both stories, children were asked if the characters (Nancy/Margie/Kenny/Mark) would do something good or bad and to explain their reasoning regarding their answers. For both stories, the majority of the six-year-old children responded with something "good" such as "good, because if they play together they wouldn't be mad at each other" (L, six-year-old girl), followed by the question of "What do you think is the right thing to do and why?" to which the girl replied, "Let her play with them, because if they didn't they would make her cry and make her want to go back to her old school." Similarly, this six-year-old boy replied, "Good. Because they might let her in to be their friends," and the right thing to do is, "Just to like be friends with her. Because that's being nice" (Q, March, 2004). Similarly, in responses to the question of why Kenny and Mark would do something good, this six-year-old boy suggested that P: Because they are nice and they are good friends (G, March, 2004).

The transcripts outlined below detail the conversations the six-year-olds engaged in regarding the Nancy and Margie Story and the Kenny and Mark Story for both six- and eight-year-old children.

Nancy/Margie Story (L, six-year-old girl; R, Researcher; March, 2004)

R: Do you think that Margie and Nancy will do something good or bad? Why?

L: Good, because if they play together they wouldn't be mad at each other.

R: What do you think is the right thing to do? Why?

L: Let her play with them, because if they didn't they would make her cry and make her want to go back to her old school.

R: So she'd want to go back to her old school.

R: What do you think is the wrong thing to do? Why?

L: Be mean to her.

R: What's being mean?

L: Like not letting her play, and making her go and not letting her come and play with them.

R: I see and why is that mean, or wrong?

L: Because that isn't very nice.

Kenny/Mark Story (L, six-year-old girl; R, Researcher; March, 2004)

R: What do you think will happen next?

L: I think Tom would come and they would pick him.

R: You think they would pick Tom?

R: Do you think that Kenny and Mark will do something good or bad? Why?

L: Good, because they're his friends.

R: What do you think is the right thing to do? Why?

L: Let him play because if you don't let him play he would get really sad.

R: What do you think is the wrong thing to do? Why?

L: To not let him play because that would be mean to him, to let him play would be nice.

R: See, why would it be mean to not let him play.

L: Because it would be mean and if they were his friends, friends always let friends play.

R: I see so friends always let other friends play.

Nancy/Margie Story (Q, six-year-old boy; R, Researcher; March, 2004)

R: What do you think will happen next?

Q: She walks over there to them.

R: And what does she say?

Q: May I play with you?

R: And what do Nancy and Margie say?

Q: Say yes.

R: Do you think that Margie and Nancy will do something good or bad? Why?

Q: Good. Because they might let her in to be their friends.

R: What do you think is the right thing to do? Why?

Q: Just to like be friends with her. Because that's being nice.

R: How will that make the new girl feel?

Q: Good.

R: What do you think is the wrong thing to do? Why?

Q: Don't let her in because that's not being very nice.

R: How will that make the new girl feel?

Q: Very bad.

Kenny and Mark Story (Q, six-year-old boy; R, Researcher; March, 2004)

R: What do you think will happen next?

Q: They'll put him in.

R: Do you think that Kenny and Mark will do something good or bad? Why?

Q: Good. Because they might let him be on the team and play hockey.

R: And that's a good thing.

Q: umhm.

R: What do you think is the right thing to do? Why?

Q: To let him. Because that's the only way you can be nice to people.

R: Nice by letting them?

Q: Be on the team.

R: What do you think is the wrong thing to do? Why?

Q: To not let him. Because that's not being very nice to people.

R: How do you think Tom would feel?

Q: Bad.

However, not all six-year-olds thought that Margie and Nancy would do something good, as this one six-year-old boy (G, March, 2004), stated in response to the question of whether or not Margie and Nancy will do something good or bad, "Bad," followed by the justification of, "Maybe they just don't like her." "Why?" "They will make fun of her."

Nancy and Margie Story (G, six-year-old boy; R, Researcher; March, 2004)

R: What do you think will happen next?

G: They will ask her to play.

R: Do you think that Margie and Nancy will do something good or bad?

G: Bad.

R: Why?

G: Maybe they just don't like her.

R: Why?

G: They will make fun of her.

R: What do you think is the right thing to do?

G: Be nice.

R: Why?

G: She is the new girl and wants to play.

R: What do you think is the wrong thing to do?

G: Not to play.

R: Why?

G: They are being like a bully.

R: What is being like a bully mean?

G: Pushing, stepping on her, tripping her. Once I was playing hockey and some-one tripped me so they could score on my net.

However, G stated that Kenny and Mark would do something good as outlined below:

Kenny and Mark Story (G, six-year-old boy; R, Researcher; March, 2004):

R: What do you think will happen next?

G: He is going to be on his team (Tom).

R: Do you think that Kenny and Mark will do something good or bad?

G: Good.

R: Why?

G: Maybe put him on their same team.

R: Why?

G: Because they are nice and they are good friends.

R: What do you think is the right thing to do?

G: Play with him.

R: Why?

G: Because that would be nice.

R: What does nice mean again?

G: Share and be friends.

R: What do you think is the wrong thing to do?

G: Not play.

R: Why?

G: Because its mean.

R: What's mean about it?

G: Mean is cheating or pushing you down when you are playing soccer ... (inaudible).

Given the longitudinal research design of our research, the ambiguous social stores were also read to the children when they were eight years of age. The responses illustrated further complexity when the children responded to the same stories and questions at eight years of age, such as the following response from an eight-year-old girl (L), "She'll sort of be nervous when they're coming because she's never spoken to them, she hardly knows anyone, and I think that the new girl and those two, one of them might know her and one of them might not" (February, 2006), and "They will invite her to play" (eight-year-old boy, Q, February, 2006), or "They're gonna ask her if she can be their new friends. The new girl will say yes" (eight-year-old boy, G, February, 2006).

To further represent the children's emotional thinking at eight years of age, outlined below are some examples of transcripts illustrating the children's responses. In general, the majority of the eight-year-old children's responses remained positive, and contained further elaboration of their reasoning underlying their decision to either choose a positive or negative outcome for the story. Outlined below are the voices of some selected eight-year-olds.

Nancy and Margie Story (L, eight-year-old girl; R, Researcher; February, 2006)

R: What do you think will happen next?

L: She'll sort of be nervous when they're coming because she's never spoken to them, she hardly knows anyone, and I think that the new girl and those two, one of them might know her and one of them might not.

R: Do you think that Margie and Nancy will do something good or bad? Why? One might do something good and one might do something bad.

R: Like what? How would that happen?

L: One might not be nice to the new girl, but one might.

R: Why?

L: Because a lot of stories that I've heard of go like that, where there would be two girls and one of them might talk to her and the other one didn't like the new girl.

R: What do you think is the right thing to do? Why? Go to the new girl and be nice, so they could make friends and have new friends not just each other.

R: How does the new girl feel then?

L: Happy.

R: How do they feel?

L: Happy.

R: What do you think is the wrong thing to do? Why? Make fun of her and stuff cause then they wouldn't be friends and they wouldn't be happy. It's wrong because it would be hurting her feelings.

R: How would Nancy and Margie feel?

L: If they were jealous I think they would feel happy that they made her cry.

R: What does jealous mean?

L: Jealous means that something is there and you really want it and your jealous that your friends have it.

R: Is it a good feeling or a bad feeling?

L: Bad feeling. Or if your mom had a baby and you used to be the only one for a few years and um Mom had a baby and you hardly get spoken to anymore, you get jealous that you don't get all the attention.

Kenny and Mark Story (L, eight-year-old girl; R, Researcher; February, 2006)

R: What do you think will happen next?

L: He'll be picked and he'll be able to play team sports with them.

R: Do you think that Kenny and Mark will do something good or bad? Why?

L: Good, because I think they're going to do something good because they've seen him doing sports that they're going to play, and they'll say he's a really good player but they always picked him last and because they always do they didn't want him to feel like they decided to pick him first all the time now so they picked him last again, but he hardly ever got picked. I think he's really happy about it that he's finally gotten picked.

R: What do you think is the right thing to do? Why?

L: Take turns picking other ones first and last. Because if you don't it'll become a fight and if everyone's on the same team all the time it won't be fair. So like if Joe and Gregg were always on the same team and they're really good players it wouldn't be fair for us. Because we always play boys against girls.

R: What do you think is the wrong thing to do? Why?

L: Pick all of the good players for your team and all of the bad players for the other team. Because all the bad players get together and make one good player.

Nancy and Margie Story (Q, eight-year-old boy; R, Researcher; February, 2006)

R: What do you think will happen next?

Q: They will invite the new girl to play with them.

R: Do you think that Margie and Nancy will do something good or bad? Why?

Q: Good, because they might play with her and ask her if she wants to be their friend or something cause she's the new girl.

R: What do you think is the right thing to do? Why?

Q: Be nice to everyone because it's a good thing.

R: How would the new girl feel if they were nice to her?

Q: Happy.

R: And how would they feel, Nancy and Margie?

Q: Happy.

R: What do you think is the wrong thing to do? Why?

Q: Laugh at her and say ha ha ha. It's making fun, she'd feel sad. Nancy and Margie would feel excited … I don't know the expression.

R: Would they feel happy?

Q: No.

R: But they'd be laughing.

Q: Yeah.

R: So they'd be laughing but it wouldn't be a funny laugh

Q: Yeah it would be a funny laugh.

R: But they wouldn't be happy?

Q: Yeah, well kind of.

R: Is it hard to explain.

Q: Yeah.

Kenny and Mark Story (Q, eight-year-old boy; R, Researcher; February, 2006)

R: What do you think will happen next?

Q: They choose him first.

R: Do you think that Kenny and Mark will do something good or bad? Why?

Q: Good because they chose him first.

R: What do you think is the right thing to do? Why?

Q: Be nice.

R: What do you mean nice?

Q: Like if you were being bullied or something you should …

R: What does bullied mean?

Q: I don't know.

R: But picked first for the team?

Q: Yeah.

R: How would Tom feel?

Q: happy and excited at the same time.

R: And how would Kenny and Mark feel?

Q: They'd feel fine I guess.

R: Is that a good feeling or a bad feeling?

Q: Good.

R: What do you think is the wrong thing to do? Why?

Q: To not pick him at all, because it's bullying.

R: And why is bullying wrong.

Q: It makes people feel picked on.

R: How would he feel.

Q: Sad.

R: And how would Kenny and Mark feel?

Q: Happy I guess, no they would feel like laughing I guess.

R: So they'd be laughing but they wouldn't be happy.

Q: Yeah.

Nancy and Margie Story (G, eight-year-old boy; R, Researcher; February, 2006)

R: What do you think will happen next?

G: They're gonna ask her if she can be their new friends. The new girl will say yes.

R: Do you think that Margie and Nancy will do something good or bad? Why?

G: Good because they want to be friends with her and friends aren't mean.

R: What do you think is the right thing to do? Why?

G: To be nice and treat her nicely. She'd feel happy. Nancy and Margie would feel happy as well.

R: What do you think is the wrong thing to do? Why?

G: To treat her badly. Because it's being mean. She'd feel sad. Nancy and Margie would feel forgiveful.

R: That's mean that they feel sorry.

Kenny and Mark Story (G, eight-year-old boy; R, Researcher; February, 2006)

R: What do you think will happen next?

G: They pick him for the team and they go play the game.

R: Do you think that Kenny and Mark will do something good or bad? Why?

G: Bad. Or good I mean because Tom is their friend.

R: What do you think is the right thing to do? Why?

G: Don't be mean because mean isn't nice. He'd feel sad. Mark and Kenny would feel happy, or no they'd feel sorry.

R: What do you think is the wrong thing to do? Why?

G: To treat people badly because it's not nice.

However, as with the six-year-olds, not all children stated that the Nancy and Margie would choose to do something good as an eight-year-old girl (M) explains below:

Nancy and Margie Story (M, eight-year-old girl; R, Researcher; January, 2006)

R: What do you think will happen next?

M: They'll ask her if she would like to play.

R: Do you think that Margie and Nancy will do something good or bad? Why?

M: Bad. They might pretend to spy on her.

R: What does that mean?

M: (No answer)

R: Why is it bad?

M: No answer.

R: Is it good or bad?

M: Bad.

R: What do you think is the right thing to do? Why?

M: Not spy, because you shouldn't spy on people.

R: What do you think is the wrong thing to do? Why?

M: Be mean. Because you shouldn't be mean to other people.

R: Why?

M: No answer

R: How would she feel?

M: Sad.

R: So that makes it wrong?

M: Yes.

R: How would they feel, the girls that are being mean.

M: Happy.

R: Why would they be happy?

M: I'm not sure.

Kenny and Mark Story (M, eight-year-old boy; R, Researcher; January, 2006)

R: What do you think will happen next?

M: They'll pick Tom.

R: Do you think that Kenny and Mark will do something good or bad? Why?

M: Good.

R: Why?

M: I don't know.

R: How would Tom feel?

M: Happy.

R: What do you think is the right thing to do? Why?

M: To choose him so that he can play soccer.

R: How would Tom feel?

M: Happy.

R: How would Mark and Kenny feel?

M: Happy.

R: Why would they be happy?

M: One of them picked him to be on the team.

R: What do you think is the wrong thing to do? Why?

M: Not pick him. Because he would feel sad.

R: How would Kenny and Mark feel?

M: Happy.

R: Why?

M: I don't know.

Socially Ambiguous Stories: Summary

In general, as the children progressed from age six to eight, as expected and in support of previous research on children's social and emotional understanding in middle childhood, the majority of the children's responses became more complex and contained a higher number of references to emotions and mental states when the children were eight years as compared to the six-year-olds. As I discussed in Chapters 1 and 2, consistent with previous research on children's understanding of the complex or self-conscious emotions, eight-year-old children discussed the complex emotions such as jealousy more often than when they were six years. The moral judgments remained similar over the years with the majority of children choosing to respond that both Nancy and Margie and Kenny and Mark would do something good with various explanations usually concerning the target child's (e.g., the new girl, Tom) emotions or sense of self.

Given the ambiguous nature of the two stories, we aimed to see whether or not children would predict negative or positive behaviors, and what they would suggest as the "right" and "wrong" things to do. Interestingly, overall, across all ages, a majority of the children offered a positive response in that they thought that the characters would do something "good" as opposed to "bad." This somewhat positive bias response could have been due in part to the problem of social desirability with self-report and interview data (e.g., Creswell, 2005), given that the children may have attempted to provide responses to "please the researcher," or to present themselves in the most positive light possible. This positive response bias has also been found when research deals with socially and morally sensitive topics (see Killen & Smetana, 2006 for a review on recent research on moral development).

Given the significant role emotions and moral sensibilities play in children's reactions to the socially ambiguous stories, we asked them to make a moral judgment regarding the social interactions of the characters. Although the stories are somewhat ambiguous regarding the relationships between the characters (Piaget, 1965, 1981), the emotional quality of peer relationships and friendships is somewhat implicated in children's growing moral sensibilities (Dunn, 2004). Similar to Dunn and Piaget, White (1994) claims, emotions help children to understand moral situations in that emotions help them to shape the course of events and make sense of the nature of social relations. Thus, the children's responses to the stories may reflect how they make sense of moral and emotional complexities within the world of the grade school classroom. As Foucault stated, "in our society the main field of morality, the part of ourselves which is most relevant for morality is our feelings" (Foucault, 1983, cited in White, 1994, p. 237).

In terms of linguistic universals of moral language, as mentioned earlier in the book, and which will be discussed in more detail in the following sections regarding educational implications, Wierzbicka's (2006) claim that linguistic universals exist on the basis of cross-linguistic research, that the concepts of "good" and "bad" can be used across a wide range of domains and they can be seen as English exponents of the universal human concept with exact semantic equivalents in other languages. However, according to Wierzbicka and her colleagues (2006), the concepts of "right" and "wrong" are not linguistic universals and need to be interpreted within the particular culture. Thus, although the majority of the children responded in that they thought the story characters would do something good, the children's responses regarding what they thought would be the "right" or "wrong" thing to do would need to be interpreted within the particular cultural frame.

Regarding the findings in terms of research related to literature on shyness and social withdrawal, the children were rated as shy or socially withdrawn, their responses also reflect that the "right" thing to do was to include either the new girl, or include Tom in the team by choosing him for the team. The present research aimed to investigate the various conceptual mechanisms that may underlie the association between social cognitions and social withdrawal. For example, as I discussed in Chapters 1 and 2, some researchers are starting to explore the possibility that for children rated as shy or socially withdrawn, global biases and deficits in sociocognitive processing may contribute generally toward social maladjustment. Such individual differences may have implications for children's social behavior within the classroom.

Researchers suggest that socially withdrawn children differ in their ability to act upon their prosocial cognitions due to poor emotional regulation and social inhibition (Rubin et al., 2002). That is, withdrawn children may process social situations similarly to their more sociable peers, but lack the ability to sufficiently regulate their emotions in the face of arousing social situations. Thus, as Wichmann, Coplan, and Daniels (2004) suggest, socially withdrawn children may show a performance rather than a competence deficit. Building on previous literature which shows socially withdrawn children to be more depressed, anxious and hold more negative self-perceptions than their non-withdrawn age mates, the present study discussed in this book explored the emotional experiences of children rated as either shy or socially withdrawn, especially regarding children's interpretations of social ambiguity.

Social-cognitive and emotional processes may also serve as a protective or exacerbating factor as well. In contrast to past research on aggressive children that suggests they attribute negative consequences that befall them to the purposeful thoughts of their protagonists, such children respond with anger and hostility (Dodge & Frame, 1982). Less is known about the social-cognitive processes that accompany and predict anxious withdrawal. For example, Wichmann, Coplan, and Daniels (2004) reported that compared with their peers, socially withdrawn children displayed a pattern of self-defeating attributions and reported lower efficacy for assertive goals, and indicated a preference for nonassertive, withdrawn strategies to deal with hypothetical conflict situations. However, as Rubin and Coplan (2004) note, little is known about how children respond to ambiguously caused negative events, and the research presented in this book aims to further this area of research as the present study asked children to discuss their emotional perceptions regarding socially ambiguous situations within a school context regarding girls and boys.

Drawings of Self and Play

Across the years (from the six-year-olds to the eight-year-olds), the majority of children's drawings depicting play included social scenes that showed the children playing outdoors in natural environmental scenes with grass, flowers, and so on. Two girls and one boy drew solitary pictures with only themselves in the drawing. Regarding emotional content, the majority of the drawings reflected positive affect. For example, all characters drawn were smiling—except one character (boy), and when children drew the sun, the sun was smiling. Aside from one six-year-old boy (W), all children across all ages used a variety of colors in their drawings. The play activities depicted across the ages focused on physical cooperative and competitive activities—outdoors including soccer, tag, swinging, skipping, playing hide-and-go-seek. When children drew themselves in solitary drawings, they depicted biking (six-year-old girl, M), standing still, or playing soccer (eight-year-old boy, W). No children drew animals or voice bubbles. The majority of children across the years drew ground or a base line such as grass, floor, and so on, although two girls consistently drew without a foundation (no grass/ground).

Across the years, all children drew full face views of themselves and in contrast to past research mentioned earlier in Chapter 2 (Malchiodi, 1998; Richer, 1990), both girls and boys drew full frontal face views and represented emotional expressions, and across the six children over the years, both girls and boys depicted drawings of physical movement, as well as stationary activities. Although the majority of children drew their friends, some children included family members such as siblings or parents. No teachers were included in the play diagrams. Interestingly, no children drew pictures of indoor games either electronic (e.g., computer games, hand-held electronic games) or nonelectronic such as board games, painting/drawing, etc. Regarding the representation of technology, no children included drawings of any electronic device such as a computer, television, radio, cellular phones, and so on.

Approximately six months after the drawings were obtained, children were shown their diagrams and then asked a few questions about their drawings such as how they felt drawing the pictures and to explain what they drew, and if they had a chance to change anything—would they—and if so, what would they change (e.g., add/delete).

All children who remembered that they drew their pictures also claimed that they were feeling happy that day because they were in a good mood, or they liked drawing, it was a good day.

A few children stated that if given the opportunity, they would change or add some things to their drawings—mainly external objects such as more grass or sun, although a few children mentioned that they would add some extra characters including their friends or family members, extra color, or grass/bushes (external objects or scenic objects). Below, I have included descriptions of the children's drawings for each year, as well as a selection of interviews with the six and eight-year-old children discussing their drawings in more detail with the Researcher.

Children's Voices Regarding their Drawings

Descriptions of Drawings for Six-Year-Olds (Girls)

L's Drawing, 1 solitary character (self)—standing still and straight on grass—smiling—1 sun (multicolor)

Self-Narrative for Drawing (Interview, April, 2004)

> R: Do you remember drawing this picture and writing this little story?
> L: Yes.
> R: Do you remember anything special that happened on that day you drew the picture?
> L: I don't know.
> R: Do you remember how you felt when you were drawing the picture and writing the story?
> L: Happy.
> R: Why did you feel happy?
> L: I don't know.
> R: That's a very interesting picture, tell me some things about it. Where are you, what are you doing?
> L: It's me playing in the grass.
> R: What are you playing?
> L: I'm not really playing anything I was just pretending that there was someone else there and playing tag with them.
> R: Oh I see so you were playing but sort of pretending.
> R: Is there anything you would like to change or add to this story? Do you like it the way that it is?
> L: Flowers and another person.

R: Who would you add?

L: My mommy.

P: Flowers in my arms.

T's, Drawing: two girls, self with soccer ball—both girls smiling (multicolor).

Self-Narrative for Drawing (Interview, April, 2004, T)

R: Do you remember drawing this picture and writing this little story?

T: No.

R: Do you remember anything special that happened on that day you drew the picture? Do you remember how you felt when you were drawing the picture and writing the story?

T: No.

R: That's a very interesting picture, tell me some things about it. Where are you, what are you doing?

T: Playing soccer.

R: Oh is that a soccer ball?

T: Yeah.

R: And who's your friend?

T: R.

R: And are you playing at school or at home?

T: No response.

R: Don't know? Oh you just know you're playing soccer. Do you like playing soccer? Is that your favorite game?

R: If you had a chance to change anything or fix anything in this picture, what would you change?

P: Don't know.

M's Drawing: 1 girl riding bike by herself—smiling, 2 clouds, 3 flours (multicolor)—no interview.

Descriptions of Drawings for Six-Year-Olds (Boys)

G's, Drawing: 4 characters—1 character on a swing, all 4 characters are smiling—all blue (1 color crayon).

Self-Narrative for Drawing (Interview, April, 2004, G)

R: Do you remember drawing this picture and writing this little story?

G: No I don't remember that … Oh I remember now.

R: Do you remember anything special that happened on that day you drew the picture?

G: I had fun playing.

R: Do you remember how you felt when you were drawing the picture and writing the story?

G: Happy.

R: Why did you feel happy?

G: Because I like drawing pictures.

R: That's a very interesting picture, tell me some things about it.

G: That's my baby V in the Jolly Jumper and that's my dad and that's my mom and that's me.

R: Where are you, what are you doing?

G: Um, I am playing with my mom.

R: If you had a chance to change anything or fix anything in this picture, what would you change?

G: I would draw my picture.

R: Is there anything you would like to change or add to this story? Do you like it the way that it is?

G: I like it the way it is.

W's Drawing: 3 characters standing beside one another, all characters are smiling, sky/grass/clouds (multicolor).

Self-Narrative for Drawing (Interview, April, 2004, W)

R: Do you remember drawing this picture and writing this little story?

W: Yes.

R: Do you remember anything special that happened on that day you drew the picture?

W: No.

R: Do you remember how you felt when you were drawing the picture and writing the story?

W: No.

R: That's a very interesting picture, tell me some things about it. Where are you, what are you doing?

W: Outside playing, I am playing with my friends.

R: What are you playing?

W: Tag.

R: If you had a chance to change anything or fix anything in this picture, what would you change?

W: Nothing.

Q, no drawing.

Description of Drawings for Seven-Year-Old Girls

L's Drawing: 2 girls, skipping, 1 boy standing, 1 sun (multicolor).

T's Drawing: 3 girls smiling, T in middle of skipping rope (full front view) with 2 girls at side-profiled holding skipping rope (multicolor).

M's Drawing: 2 girls playing in the leaves and smiling, 1 sun (multicolor).

Description of Drawings for Seven-Year-Old Boys

G, no drawing.

W's Drawing: 1 character standing alone smiling, sky/grass/clouds/birds/sun (multicolor).

Q's Drawing: 4 characters playing hide and go seek and smiling, 2 doors/1 house (multicolor).

Descriptions of Drawings for Eight-Year-Old Girls

L's Drawing: 1 character smiling (solitary), standing still on grass, 1 sun, 1 flower (multicolor).

Self-Narrative for Drawing (Interview, February, 2006, L)

> R: Do you remember drawing this picture and writing this story?
> L: Yes.
> R: Do you remember anything special that happened on that day you drew the picture?
> L: I remember when I got home my brother and sister raked the leaves in a pile so I jumped in it.
> R: Do you remember how you felt when you were drawing the picture and writing the story? Why did you feel this way?
> L: Happy because when I jumped in the leaves I thought it was sort of fun. Drawing it made me feel like I was actually doing it.
> R: That's a very interesting picture, tell me some things about it. Where are you, what are you doing?
> L: Jumping in a leaf pile in the fall and the sun is shining over my head.
> R: If you had a chance to change anything or fix anything in this picture, what would you change?
> L: I'd add my friend beside me and make the leaf pile bigger.

R: Is there anything you would like to change or add to this story? Do you like it the way that it is?

L: I like the way it is.

T's Drawing: two girls—all smiling, (full front view) with two girls at side, T holding football (multicolor).

M, no drawing.

Descriptions of Drawings for Eight-Year-Old Boys

G's Drawing: two characters (G and Dad), both playing soccer and smiling, grass/clouds (multicolor).

Self-Narrative for Drawing (Interview, February, 2006, G)

R: Do you remember drawing this picture and writing this little story?

G: Yes.

R: Do you remember anything special that happened on that day you drew the picture?

G: No.

R: Do you remember how you felt when you were drawing the picture and writing the story? Why did you feel happy?

G: Happy because I was drawing.

R: That's a very interesting picture, tell me some things about it. Where are you, what are you doing?

G: It's soccer. That's my friend going at the net cause I'm going to kick it at him. That's my friend Y. We're playing soccer in the field.

R: If you had a chance to change anything or fix anything in this picture, what would you change?

G: Leave it the way it is.

W's drawing: one character, smiling and playing soccer, sky/grass/clouds/soccer ball/sun (multicolor).

Self-Narrative for Drawing (Interview, February, 2006, W)

R: Do you remember drawing this picture and writing this little story?

W: Yes.

R: Do you remember anything special that happened on that day you drew the picture?

W: I don't think so.

R: Do you remember how you felt when you were drawing the picture and writing the story? Why did you feel this way?

W: Happy because I was having a good day.

R: That's a very interesting picture, tell me some things about it. Where are you, what are you doing?

W: This is me playing soccer at the park. This is a stream. This is the sky and sun, I'm playing with my friends.

R: If you had a chance to change anything or fix anything in this picture, what would you change?

W: No response

Q's drawing: 5 characters playing hide and go seek, 4 smiling (including Q), 1 character frowning, 2 doors/2 trees/grass. sun/sky (multicolor).

Self-Narrative for Drawing (Interview, February, 2006, Q)

R: Do you remember drawing this picture and writing this little story?

Q: Yes.

R: Do you remember anything special that happened on that day you drew the picture?

Q: No.

R: Do you remember how you felt when you were drawing the picture and writing the story? Why did you feel this way?

Q: A bit happy because I was drawing something.

R: That's a very interesting picture, tell me some things about it. Where are you, what are you doing?

Q: Me and my friends together playing hide and go seek and we're hiding. He's counting.

R: If you had a chance to change anything or fix anything in this picture, what would you change?

Q: I'd put more bushes and more colors into the people.

Drawings of Play and Self: Summary and Silences

Regarding the silences in the data obtained from the children's drawings of play and self. Interestingly, regarding the illustration of imaginative or pretend play, only one six-year-old girl described her drawing as an example of her "I'm not really playing anything I was just pretending that there was someone else there and playing tag with them." (L, March, 2004). Similarly, no drawings reflected inner thinking or self-talk or private speech, no children drew voice bubbles to illustrate thinking or mental states and imagination.

Additional silences in the data showed that children did not draw teachers or explicit drawings of the classroom (e.g., desk, chalkboard) were included in the play diagrams. Furthermore, no children drew pictures of indoor games such as board games, painting/drawing, etc. Interestingly, no child drew a picture of a computer or any electronic device (e.g., electronic hand-held games, cellular phones, etc.) These gaps in the data were are consistent with previous research on children's (ages six to nine) drawings of play (Richer, 1990) in that previous research has found that children are more likely to draw pictures of physical activities, either autotelic (or done for your own sake, they are ends in themselves) such as biking or swimming, solitary (skipping) or cooperative (such as group-skipping, collaborative building a playhouse), or competitive (e.g., soccer, basketball). Our findings support this past research, in that the majority of children drew physical (cooperative/competitive), or autotelic activities.

Another interesting silence in the drawing data involved the lack of illustration of technology or electrical equipment. Given the technologically advanced classroom, and the availability of televisions and computers in most homes, many children find that both their school and home worlds are filled with noise and various machines (e.g., TV, computer, radio). For many children, solitary play or time alone may have been a time when she or he enjoyed some "quiet time" to themselves, but research shows that an increasing percentage of children and adolescents are spending their solitary and/or leisure time either on the computer or using some electronic device (Ward, 2004). However, despite these past research findings, given the increasing role technology plays in children's learning contexts and exposure to the electronic media such as television, videos, videogames, computers, and so on, in our study, all six children chose not to draw any technological or electronic devices or games across the years.

This lack of illustration of technology may have been due to a fear of drawing a technological device. For example, how would one draw a cell phone or a computer? Another explanation could be that in the present study, children's perceptions of playing do not include references to electronic play such as technological or electrical devices (e.g., televisions, computers, cellular phones, etc.) and games (e.g., electronic, hand-held games, etc.). Perhaps children of this age (six to ten years) perceive playing as technology-free games, and as the drawings suggest, more physical activities including the natural environment.

Future research needs to continue to explore this in more detail, and to seek ways to assess children's perceptions of "play." For example, if children's perception of play fails to include technology, what does this mean for their definitions of the Internet or anything electronic. Perhaps the children described in this book viewed these electronic devices as either entertainment, or perhaps as communication and learning tools as opposed to sources of play? As Scarlett et al. (2005) suggest, given that technology such as the personal computer may provide different opportunities in the classroom for learning, perhaps educators need to work on strengthening the connection between the integration of computers in the classroom and children's play and imaginative lives. As I further discuss in Chapter 5, future research should continue to explore the connections between the use of technology, emotions, and play in middle childhood.

Also, given the children's level of cognitive development, although we expected to find evidence of imaginative play, only one child (six-year-old girl) drew a picture of herself "… pretending that there was someone else there and playing tag with them." No children drew voice or thought bubbles, children did not choose to include these bubbles in their drawings of play (Flavell, 1998, 2000). Also, given past research on children's drawings of play, we expected some children to draw pictures of themselves playing board games or painting/drawing (Richer, 1990) although across the years of the study, no such drawings were found among the six children.

The finding that children did not include drawings of their teachers or draw-ings of the school classroom such as a desk, books, or chalkboard suggests that they do not perceive these objects as representative of their play experiences. Given the vague direction we offered to the children "Draw a picture of yourself playing and circle yourself in the picture," consistent with past research on children's drawings, (Richer, 1990; Willat, 2005), children may have included in their spontaneous drawings objects and scenes regarding what they knew or thought, as opposed to what they perceived visually (e.g., what they see). Thus, perhaps the children's drawings represented their thoughts and feelings about their ideas around play experiences as we also found this in their interviews. As explained earlier in the chapter, when asked to discuss their drawings either in the stories or in-person dur-ing the interviews, children also explained their perceptions of play and self. Overall, the lack of drawings of academic-related materials in their drawings suggest that children do not include academic material or indoor games such as board games, drawing/painting, and so on, in their perceptions of play within the school context. Although this may be representative of their abilities to draw such activities, this finding could also be due to their thoughts regarding their concept of play.

In a different approach to exploring what the drawings did reveal regarding emotional expressions, the diagrams did not reveal any negativity in either the faces of the children or their playmates. This positivity bias has been found in the previous research with children given the possible social desirability factor in that some children may have drawn what they thought the researcher would have wanted (e.g., Richer, 1990). The lack of negative faces could also suggest that children perceive play to be a positive experience and that when they think of themselves playing, they may see themselves and their playmates as smiling and happy.

4.3. Communicating with Self and Others

As mentioned in Chapter 3, to explore children's interest in communicating with oneself and others, as part of our ongoing research project, we asked some children to continue to help us to understand how they think of themselves in terms of their friends and family, and to understand what talking and listening means to them with their friends as well as their family. For example, we asked them questions regarding their sense of self, as either talkers or listeners, as well as their thoughts on their peer relations and communication. We also asked questions concerned with their preferences and habits regarding talking and listening with their peers and family. Regarding the peer relations communication, children were asked "When you're with your friends, what do you like do better, talk or listen, and why?" (see Chapter 3 for the list of interview questions).

The majority of children across both genders were more likely to choose listening for the main reason of learning from the conversations. We also asked, "When you're with your friends, how do you feel when you are talking with others, listening to others, and how do you feel when you are silent or being quiet? As described below, some of the children's common responses across provided very positive and engaging experiences and the majority chose either to talk or listen. However, we asked children to make a decision as to whether they preferred talking or listening (with friends and family). Overall, when asked how they feel when quiet or silent, most children reported mixed feelings regarding being silent or quiet, with some children reporting that they felt fine, although some reported feeling nervous. I've outlined below some excerpts of transcripts from the interviews.

Children's Voices (Girls) M, nine years old; (February, 2007)

Peer Relations/Communication

R: When you're with your friends, what do you like to do better, talk or listen? Why?

M: Both.

R: When you're with your friends, how do you feel when you talk with others.

M: Happy because I like spending time with my friends.

R: How do you feel when you are silent or being quiet.

M: Don't know. In between.

R: How do you feel when you are listening?

M: In between.

R: What do you like best about listening to your friends?

P: I get to hear what they want to say to me.

R: What do you like best about talking with your friends?

M: Talking about each other.

Talking/Listening

R: Would you call yourself or think of yourself as more of a "talker" or a "listener?" (with friends/family) Why?

M: Friends—Listener, I'm more like a quiet one.

M: Family—Both, I don't know why.

R: Are listening and talking the same thing?

M: No.

R: If not how are they different?

M: Don't know.

R: For example, what does someone mean when they say "I hear you." Are they listening to you—how do you know? When you are talking with someone, how do you know that she or he is listening to you?

M: They look at you, they're not talking over top of you.

R: What evidence would make you think that he or she are listening to you? For example, what are the clues or signs that help you think that he or she is listening to you? How do you feel when you think that he or she is listening to you?

M: Good. Because they're interested in what I'm saying.

R: What are you thinking?

M: I'm thinking that they want to hear what I'm saying.

R: How do you think s/he feels when he or she listens to you?

M: Interested.

R: What do you think s/he is thinking?

R: When you are talking with someone, how do you know that he or she is not listening to you?

M: They might be talking to someone else, they could be playing with something.

R: What evidence would make you think that he or she are not listening to you? For example, what are the clues or signs that help you think that he or she is not listening to you? How do you feel when you think that he or she is not listening to you?

M: I feel upset because the person is being rude.

R: What are you thinking?

M: That the person doesn't really want to hear what I'm saying.

R: How do you think he or she feels when he or she does not listen to you?

M: Not sure. They would feel Ok.

R: What do you think s/he is thinking?

M: Don't know. Maybe that I'd be upset.

Children's Voices (Girls) L, nine years old; (February, 2007)

Peer Relations/Communication

R: When you're with your friends, what do you like to do better, talk or listen? Why?

L: Talk because I like to talk a lot I don't know why. I like listening too because I can learn more.

R: When you're with your friends, how do you feel when you talk with others?

L: Happy because they're always saying positive things not negative.

R: How do you feel when you are silent or being quiet?

L: Like I want to do something else. For example if someone made a mistake on something I want to blurt out the right answer. It's annoying when I'd rather be talking.

R: How do you feel when you are listening?

L: During class in lesson I don't mind because I know everything is right from the teacher or if they're doing speeches they've researched it. With my friends sometimes I don't know if it's right so I ask them questions. I feel happy when they're saying nice things, sad if they're saying mean things.

R: What do you like best about listening to your friends?

L: You get to learn new things.

R: What do you like best about talking with your friends?

L: They get to learn what you know about and your favorite subject.

Talking/Listening

R: Would you call yourself or think of yourself as more of a "talker" or a "listener?" (with friends/family) Why?

L: Friends—Talker because most of the time I play with kids that don't really talk and they're shy so lets say we were playing a game when someone had to talk all the time, I'd probably be the person talking. They're shy because, she for example doesn't like talking in front of people, she's nervous in class.

L: Family—Listener, because my mom and dad always tell me stuff I have to do. I always have to baby-sit my brother and sister and they do most of the talking, and I say can you be quiet a little bit because I'm trying to do my homework.

R: Are listening and talking the same thing? If not how are they different?

L: Sort of because in talking you learn because people correct you, and in listening you learn new things.

R: What does someone mean when they say "I hear you." Are they listening to you—how do you know? When you are talking with someone, how do you know that s/he is listening to you?

L: They're looking at you and they're actually interested and asking questions. My teacher was talking about math, and I raised my hand and asked questions.

R: What evidence would make you think that s/he are listening to you? For example, what are the clues or signs that help you think that s/he id listening to you?

R: How do you feel when you think that he or she is listening to you?

L: Happy and appreciated.

R: What are you thinking?

L: Wow, they think I'm not boring.

R: How do you think he or she feels when he or she listens to you?

L: Interested in the subject.

R: What do you think he or she is thinking?

L: Depends, say we were in math class they'd be thinking about math.

R: When you are talking with someone, how do you know that he or she is not listening to you?

L: They're looking around the room, like at hockey, our coach was trying to talk to us and a puck fell and everyone looked at the puck.

R: What evidence would make you think that he or she are not listening to you? For example, what are the clues or signs that help you think that he or she is not listening to you? How do you feel when you think that he or she is not listening to you?

L: Disappointed because it's like the entire time you're trying to tell them something important and they weren't listening.

R: What are you thinking?

L: I think why can't they listen to me, am I so boring that they mind?

R: How do you think he or she feels when he or she does not listen to you?

L: Sometimes they're bored, and sometimes they don't like me or something.

R: What do you think he or she is thinking?

L: They're thinking this is boring, I'm going to look around for something else interesting and hopefully she doesn't notice.

Children's Voices (Boy) Q, nine years old; (February, 2007)

Peer Relations/Communication

R: When you're with your friends, what do you like to do better, talk or listen? Why?

Q: Talk because sometimes I make jokes and sometimes I just talk about other things like what we've done over the weekend.

R: When you're with your friends, how do you feel when you talk with others.

Q: Good because I'm with my friends.

R: How do you feel when you are silent or being quiet, how do you feel when you are listening?"

Q: I don't really feel anything, because I'm silent.

R: What do you like best about listening to your friends.

Q: When we're together we like to talk about the same things.

R: What do you like best about talking with your friends?

Q: I like when people tell jokes.

Talking/Listening

R: Would you call yourself or think of yourself as more of a "talker" or a "listener?" (with friends/family) Why?

Q: Friends—In between because sometimes I talk and usually someone else will talk and I'll just listen.

Q: Family—Listener because usually at dinner my parents talk about their day at work and my sister will talk about school and usually I just listen.

R: Are listening and talking the same thing? If not how are they different? For example, what does someone mean when they say "I hear you." Are they listening to you—how do you know?

Q: No response.

R: When you are talking with someone, how do you know that he or she is listening to you?

Q: They're looking at me and they might talk back.

R: What evidence would make you think that he or she are listening to you? For example, what are the clues or signs that help you think that he or she is listening to you? How do you feel when you think that he or she is listening to you?

Q: Good because they're listening and they know what I'm talking about.

R: What are you thinking?

Q: That they're listening to me.

R: How do you think he or she feels when he or she listens to you?

Q: Good because we might be talking about something that they like.

R: What do you think he or she is thinking?

Q: About whatever I'm talking about.

R: When you are talking with someone, how do you know that he or she is not listening to you?

Q: They're looking away and not talking.

R: What evidence would make you think that he or she is not listening to you? For example, what are the clues or signs that help you think that he or she is not listening to you?

R: How do you feel when you think that he or she is not listening to you?

R: What are you thinking?

Q: I'm thinking that they should just go because they have better things to do then listen to me.

R: How do you think he or she feels when he or she does not listen to you?

Q: Rushed, they have to go somewhere and I'm talking and they want me to finish.

R: What do you think he or she is thinking?

Q: They're thinking why don't I just stop talking, cause they have to go somewhere.

Children's Voices (Boy) G, nine years old; (February, 2007)

Peer Relations/Communication

R: When you're with your friends, what do you like to do better, talk or listen? Why?

G: Talk. Because it's more like me to talk.

R: When you're with your friends, how do you feel when you talk with others?

G: Happy. Because I like to talk.

R: How do you feel when you are silent or being quiet?

G: Bored. It's an in between feeling.

R: How do you feel when you are "listening?"

G: Bored because the teacher says boring stuff in the class.

R: What do you like best about listening to your friends?

G: Sometimes they say stuff that's funny.

R: What do you like best about talking with your friends?

G: You can communicate about stuff.

Talking/Listening

R: Would you call yourself or think of yourself as more of a "talker" or a "listener?" (with friends/family) Why?

G: Friends—Listener, because I have some friends that talk for a while and I just get to listen.

G: Family—Talker because I like talking with B.

R: Are listening and talking the same thing? If not how are they different?

G: Sort of, but not really. Sometimes I listen and talk. They're different things.

R: For example what does someone mean when they say "I hear you." Are they listening to you—how do you know? When you are talking with someone, how do you know that he or she is listening to you?

G: Standing right in front of me.

R: What evidence would make you think that he or she are listening to you? For example, what are the clues or signs that help you think that he or she is listening to you? How do you feel when you think that he or she is listening to you?

G: Good.

R: What are you thinking?

G: I forget and then I tell them.

R: How do you think he or she feels when he or she listens to you?

G: Happy because when I say funny stuff it makes them happy.

R: What do you think he or she is thinking?

G: I don't know.

R: When you are talking with someone, how do you know that he or she is not listening to you?

G: That B.'s just like not looking at me.

R: What evidence would make you think that he or she are not listening to you? For example, what are the clues or signs that help you think that he or she is not listening to you? How do you feel when you think that he or she is not listening to you?

G: I just wish they'd listen because sometimes it's important and I think "come on, listen!"

R: What are you thinking?

G: I'm just thinking of other stuff trying to get their attention. Just like saying it loud.

R: How do you think he or she feels when he or she does not listen to you?

G: They wouldn't really care.

R: What do you think he or she is thinking?

G: They might be thinking about playing.

Communicating with Self and Other: Summary

Given the age of the children (approximately nine years of age), their responses regarding descriptions of the self concerning talking/listening and their communication with others involved a greater number of references to psychological dimensions as compared to interviews with the six-year-olds. These findings reflect past research which shows that children's conceptions of self and others develops from physical, behavioral descriptions, to more psychological and mentalistic descriptions. As past research shows (Damon & Hart, 1988; Harter, 1999), as children grow from early childhood through to middle childhood, they are more likely to include both behavioral and mental state information as they develop understandings of other's minds and as they come to think of themselves and others as intentional, psychological beings (Boseovski, Marcovitch, & Love, 2007; Gelman & Heyman, 1999; Kamawar, Ridgeway, Holock, & Glennie, 2007). For example, almost all children mentioned the importance of their "personality" or the kind of person that they were—including both behavioral activities and psychological traits.

The conversations regarding the talking and listening illustrated the important role emotions play in the social communication process with both family and peers. Children also noted that their role in the conversation was usually contingent upon the social context of the conversation. That is, their role and preference for talking/listening varied as a function of whether they were speaking with their family or their friends. For example, the majority of children switched between roles of listener and talker such that they would think of themselves as a talker with their friends, but a listener with their family, or vice versa. Interestingly, no child thought of her/himself as a listener or a talker in both contexts, suggesting that they defined their roles as a function of the conversation partner, be it a family member or a peer. These findings support past research that suggests the role of the emotional and moral context of relationships plays a key role in the communication process between children and adults (Isaacs, 1937; Maccoby, 1998).

Throughout the conversations, the importance of emotional connections and caring relationships with others played a role in how they perceived their roles as either a talker or a listener. Many children mentioned the importance of being able to "be myself" with my friends and family, and to trust and feel comfortable with those that they care about. For example, when asked how they feel when talking with their friends, all children expressed positive feelings, as this nine-year-old boy stated, "Good. Because they're my friends and they won't do anything bad to me." Such findings support past research that suggests relationships with peers and family help children to learn about the emotional worlds of others (Denham, 1998; Harris, 1998; Saarni, 1999). As Dunn (2004) notes, when asked to talk about their experiences with their peers, many children as young as six and seven years begin to develop the ability to understand the subtleties of the human connections and communication between two beings that care about each other. Such research shows that by the ages of six to nine years, many children begin to develop the understanding that these exchanges are information-laden packed full with emotional and moral content, and involve many more pieces than the mere verbal aspect of the conversation (e.g., Dunn, 2006; Tannen, 1994).

Regarding the specific emotional reactions to the conversations, all children noted the strong positive feelings associated with the experience of being listened to, and were able to detect whether or not people were listening to what they were saying during a conversation. All children noted the negative feelings associated with the experience of not being listened to, and this reflects the important role language and social communication play in their self and emotional development. When asked to imagine what the listener was thinking as they were not listening to them, many children thought that the listener, maybe, thought they were boring, or that they would rather be somewhere else. Children's feelings around the experience of being quiet or silent were mixed, with some children expressing negative emotions such as boredom or nervousness, while others mentioned more positive feelings such as patience. Aside from emotions playing a key role in children's perspectives of talking and listening, another key theme that emerged involved the educational value of listening and talking with others—almost all children stated that they enjoyed talking and listening to others because they were able to learn from the conversations. That is, most children noted the educational importance of conversation and found it to be a learning experience. In sum, the positive and negative emotional experiences associated with the experiences of being listened to (or not) holds many educational and clinical implications for socially withdrawn children which will be discussed in the next chapter.

4.5. Silences among the Shadows

Given the complexity and ambiguity of emotional issues (Harris, 1989, 2000), the six children provided responses to questions of self, ambiguous social events, and emotional issues. Reading across the various tasks over the years (six to ten years of age), the interviews and the drawings of the self and play experiences revealed key themes of an increasing focus on peer relations and a declining participation of adults in the children's lives. This finding supports past research that suggests that as children enter middle childhood and early adolescence, although the family remains an important factor in self-development, the peer group begins to play an increasingly important role in the children's developing sense of self (Schaffer, 1996). Such a finding may also hold particular relevance for children rated as shy or socially withdrawn by their teachers as relational issues may play a key role in shy children's emotional learning experiences (Rubin, Burgess, & Coplan, 2002). Across the various tasks, responses illustrated a focus on positive emotions and illustrations of positive experiences regarding play. Although these responses could have been due in part to the influence of social desirability in that perhaps the participants wanted to "please the researcher," these findings also support past research that shows that for some contexts, children are more likely to refer to positive emotional experiences as opposed to negative (Denham, 1998).

In addition to main themes, what the children did not discuss during the conversations or what was missing from their drawings also provides us with insightful information regarding the children's perceptions of emotional experiences within the classroom. Also, given the gaps in the conversations and drawings, how can we explain these silences within the context of existing empirical evidence, and what do these silences mean for educational implications?

In general, across the self-understanding, social stories, and emotional understanding interviews, children did not discuss aspects of spirituality or issues of culture and language. Such a gap in the conversation regarding issues of ethnicity and culture are interesting in that the silence may reflect the difficulty in discussing sensitive issues such one's cultural background and how this connects to emotional learning (Basso, 1970; Behrens, 2004; Briggs, 1995; Kahima et al., 1995). Alternatively, the silences could represent the fact that children did not think about these issues within the context of the questions, or the issues may not play a relevant role in these particular six children's emotional lives within the classroom given the cultural context of the school and the children's homes.

In addition, through the conversations, aside from some responses referring to emotions of pride, children did not explicitly discuss relationships with teachers or aspects of school/academic tasks. This lack of conversation regarding academic issues may suggest that the importance of relationships and connections with friends and family play a crucial role in self-development and emotional experiences within the classroom. This focus on the relational and emotional aspect of education supports holistic approaches to learning (e.g., Bruner, 1996; Drake, 1992; Goldstein, 1997), and emphasizes the importance of personal engagement and social and emotional experiences within the classroom. Finally, as I mentioned earlier, the majority of children did not discuss the Internet or any use of electronic or virtual communications with peers or their family members. Two nine-year-old boys mentioned that they played on the computer and video games as they describe what they liked to do. Thus, this absence of illustrations of technological devices within the context of play and also within the conversations regarding self-concept and social and emotional experiences may reflect the children's thinking regarding whether or not the role of technology and media play a role in their inner world.

4.6. Key Lessons Learned

In sum, this chapter described the key findings regarding the six children's emotional experiences over the years (six to nine years) regarding the contexts of the interviews regarding self-understanding, social understanding, and emotional understanding (happy, sad, proud, embarrassed). Summaries of the key findings of their drawings regarding self and play were also discussed. Across the six children's responses, key underlying themes were discussed that emerged from the conversations over the years, and these commonalities or themes may suggest that peers and family may play a crucial role in shy or socially withdrawn children's emotional experiences within the classroom. In addition to the role the family and friends play in self-understanding and emotional experiences, participants across all ages and genders discussed the role of a religious or spiritual Deity or presence such as God.

Regarding children's thoughts on listening and talking, the majority of children discussed the complex relations between talking and listening with both friends and family, noting the emotional complexities of realizing when someone is listening to you and not listening to you. Most children also noted that they played different roles in their families as compared to their peers—either they were more of a talker with their family and listener with their friends, or vice versa. Across all of the interviews regarding listening and talking, both emotional and educational experiences were a crucial component of the communication process. That is, the children's perspectives revealed their growing understanding of how a conversation between two people is a multifaceted learning experience that involved more than mere "verbalization" as it included nonverbal cues such as eye contact, facial expressions, body language, and so on. In sum, at the ages of approximately nine years, the children in our study appeared to be skilled at reading the thoughts and emotions of others, particularly during conversations.

As mentioned earlier in the chapter, consistent with past research (Bosacki, 2005), various factors may help to shape children's understanding of religiosity and spirituality including social interactions within various social contexts (family, peers, etc.). Finally, the silences or gaps in the conversations were also noted including issues of culture, language, and technology. Possible explanations were provided to help explain these themes and silences, and I discussed how such findings could help us to further understand children's emotional experiences within the classroom. In the next chapter, I will discuss the theoretical, psychosocial, and educational implications these key themes and silences have for children's emotional experiences within the grade school classroom.

Applications: How Can We "School and Research the Emotions?"

5.1. Introduction: Who Learns from this Research?

This chapter builds on the previous chapter in that it will discuss how the present findings help to further advance developmental theory regarding the emotional lives of children in middle childhood. That is, how do the findings discussed in Chapter 4 further the discourse on current educational and developmental literature? This chapter will describe the three main audiences that will benefit or learn from the findings including: (1) developmental social cognitivists, (2) educators, therapists, policy makers, and learners, and (3) future researchers. Each audience or community of learners will be discussed in turn.

5.2. Developmental Social-Cognitivists

The research discussed in this book extends the existing theoretical and conceptual literature regarding developmental social cognition by exploring the little-known topic of the emotional lives of socially withdrawn children within the middle school grades. As many researchers have noted (Dunn, 2005; Harris, 1989, 2000), during the past two decades, researchers in the field of child development and education have become increasingly concerned about the emotional lives of those children they work with, in addition to themselves as well. Although many exciting new initiatives exist and continue to be developed, given the scope of this book, I will focus on three main areas of development or growth for theorists that focus on promoting children's overall emotional health. As Berkowitz, Sherblom,

Bier, and Battistich (2006) suggest, given that the goal of promoting children's psychological and emotional health cuts across various disciplines and is relevant to both theorists and practitioners, for the purpose of this book, I will focus on the following lines of inquiry in developmental research: positive psychology and applied developmental social cognitive science including the specific research areas of social competence and self-development, and recent work in developmental social cognitive neuroscience. Building on the existing research and literature concerning adolescents and children, consistent with the theme of this book, I will discuss these areas of inquiry in terms of middle childhood and shyness or social withdrawal.

As mentioned in Chapters 1 and 2, children's capacities for internalizing and acting morally and ethically depend upon the many basic aspects of emotional and cognitive development, including the use of language and the development of empathy, etc. (Kagan, 2005). As Dunn (2006) reminds us, the majority of social cognitive theories of moral development state that emotional relationships play a key role. This importance of emotions and the emotional relationships we have with ourselves and others provides the theoretical foundation of the research discussed in this book, and it is my hope that the one "take-away" message or thought that I would like the reader to finish this book with would be the importance of emotions in our everyday lives, particularly the importance for school children.

Given the recent move for educational and developmental research and theory to focus on children's and adolescents' emotional worlds (Dahl, 2007; Selman, 2007), and on the social and cognitive processes of internalization difficulties (Hastings, Utendale, Sullivan, & McShane, 2007; Kuhn, 1989; Seroczynski, Jacquez, & Cole, 2003), there has also been a trend over the past 10 to 15 years regarding the focus on emotional experiences of children in the classroom, and how this relates to their label as either shy or socially withdrawn, aggressive, or "typical"? (Arbeau & Coplan, 2007; Wojslawaowicz Bowker, Rubin, Rose-Krasnor, & Booth-LaForce, 2007). Many researchers also claim that emotional development is also contingent upon aspects of the self and identity, and that morality may develop as part of, or in parallel with the self-system (Hinde, 2002).

Positive Psychology for Children

Regarding the recent movement of positive psychology (Rich, 2003), the theme of this recent developmental approach includes the investigation of positive characteristics of human nature and our social worlds. Drawing on the theories of humanist psychologists (Allport, 1960; Maslow, 1971; Rogers, 1961), and various other developmental and prevention-oriented psychologists (Greenberger & Sorenseon, 1974; Jahoda, 1959), positive psychology aims to promote emotional and mental health and to examine the positive features of human life that make our life meaningful, including the study of such topics as optimism, future mindedness, hope, wisdom, creativity, spirituality, emotionality, and various inter- and intrapersonal skills.

According to Seligman (2002), to promote authentic happiness, a renovated science of prevention needs courageous and forward-minded researchers who are willing to address issues of the mind, morals and the meaning of life to help create a better society and personal health. Although this positive psychology draws on mainly research with adults, this approach which combines both initiative and personal autonomy and social connectedness could help to promote emotional development in children and extend to research on emotional aspects of learning including topics of play and flow (e.g., Csikszentmihalyi, 1990).

This recent movement of psychology focuses on a holistic approach to development in the sense that it includes the investigation of all aspects of our human nature and our social worlds. Seligman and Csikszentmihalyi (2000) describe the movement as a response to psychology's history of focusing on pathology and health problems only. In contrast to this negative focus, positive psychology aims to prevent risky or self-harmful behaviors by examining the positive features of human life that make our life meaningful, including the study of such topics as wisdom, creativity, spirituality, responsibility, and perseverance, hope, future mindedness, and so on (Radford, 2006). Given that positive affect or emotion is listed in the mandate for this research movement in psychology, the focus on both initiative (a characteristic that is associated with individualism and autonomy) and social connectedness could help to promote spiritual development in children and adolescents, and extend to research on play and flow (e.g., Csikszentmihalyi, 1990; Pearce & Van Ryn, 2007).

Although the majority of past research in positive psychology focused on the psychological health in older adolescents and young adults, researchers have also recently started to explore the significance of positive experiences within parent-child relationships for moral development (Dunn, 2006; Hinde, 2002). Similarly, focusing on the concept of happiness, researchers have also started to work on educational programs that promote well-being in children (Layard, 2005; Nodding, 2002). Also, given the interdisciplinary discourse surrounding the psychological and emotional health of the child (Berkowitz et al., 2006), positive psychology also relates to terminologies regarding relevant areas of education and intervention including positive youth development, social and emotional learning, and prevention science which will be discussed further in the chapter.

As collaborative, transcultural applied research that partners spiritual and religious issues with cognitive science, positive psychology would help to prevent mental illness by recognizing and developing sets of strengths, competencies, and virtues in young children, such as future-mindedness, hope, interpersonal and intrapersonal skills, the capacity for playfulness, faith, and a positive or optimistic work ethic. Building these strengths as a buffer is alien to the disease or deficit model that focuses on remedying deficits; the application of such research to educational and clinical settings would promote changes in both mind and behavior. According to Seligman (2002), to promote authentic happiness, a renovated science of prevention needs courageous researchers and educators who are willing to address issues of the mind, morals, and the meaning of life to help create a better society.

As Haidt (2006) suggests, to promote a notion of balance and happiness, we need to help children to first learn how to recognize and become aware of their emotional needs and the emotional needs of others, and then to learn how to balance their needs and the needs of others in a personal, meaningful way that leads to effective social functioning. The question remains as to what is the best way to do this and how can we develop effective models of "best practice" to encourage emotional health in children? For example, to develop children's emotional understandings, also referred to as SEL or social-emotional learning, Bocchino (1999) suggests that educators try to incorporate a classroom procedure referred to as "SAFE" (speak and feel exchange) where students group themselves in pairs, where one learner guides the other in their description of emotional reactions to a particular event. For example, two learners can get together to discuss their emotional reactions to a particular book, film, discussions which occurred from the classroom context.

Applied Developmental Social-Cognitive Science

The second main area of psychological and educational research that may provide particular insight into the emotional experiences of children involves the theory-of-mind (ToM) or psychological understanding research within the larger frame of social cognitive research and cognitive neuroscience. As previously explained, as developmental social cognitive neuroscience gains increased understanding of the social cognitive and neural processes that underlie emotional awareness (Dahl, 2007; Killen & Fox, 2007), it may become clear which brain processes help children in the middle school grades to think in ways that are in tune with themselves, others, nature, and beyond. However, as Bruner (1996) cautions, we need to remain "perspectival" in that the two visions of the mind as either humanistic or naturalistic remain different yet complementary.

As already stated in previous chapters, higher order ToM, or the ability to "read" others' mental states in the context of social action can also be referred to as psychological understanding (Bruner, 1996). This ability to read others' mental states enables children to understand multiple perspectives and to communicate with others (Nelson, Henseler, & Plesa, 2000; Watts, 1944). Although past ToM research focuses on young children (four-and five-year-olds) to show that people have desires that lead them to actions, and these actions are based on beliefs, little is known beyond the age of five, however, little is known about the links between this kind of psychological understanding and social experience. Given that children who possess high levels of psychological understanding are more likely to "think about their own and others' thinking" during the school day, such an ability has important educational implications (Wellman & Lagattuta, 2004). Moreover, research has shown that the ability to "read others" may be connected to children's self-conceptions and their social interactions. Thus, the findings discussed in the present book extends the new areas of ToM research that are beginning to explore 8- to 13-year-old children's ToM abilities by exploring shy children's ToM abilities in that they were asked to make sense of hypothetical socially ambiguous statements by imagining what the children might be thinking or feeling, within the elementary school context. In particular, the research presented in this book explored the connections among higher-order reasoning and children's understanding of simple and complex emotions, their self-concept, and social interactions.

Regarding the further development of higher-order mentalizing ability during childhood, the present research adds to the growing evidence that suggests that emotion understanding and experience continue to develop in complexity during this time, particularly regarding complex and ambiguous emotions (Pons, Lawson, Harris, & de Rosnay, 2003). In contrast to the simple or basic emotions (e.g., happy, sad), to understand complex emotions (e.g., pride, embarrassment), children must hold in mind two separate pieces of information, other people's and societal norms (Lewis, 1995; Lewis, Sullivan, Stanger, & Weiss, 1989; Saarni, 1999). Given that at the time of writing this book, few studies have investigated the links in socially withdrawn children among self-perceptions, second-order ToM (Lalonde & Chandler, 2002, 2007; Lewis & Carpendale, 2002; Mansfield & Clinchy, 1997) and the understanding of complex emotions (Carpendale & Shelton, 1999), and future researchers need to investigate the links between the understanding of complex emotions and higher-order or an interpretive ToM.

Furthermore, future studies should also explore this relation longitudinally, including investigating gendered differences within the school context during middle and late childhood.

Consistent with the book's common theme of emotionality, by focusing on the emotional aspect of development in previously unconnected fields of research such as ToM research (e.g., Astington 1993; Cutting & Dunn, 2002), and the psychosocial literature regarding sensitivity and self-concept (e.g., Dabrowski, 1964; Harter, 1999), the research presented in this book may provide new and innovative possibilities for connecting exploring the emotional lives of children. It is my hope that this research may continue to encourage the connections among these similar areas of research, although in different fields, researchers can come together in future programs of research to promote emotional health and a positive self-concept in emotionally sensitive children in the middle school grades, particularly those children who are labeled as shy or socially withdrawn in the classroom.

The application of the two growing areas of theory and research mentioned above include multidisciplinary, holistic, therapeutic, and educational programs that draw on other cultures for their sources of expertise. As Sternberg notes (2007), although academic knowledge and skills are a foundation for the development of life skills which can apply to all cultural contexts, adaptive success in life depends on much more than the conventional assessments academic knowledge and skills promoted in school. An integrated, transformational learning model that connects education to therapy could provide a useful foundation within which holistic educational and therapeutic programs can be developed. Research findings from the areas of both cognitive science and positive psychology could be used to help create developmentally appropriate educational and clinical programs. For example, findings from applied developmental social cognitive research, such as studies that explore children's ToM understanding could be used to help create a developmentally appropriate curriculum for children in the classroom that aims to promote both inter- and intrapersonal competencies. As such, in the following sections below, I will outline some examples of educational and therapeutic intervention programs that aim to promote emotional health in children.

5.3. Educators, Therapists, Policy Makers, and Learners: "Schooling the Shadows"

In the following sections, I will outline how can the present research findings help educators who work with children to learn how to encourage children to learn about happiness and self-faith and self-knowledge? In agreement with many psycho-education and developmental interventionists (e.g., Bruner, 1996; Jones & Cooper, 2006; Noddings, 2003; Olson, 1994, 1997, 2003; Paley, 2004; Pellegrini, 2005, etc.), I agree that developmental research and educational programs need to be developed in tandem, collaboratively with researcher-educators working together to develop developmentally appropriate curriculum grounded in developmental empirical research. Moving beyond the notion that research and theory should drive educational policy and practice, the fields of psycho-educational practice and developmental research need to work together and learn from each other to co-develop programs of research and education. Such a partnership would ensure that children will learn from educators and therapists who work with children and also are familiar with the experiences of the child across the ages. Most importantly, as Paley (2004) among others advocate, researchers and policy developers need to listen to the voices of the learners and work with the children in that what is reflected in the curriculum represents as closely as possible, the emotional and social and mental worlds of the child.

Consistent with Noddings' (2006) and following the Socrates method, we should teach for self-knowledge, and investigate the selves in connection to others, world, and beyond. I will now discuss educational implications for moral, inclusive, humanistic approaches to education including the use of educational activities to promote children's emotional health. In particular, I will outline below some practical applications that psycho-educators can use to promote children's emotional literacy skills and mindfulness in the middle school grades.

Emotional Language

As I've outlined earlier, according to Wierzbeka's (1999, 2006) work on cultural construction of language and emotion, to help children further understand the connections among culture, language, and emotion, she has developed natural semantic meta-language (NSM) as a research and psycho-educational tool to create universal language and to further our understanding of emotions and language (Wierzbecka, 1999, p. 33, 2006). According to Wierzbecka (1999), emotional concepts can be defined as cognitive scenarios (Wierzbeka, 1999; Notes 2), and this mini-language of universal human concepts derived from empirical cross-linguistic investigations aims to help children create cognitive people-based scenarios (p. 307).

This NSM is similar to the universality of a mentalistic/mental state language that is often used to describe mental state and emotion terms regarding ToM research (Astington & Pelletier, 2005). Similar to NSM, mental state, ToM, or social understanding vocabulary is also based on human experiences and emotions. For example, according to Wierzbicka (1999), the phrases, "I think, I want, I feel" may be universal for all languages (p. 286). Thus, according to Wierzbicka, different languages "choose" different cognitive scenarios as reference pints for their emotional concepts, and no such scenarios are universal. Although at the same time, there are certain components of the cognitive scenarios which appear to be universal as reference points for emotion concepts. For mnemonic purposes, these components could be described as fear-like, anger-like, and shame-like.

According to Wierzbicka (1999, p. 288), it could be suggested that all cultures have a word (or words) referring to the "social emotions" or words referring in their meaning to "people" and to what people may think about us. In particular, these words convey a concern about "bad things" that people may think about us. More specifically, the cognitive components in question can be represented as follows: "People can think something bad of me and I don't want this to happen"—the lexicon suggests that there is a cognitive concern or mental state understanding that is connected to an emotion. Weirzbicka (1999) suggests that although positive emotions or "good" feelings may not include a common assumption that "love" is a universal human emotion, all languages may nonetheless recognize lexically a distinct type of feeling linked with the semantic component "person X wants to do good things for person Y." But many researchers suggest that this issue requires further investigation.

As researchers and educators, we need to wonder why all languages have a word linking feelings with other people's (real or imagined) disapproval, and how do children learn these emotions such as shame, embarrassment, and shyness across different cultures? Whereas anger-like words document a universal human impulse, and need, to "act" (to do something) in order to prevent the repetition or occurrence of some undesirable event. Unlike anger and fear which are considered by some to be "basic" or "simple" emotions (Plutchik, 1994), "shame-like" emotions, in line with the focus of this book on sensitivity and interiority, become more complex in that they involve a more social focus, and are connected with concepts of embarrassment, and shyness. However, some cultures suggest that the emotion concept of fear and shame are similar, with the common theme the strong impulse to retreat from the stimulus (Hiatt, 1978). Furthermore, consistent with the theme of this chapter, what are the implications of such emotion knowledge, particularly regarding the emotions of sadness and embarrassment (those which were included in the research discussed earlier), for how we think and feel about ourselves, and how we interact with others within the school context. The sections below will address these possible implications for education and therapy.

Psycho-educational Activities to Promote Mindful Awareness

Given that Wierzbicka's (1999) NSM and ToM, or metacognitive language can provide educators with a language tool to help promote emotional awareness in children through the awareness of emotion and mental state language, this language could be used to help create literacy activities within the classroom. Such classroom activities would aim to promote intrapersonal and interpersonal competence by means of emotional literacy through the use of NSM and ToM language which would be integrated into the various classroom activities.

For example, NSM and metacognitive language could be used in the classroom to promote the intrapersonal skill of "mindfulness or self-awareness"—as Varela (1992) notes, in Buddhist teaching/learning traditions, the practice of recognizing the emptiness of the self is the very foundation of training, including ethical teaching and learning practices. This practice of recognizing emptiness in every moment is referred to as the practice of mindfulness/awareness or *samatha-vipassana*. Basically, a radical not-doing, it is traditionally understood as a universal practice, but despite having been refined and explored for over 2,500 years by over half the world, it was never discovered independently in the West. Thus, this *samatha-vipassana* creates the space through nonaction, which included nonresponse to language which may be a useful activity to help children cope with silence or encourage children to wait before attempting to respond immediately in class conversation.

As outlined in Table 5.1, educators need to incorporate educational activities that promote emotional understanding and mindfulness throughout the curriculum. To illustrate, the student/practitioner learning mindfulness/awareness may first begin by observing, in a precisely prescribed fashion, what the mind is doing, its restfulness, perpetual grasping, from moment to moment. This classroom activity is consistent with Rudolph Steiner's (1976) notion of eurythmy, guided imagery, collaborative role-playing activities, etc in that all activities aim to promote children's ability to remain aware of being mindful of the moment, focusing on the present task alone, not thinking about the past or future events. This activity may enable some students to free themselves from some of their habitual patterns of thought, which in turn, may lead to further mindfulness and feelings of warmth toward others, inclusiveness, and relatedness (Steiner, 1976).

This classroom activity may also aim to promote children's ability to develop compassion or the Sanskrit term "*karuna*" claims that mindfulness or awareness requires this warmth or compassion, and this "ethical know-how" is based on

Table 5.1 Curriculum Framework for Children's Emotional Lives (6–12 yrs)

Metacognitive Skill	Learning Goals	Learning Activities
I. Social and Transcultural Connections **Learning Question: What are others thinking? Why?**		
—interpersonal understanding	—develop ability to attribute mental states to others mental states within transcultural context	—critically read, reflect, and respond to novels and poetry that focus on the attribute psycho emotional aspect of interpersonal and transcultural, natural relationships (peers, family, teachers, animals, environment/nature)
1. Conceptual Role-Taking	—understand multiple perspectives/points of view —understand the beliefs and intentions of others	—dramatic role-playing (psychodrama) —painting and writing from multiple perspectives —critical dialogue, debate —cooperative games, peer teaching and learning
Learning Question: What are others feeling? Why?		
2. Empathetic Sensitivity	—understand the emotional worlds of others	—dramatic role-playing —creative writing —conflict mediation
3. Person Perception	—to view others as psychological, emotional beings (i.e, understand personality traits)	—creative writing/film, tv, Internet —critical bibliotherapy (emotions) —painting others' portraits, people sculpting —create comics, characters
Learning Question: Is there another way to think about this? Why?		
4. Divergent Thinking	—create alternate solutions (divergent thinking skills) —promotes cognitive flexibility	—critical media analysis (tv, radio, magazines, film, etc.) magazines, Internet/websites
II. Self Connections **Learning Question: What am I thinking? Why?**		
—intrapersonal understanding	—develop ability to attribute mental states to self on novels that focus on the intrapersonal relationships	—read and reflect on novels with psychoemotional focus (self-discovery, self-journeys)
Learning Question: What am I feeling? Why?		
1. Affective	—develop ability to trust, care, and accept oneself	—guided imagery focused on body-mind-world connection —guided meditation/mindfulness —eurythmy —self-portrait of face/body

Metacognitive Skill	Learning Goals	Learning Activities
2. Cognitive	—understand mental world (thinking process and narrative and visual creation of mental scripts)	—critical bibliotherapy —journaling, dream work —self-portrait of the mind —self-narrative/dialogue and autobiographical writing (thinking using various mediums)

Notes. Overall Learning Goals 1. to advance the critical understanding and care of self and other as psychological beings within the cultural and global context; 2. to promote personal, social, and transcultural competence; 3; to foster the metacognitive abilities that underlie the ability to critically understand one's personal, social worlds, and cultural worlds (i.e., encourage critical emotional and cultural literacy skills). Activities within each domain (social and self respectively) are interchangeable. Learning activities can be applied to a variety of psychocultural themes (gender, ethnicity, social status/popularity), and can serve as both individual and cooperative group assignments.
Source: Adapted from Bosacki, 1998; Bosacki, (2005, p. 131).

our responses to ourselves and others as sentient beings or capable of responding emotionally rather than intellectually. Compassionate action or "skillful means" (*upaya*) in Buddhism is inseparable from wisdom and is somewhat comparable to a cognitive skill in which the learner practices or "plants good seeds"—that is, avoids harmful actions, performs beneficial ones, meditates (Varela, Thompson, & Rosch, 1991).

Drawing on Selman's (2003) activity of asking children to create an emotionally persuasive letter regarding an ethical or sociomoral issue such as a peer conflict or social problem in the school, I suggest that we could ask children in the middle school grades to write about an emotional issue to persuade the principal or teacher to take social action, for example, either to change her mind about an issue or to be sufficiently persuaded that an issue is important enough to warrant their immediate attention. That is, to ask students to encourage others to solve a particular social problem such as how to include another child in a circle or dyad of friends. To incorporate the role of emotional understanding, I would ask the children to think about how they and others would feel in this scenario.

Regarding emotions, children could be asked how they would make someone feel better who is feeling emotionally in pain or feeling down (e.g., hurt, ignored, victimized), and what would they do to help the other person feel better? Children could be asked what is the right and wrong thing to do and why and to elaborate on the issue of what scenario would reveal kindness to both others and self, and which scenario would illustrate cruelty. We could also ask children to explain what they would do to make themselves feel better and what would be the kind and cruel thing to do to themselves and why? Children could be asked to first address the letter to themselves, and then to write a second letter to another person of their choice. That is, they would be asked to decide to choose someone they would like to help such as a family member, teacher, friend, and so on. Children could then compare the two letters and discuss how the letters were the same and/or different and why? Such an activity would promote the development of caring and comforting others, in addition to caring and comforting oneself.

Given the focus of this activity on both self and other, this learning experience would promote both inter- and intrapersonal competencies within the context of stories that are created by the children themselves. By providing the children with this opportunity to create these stories or dilemmas themselves, the stories would be personally relevant to the children at the particular time in their emotional lives. According to Selman (2003), persuasive writing depends upon both the students' capacity to coordinate perspectives and their ability to use their literacy skills to craft a convincing argument. A social developmental lens offers a crucial insight into how students' capacity may be influenced by their understanding of relationships and others' points of view. Thus, a social and emotional developmental perspective might help to shed light on the field of literacy.

Building on the persuasive writing activity, to provide an opportunity for children to express themselves aside from writing, educators could also provide children with the option of drawing a poster or advertisement to encourage people to act in caring, kind, and ethically and socially sensitive ways (persuasive poster)—no text (visual aids only) or to draw a comic strip showing action depicted through social interactions. Further alternative methods of expression could also include sculpture, music, or dramatic art such as role-playing or puppetry. Following the creation of these letters (to self and other), children would then be asked to share and compare the letters in either individually, cooperatively, or both.

In agreement with Selman's (2003) emphasis on encouraging practitioners and researchers to pursue practice, theory, and research simultaneously, I suggest that developmentalist research attitudes and activities need to be co-created with practitioners and researchers within the classrooms in the hope that such research attitudes and activities become part and parcel of regular classroom practice and becomes integrated into school curricula and policies.

Critical Media and Emotional Literacy

Also, given that middle childhood is a time where children are entering preadolescence and their engaging in frequent media use and they may become increasingly in contact with popular media messages as described earlier in the chapter (Elliott,

Woloshyn, Richards, Bosacki, & Golden, 2002; Linn, 2005). Given that popular culture media such as magazines, Internet, and videos may have emotional implications for children who read these articles, educators need to develop critical media literacy programs that encourage children to question and read media from a critical and thoughtful perspective (see Table 5.1). As I have mentioned throughout this book, past research has suggested that particularly emotionally sensitive children may be sophisticated in detecting subtle mixed messages and make sense of ambiguous messages (Cutting & Dunn, 2002; Rudolph & Conley, 2005).

For example, children should be encouraged to read various forms of media and to critically explore the text and reflect and engage in conversations about what are the emotional and moral implications of the content (text or graphics). To illustrate, an example classroom activity could involve children critically reading the advertisements or articles found in a variety of popular magazines targeted for preteens focused on fashion, music, and so on, and explore the content of these magazines and identify key emotional or social messages that they believe would make sense for them around issues of values and character including issues of maybe identity, body image, peer relationships, and so on. Following this critical content analysis, children could then work in groups to discuss the main themes they viewed across the magazines and articles, summarize and document the themes as a group, and they could write a brief critical reflection after the activity to explain what they learned the most from that activity, and to write about their emotional experiences during the activity.

I have used multiple versions of this activity with learners of all ages (grade school to graduate school), and over the years I have found that all learners tend to come away from this activity with something that they need to learn at that moment in their emotional learning journey. Such a curricular assignment for the middle school grades would be consistent with Nucci's (2006) example of education for critical moral reflection which states that education for critical moral reflection needs to include the social-cognitive domains in a curricular assignment and also an exploration by the teacher of whether or not disagreements about the morality of the focal issue is a function of differences in the informational beliefs maintained by students and members of the broader society.

In addition to encouraging children to critically question and discuss the media, educators could also encourage children to be cognizant of their usage of electronic media in their lives and encourage the children's parents to become active participants as well. Children could be asked to keep an emotional media life diary or journal in which they could list the activity, the amount of time spent on the activity, who they were with (alone, friends, family) and the thoughts and feelings that they had while engaging in the activity. This emotional life diary could also be applied to children's play life as well—that is, children could be asked to document when they play, whom are they playing with, what they are doing, and again, list the emotions and thoughts that they are experiencing during the activity.

Example: Play Activity Reflection Journal (Worksheet could be adapted for various age levels)

What are you doing? Why?
Where are you? Time? How long did you play for?
Who are you with and why? (Before, During, After)
How did you feel? (Before, During, After)
What were you thinking? (Before, During, After)
Would you do this again—why/why not? Or would you do something different—why /why not? With the same person—why/why not?
What was your favorite lesson that you learned from playing this today? Why?
What did you enjoy the most about this activity? Why? What did you enjoy the least about this activity? Why?

Consistent with some Ontario schools which are beginning to impose boundaries on viewing of television, movies, video games, and computers, these schools are encouraging children to find alternative amusements for themselves after school hours. To illustrate, a recent Canadian national newspaper the *Globe and Mail* article entitled, "Childhood unplugged" (Kelly, 2007, M1, 5) describes a recent movement in Ontario schools (both public and private such as some Waldorf schools) to encourage children to engage in activities not related to the TV or computer such as playing outside or reading, drawing, knitting, and so on. Thus, by encouraging children to limit their engagement in electronic media, and when they do engage, to critically question and discuss what they experience, schools can help to foster creative and imaginative thinking in the classroom. This approach to making wise media choices and to question the media may also help children to engage in healthy learning activities that may help them to cope with the emotional issues connected with the use of electronic media (Hutchison, 2007).

Consistent with emotionality in the classroom, drawing on research in spirituality and religiosity, given the complex and sensitive nature of the topic of spirituality and religiosity, although research on the role of religion in children's lives is of particular political and ethical sensitivity, it remains an urgently needed area of study (Bosacki, 2001, 2005c; Dennett, 2006). Thus, adults who work with children in learning contexts need to be aware that they have a responsibility as educators to provide a psychologically and emotionally secure learning atmosphere to explore sensitive issues in the classroom, including issues of culture and faith, especially given the increasingly diverse student population in North America and the general globalization of the world population. To help children build both emotional and cultural competence, they need to feel emotionally secure to engage in such sensitive conversations within the classroom.

Religiosity/Spirituality

To help sensitive children make sense of their selves and emotional worlds within the context of the grade school classroom, school programs can draw on programs of both critical media literacy and character education by engaging in a conversation with learners about the emotional, moral, ethical, and spiritual implications of living within the consumer culture. The present findings discussed in this book suggest that perhaps asking children to articulate their thoughts and feelings about their emotional and social worlds may provide them with an opportunity to explore ways to engage in developing a strategy for a healthy "emotional diet or guide." Such a guide would consist of emotional, cognitive, and behavioral choices to children achieve a balanced emotional life with themselves and others.

Given that emotions are connected to all areas of life, this emotional guide could also be connected to issues of spirituality and religiosity. Although an in-depth discussion of spirituality and religiosity within the context of child development is beyond the scope of this book, as Radford (2006) notes, perhaps educators need to conceptualize spirituality and spiritual development in the same lines as intellectual, aesthetic, moral, physical, and social development that they are all, in a sense, involve public forms of articulation that share the common focus of human experience. Thus, according to Radford, the spiritual development of children may be seen in part as a process of identifying of those underlying features of the human condition for which for some, find articulations in religious teaching, but which are important to learners in terms of our ability to understand how we need to be kind to and care for ourselves and all living beings.

For example, Bering, Blasi, and Bjorklund (2005) suggest that educational programs should aim to address the possibility that instruction/exposure to diverse faith and belief systems, and universal ontogeny of cognitive abilities may play a role in the development of children's afterlife beliefs. The present findings discussed in this book also highlight the important role family plays, especially the parents, in children's developing sense of self and their emotional experiences, even within the context of the peer group and also given the ongoing exposure to mass media. Perhaps by listening to children's voices, and integrating critical discussions of popular forms of media such as popular music into the curriculum, researchers and educators could work together to co-create developmentally appropriate curriculum (e.g., media literacy programs, character education). Given the connections among emotions,music, and language (Sacks, 2007), such educational and therapeutic programs that incorporate music into the curriculum may encourage children to find more personal meaning and emotional connections in their learning (Sacks, 2007), Thus, given the challenge of finding meaning in our the increasingly diverse and technological advanced society, this may help to immunize children against the "emotional and spiritual emptiness" that writers and educators warn us against (Hudd, 2005; Postman, 1995, 1999).

Given the focus of this book on emotionality and the relevance emotional development has for the whole child involving all areas of development including religiosity and spirituality, research on religiosity and spirituality in older youth could benefit from drawing on research findings on children's emotional and self-development. For example, Hazel and Mohatt (2001) integrated cultural and spiritual coping into their treatment programs aimed to prevent alcohol abuse and addition, and to understand the learning and healing processes involved among American Native youth and adults struggling with alcohol addiction. Further clinical applications of children's emotional development involve the use of emotions in the lives of adolescents to repair problematic or disrupted attachments to peers and parents (Lovinger, Miller, & Lovinger, 1999). Attachment research and therapy can be applied to aspects of religiosity and used to understand the connections between the quality of children's interpersonal relationships and their relationship to religious figures. Ream and Savin-Williams (2003) suggest that to some degree, religiosity can be viewed as a process of emotional attachment, to the larger community, community members, and to the divine. Thus, consistent with Watts and Williams'(1988) focus on the importance of religiosity, further research on the connections among children's spirituality, religiosity, morality, and emotionality may also investigate children's societal attachment or connection that may include the institutions and norms of school, religion, and parents (Bosacki, 2005b).

Clinical and Therapeutic Implications

Similar to the school setting, the emotional dimension can be applied to a therapeutic setting, in which therapists and psycho-educators can draw on theory and research in emotional development to help children create a healthy, balanced, emotional world. The use of language and art, particularly the use of metaphor may be useful in psychoeducational programs that follow cognitive behavior therapy models (e.g., Beck, 1976), in that it may help promote accessing unconscious sensory system within the child. For example, such activities that incorporate the use of emotional language could be applied to children who may experience internalizing and sociocommunicative difficulties (e.g., social anxiety, depression, selective mutism), and also difficulties understanding and using emotions such as alexithymia (Boden & Barenbaum, 2007). During therapy, socially ambiguous narratives discussed in this book may be offered to the child that may enable her/him to relate to hypothetical social and emotional experiences. Such hypothetical, ambiguous narratives may be similar to, but not identical to the personal experiences of the child which may become problematic in that they are too powerful and emotionally overwhelming. Metaphor may also be useful in that it may help the child or adolescent to conceptualize an abstract concept in a concrete manner. Learners of all ages could be encouraged to co-construct metaphors through the use of writing, drawing, sculpture, drama, etc.

According to various holistic educators (e.g., Hutchison, 1998; Kessler, 2000; Levine, 1999; Miller, 1993; Palmer, 1999; Winston, 2002), the use of literature and art during children's cognitive behavior therapy may help the child to develop a willingness to explore personal feelings and beliefs. According to (Meehan, 2002), the use of literature provides the structural organization which mirrors the child's spontaneous cognitive processes and allows for accessing unconscious resources. The result is that through the interpretive process, the child in therapy may tap unconscious knowledge and emotions that can offer creative ways to resolve problems and enhance spiritual and religious growth. Given that children's cognition may help create creative healing it may also help to unfold the unconscious resources and promote the understanding of religious issues.

Furthermore, through holistic education methods such guided imagery/visualization and meditation, the self-conscious, complex emotions which may sometimes be difficult to articulate and make sense of (e.g., shame, guilt, pride, embarrassment, jealousy, compassion, and obligation), could be represented by an object that the child can visualize and address directly such as a particular color or shape or object (e.g., stone, weed, etc.). Focusing on a neutral object can thus help the client to reflect upon the painful experience or thought in a manner that is more comfortable and familiar. For example, bibliotherapy can also be used to help children and youth to understand their emotional worlds. Similar to journal keeping, children could be encouraged to develop personal libraries of books that they found they learned the greatest emotional lessons from. Children could then keep an ongoing response journal where they could respond to the particular book by either writing and/or drawing.

Bibliotherapy can serve as an educative and therapeutic vehicle in that the literature offers material in both context and form which allows for easy in applying the child's cognitive abilities. Bibliotherapy with children is a valuable method because the form of the therapy is issue to the cognitive skills for children. For example, children's picture books such as Ed Young's (1992) *Seven Blind Mice* and Leo Lionni's (1970) *Fish Is Fish* could be read to children of all ages followed by a class discussion on the importance of understanding multiple perspectives and worldviews. To help children develop a sense of courage and cope with issues of fear and control in positive ways, the book by Mélanie Watt (2006), *Scaredy Squirrel* is another valuable resource for children and adults of all ages. The exploration of such texts allows exploration of human experiences and can promote a pondering of human ideals and human predicaments.

Furthermore, given that the majority of these books are mainly illustrations, children's understandings of the texts will not be influences by individual differences in language ability. For example, Saxton Freymann and Joost Elffers (1999), *How Are You Peeling? Food With Moods?* is a valuable tool which could be applied across various ages and ethnicities given that it is a humorous picture book of vegetables developed to help children understand the complex concepts of emotions. Thus, language skills are not necessary as children will be able to explore the photos of the vegetables depicting various emotions and scenarios. Such an understanding of emotions and perspectives may also help children to develop moral, spiritual, and cultural understandings.

To help children develop the ability to further explore the private emotional worlds and inner voices of children during the elementary school years, books such as Judy Blume's (1972) *Tales of a Fourth Grade Nothing*, and Sylvia Plath's (1996) *The It-Doesn't-Matter Suit* may encourage children to develop their emotional landscapes and perspective-taking abilities by providing them with the opportunity to examine the thoughts and emotions of characters in a novel. In addition, more advanced reading material excerpts and poems from Dan Millman's (1995) book *The Laws of Spirit: A Tale of Transformation* can be read daily to students in class as short life lessons which promote reflection and contemplation. Consistent with Levine's (1999) notion of creative healing, the use of such narratives can help adolescents deal with the personal struggles and challenges experienced during time of change and emotional and personal growth.

Similarly, children's dreams can also be explored through similar concepts with the use of visual art, drama, narrative and metaphor. Given the importance dreams play in children and adolescent psychological development (e.g., Kagan, 1984), therapy that helps to promote children's understandings of dreams may also lead to further growth in self-development and self-knowledge. Growth in self-knowledge may also encourage social connections to develop with both peers and adults as well, leading to a greater sense of spiritual awareness.

Regarding psycho-educational programs that are both educative and therapeutic, Taylor and Carlson's findings (2001) regarding parents' religious beliefs and their children's pretend play also have practical implications for early childhood programs that integrate play therapy into the curricula (Faulkner, 2001). For example, children who experience emotional difficulties may be encouraged to participate in role-play activities regarding social situations with their peers. Furthermore, children's pretend and imaginary play may help to promote their emotional development, as well as their societal and cultural knowledge (Scarlett et al., 2005). That is, fantasy and imaginative play has particular relevance for schools with multiethnic and multifaith population in that thematic fantasy play can help to develop children's understandings about power, status and ritual in their diverse society (Furth & Kane, 1992).

A major implication of the present research is that children rated as socially withdrawn by their teachers in grade school may present a disconcerting combination of psychosocial risks that seem to reflect their sensitivity to emotional issues, illuminating the need for comprehensive interventions that address the broad range of difficulties experienced by these children (Markway & Markway, 2005; Marini et al., 2000). Practitioners should be vigilant to ensure that clinical services address the full range of adjustment issues, including internalizing problems such as social anxiety and depression. Targeting only one set of potential risks may decrease the effectiveness of the intervention.

The complexity of the emotional experiences of children in the present study suggests that it may be critical to target possible social-cognitive bias in psychosocial interventions such as problem-solving skills training (PSST) programs that have been empirically supported as effective interventions for adolescent conduct problems (Kazdin, 2003). To address normative beliefs legitimizing antisocial behavior comprehensively and effectively, it may be beneficial to expand PSST programs to include cognitive-restructuring strategies designed to reduce the extent to which child victims apply problem-solving skills learned in PSST to the pursuit of antisocial rather than prosocial ends (Marini, 2001; Sutton et al., 1999).

The results also suggest that emotionally sensitive children may present problems related to parent-child attachment and parental monitoring that could be addressed by empirically supported parenting interventions for conduct problems, such as parent management training, multisystemic therapy, and family therapy (Henggeler, 2003; Kazdin, Siegel, & Bass, 1992; Robin & Foster, 1989;

Shadish et al., 1993). Family systems interventions that emphasize reducing care-giver-child conflict through constructive communication may help to reduce alien-ation in the maternal-child attachment relationship (Robin & Foster, 1989), and further may facilitate the child's self-disclosure that may foster effective parental monitoring (see Stattin & Kerr, 2000).

For therapeutic programs involving older children and youth, combinations of both positive self-talk and religiosity and/or spirituality that incorporate the use of emotional vocabulary, could be viewed as a healthy coping strategy to assist chil-dren and youth to cope with the possibility of engaging in risk-taking and harmful behaviors such as alcohol and abuse. Further, research on addictions and substance abuse in adolescents and young adults, could also benefit from studies on younger children's emotional worlds. By exploring some of the underlying emotional fac-tors that play a role in later life's choices, communication should increase educators and researchers of grade school children, and psycho-educational therapists and researchers working with young children regarding emotional development and also researchers working with older adolescents and young adults regarding iden-tity and self-concept issues, addictions, social problems, etc. Children's emotional lives within the classroom will benefit from stronger connections between the edu-cational and clinical fields in that both fields of expertise and share a common goal to promote emotional health in children and adolescents. Thus, a future question for researchers and educators who work with shy or socially withdrawn children is: How can educators, clinicians, researchers, and policy makers learn from each other and work together to create multidisciplinary, holistic psycho-educational programs that share the goal of promoting emotional health and self and social knowledge among all children?

In sum, effective educational and therapeutic practices need to pay careful attention to children's emotions in both clinical and non-clinical populations. Although we tend to think of education as a purely "intellectual process"—many educational thinkers warn us against this (Bruner, 1996; Noddings, 2006). Real (Authentic) thinking and learning involves curiosity, excitement, and passion. Many believe that these emotions are the driving force behind the growth of the mind. When children become engaged in tasks (is all engagement emotional?) they think reflectively, critically, deeply, and imaginatively and their minds expand. As I've mentioned through this book, a key goal of our schools today should be to ensure psychological and emotional safety for our children—that is, to try to minimize negative emotions such as anxiety, and boredom which research shows many children experience in school, particularly during testing situa-tions (Crain, 2007; Markway & Markway, 2005). If the main goal of education is to improve academic test scores, how does this goal benefit children if they conclude that learning is an odious process? As Crain advocates (2007), to child-centered educators, emotional attitudes are important because they indicate the kinds of experiences children need to develop fully. When children find tasks that they enjoy or are meaningful, they take great interest and work on them with great energy and concentration.

Learning Programs aimed to Promote Emotional Development

Many educators and therapists agree that the emphasis of quality, effective learning programs promote inquiry and dialogue, particularly the skills of questioning and listening. Although much has been written about critical education and critical approaches to learning in adolescence and adults (see Noddings, 2006; Postman, 1999), a critical and caring approach could easily be applied to educational programs for all ages, including middle childhood. All programs that promote children's psychological health need to be comprehensive, multifaceted, and methodologically diverse.

As noted earlier, the need to teach for self-understanding and self-knowledge is also referred to as the Socratic approach in that it focuses on dialogue and inquiry (see Haynes, 2002). According to Berkowitz et al. (2006), there are several traditions that aim to help children to develop into psychologically healthy adults. Prevention science or positive psychology, character and moral education, and applied developmental social cognitive science including social-emotional learning programs all have created theory, conducted research, and crafted interventions to support psychological health among youth. All three approaches advocate a holistic, multifaceted approach to positive development and learning because they see that whichever parts of youth development they support depend on the success of other parts, and ultimately, on the success of the whole child. More specifically, those concerned with prevention science or positive psychology and youth development focus on children's ability and tendency to choose healthy actions and lifestyles. Character or moral educational programs focus on the development of the multiple aspects of children's moral personality and behavior. Finally, those programs that fit within the applied developmental social cognition area include programs that involves social-emotional learning, and are more centrally interested in the development of children's social and emotional competencies. Both positive psychology and applied developmental social cognitive science categorize the psychological strengths youth need to develop, and integrates a number of theoretical perspectives within developmental psychology useful to understanding children's development. All programs are necessary to create a well-rounded understanding of children's psychological development.

In the sections below, I will outline educational approaches below within the context of emotional health and development. Across all approaches, the most commonly shared implementation strategies are professional development for those implementing the initiative; student-centered peer discussions; interactive strategies such as class meetings student governance, and peer tutoring that contribute to perspective-taking experiences; problem-solving and decision-making training; direct training of social, emotional, and personal management skills (such as emotional self-regulation, conflict resolution, or anger management); cooperative learning; self-management, and self-regulation skills training and awareness; parent training and involvement. Most programs include activities that include language art activities including emotional language, and involve individual and cooperative activities that promote inquiry and dialogue (e.g., shared reading/story telling, cooperative learning games, puppets, role-playing, etc.).

Preventive Science

According to Berkowitz et al. (2006), the majority of research in the various fields of prevention is guided by the goal of preventing specific or targeted problem behavior or difficulties such as delinquency, depression and social anxiety, early substance abuse, antisocial behavior, conduct disorders, school failure, and dropout, teen pregnancy. Although in the past, research funding may have been problem-driven, this is now changing to incorporate a process and team based model that involved holistic assessment and intervention into the child's overall well-being. As a number of authors have suggested (e.g., Bukowski & Adams, 2005; Cummings et al., 2000; Marini, Bosacki, Dane, & YLC-CURA, 2005; Willoughby, Chalmers, & Busseri, 2006), it is critical to examine process-oriented models to better understand why and how a given form of psychopathology emerges. Regarding this book's focus on children who are considered to be socially withdrawn, current research findings suggest that a possible pathway or chain of events that may culminate in the development of internalizing difficulties social anxiety and depression (Bosacki, Dane, Marini, & YLC-CURA, 2007). This evidence has important implications for the prevention and treatment of internalizing problems that will be discussed later in the chapter.

Furthermore research suggests that the present findings suggest that self-esteem plays a critical intervening role with regard to adolescent psychosocial adjustment (e.g., Bosacki et al., 2007; Dubois & Tevendale, 1999; Grills & Ollendick, 2002; Harter, 1999). The risk of internalizing problems, particularly depression, among youth with problematic peer relationships may also be addressed by seeking alternate means to bolster self-esteem, such as interventions directly targeting low self-esteem through assertiveness training, attribution restructuring, and social reinforcement of positive self-statements (Shirk et al., 2003), or by facilitating involvement in extra-curricular activities that instill a sense of achievement and pride (Harter, 1999).

According to Battistich (2001), interventions that are effective typically support core competencies: inclinations and abilities that are relevant to success in a winder range of situation, such as understanding of self and others, communication and social interaction skills, and abilities to think critically and resolve interpersonal problems. Overall, although the programs are different in that they have their own language and emphasis, they are all moving toward a more holistic, approach to development and situates youth development ecologically in the surrounding social and emotional environment. All prevention programs aim to have their interventions move from targeted behavior problems in the individual to larger community health issues, and from a deficit model focused on prevention to a positive model promoting the development of self-esteem, self-control, intra and interpersonal skills, connections to friends and institutions, and a prosocial orientation and a positive identity.

Regarding the issue of best practices, Greenberg and colleagues (2001) reviewed primary prevention programs to determine which interventions have been found effective in reducing systems of psychopathology in school age children. Their summary of best practices revealed that those programs focus on longer term over short-term intervention, developmentally earlier rather than latter problem behaviors, and those programs aimed at changing environments and learning communities and not just individuals. Greenberg et al., also recommended packages of coordinated strategies over individual programs and recognized the strength of integrated models of intervention across school, home, and community.

School-based crime prevention is another area of prevention science in which there are similar changes. Such programs aim to support safe, peaceful, and drug and violence free schools through violence reduction programs, promoting conflict resolution, and so on. Gottfredson's (2001) review of effective delinquency prevention programs cites similar trends in school-based crime prevention toward involving whole schools rather than focusing on individual students, achieving consistency and clarity in communicating norms about acceptable behavior, and favoring comprehensive instructional programs that focus on a range of social competency skills. Such skills include developing self-control and learning stress management, responsible decision making, thinking, social problem solving and communication skills. In summary, similar to social science, prevention science has become more holistic in that it focuses on sustained engagement rather than one-time interventions, and situates child development ecologically in the surrounding social environment.

Another recent prevention-based program to help children to think and act responsibly is EQUIP for Educators (DiBiase, Gibbs, & Potter, 2006). Adapted from the treatment program EQUIP (Gibbs, Potter, & Goldstein, 1995), the EQUIP for Educators: Teaching Youth (Grades five to eight) program was developed into a broader-based prevention curriculum to encourage children to think and act responsibly. In particular, this prevention-based, psycho-educational program research-based curriculum can be used with students who have emotional and behavioral disorders in the later grade school years (Grades 5 to 8). The emphasis is on cultivating positive youth culture, and on helping students learn to understand the perspectives of others and to help them to identify and correct self-serving cognitive distortions.

Character Development and Moral Education

The movement to blend aspects of emotional and affective development and moral development has been addressed by a movement by educators stated as "Character Development or Education." Drawing on the various fields of social, emotional and moral psychology, one of the aims of Character Education is to encourage children to develop into caring and compassionate thinkers who are morally and ethically responsible (see Killen & Smetana, 2006). Character education models aim to develop children's awareness of the connections between themselves and others, and encourages children to think and ethically and responsibly, and to engage in respectful and compassionate interactions that benefit others and the larger society.

To illustrate a recent example of the integration of Moral Education into everyday school curriculum is the new initiative in the Canadian province of Ontario aimed to promote character development in children aged 4 or 5 to 17 or 18 years (kindergarten to Grade 12; Ontario Ministry of Education, 2006). This particular Character Education program within the cultural context of Ontario, Canada, aims to promote children's developing sense of selves and their connections with others, and suggests that educational programs in general need to address the whole child, including the heart as well as the head including all aspects of development (e.g., cognitive, affective, behavioral domain) (see Ontario Ministry of Education, 2006 for further details). From a global perspective, in agreement with Yon's (2000) work on schooling in global times, this study could help to provide empirical evidence for educational programs that aim to encourage children to develop empathy and respect for people within their increasingly diverse communities.

Another example of a developmental moral educational program that promotes social, emotional, and moral growth through social and emotional interactions is the extension of school-based social experiences to include community service activities. Efforts to promote youth engagement in community service are not new, and in the United States can be traced back to William James (Killen & Horn, 2000; Nucci, 2006). Community service is linked to the school curriculum in the form of mandated requirements is labeled as "service learning."

Programs for service learning are diverse and include a range of activities from tutoring or coaching youth sports to working in a local hospital, community soup kitchen or a community shelter for the homeless, and so on. For this reason the impact of service learning has been difficult to evaluate, although some research suggests that effective service-learning programs lead to an increased level of civic engagements and an increase in positive oral action and a decrease in rates of delinquent behaviors (Youniss, McLellan, & Mazer, 2001).

Past research suggests that the important factors that are important for service learning to positively impact students' social and emotional growth is that the child must have some degree of choice for the activity to have a positive benefit in that it holds personal relevance or meaning for the learner. The importance of personal agency and choice is linked to both student motivation as well as healthy self-development. That is, if a learner does not have a choice and engages in a service-learning activity in which she or he does not feel emotionally connected, then one needs to question the authenticity of the community experience and wonder who benefits and learns from the experience (Hart & Fegley, 1995; Leming, 1999). Although in the past, the majority of service-learning programs have been a part of secondary schools, service-learning programs that promote emotional and social connection with others could be integrated into grade school classrooms by the implementation of routine field trips to hospitals, community centers, pen-pal club with children or the elderly in a long-term care facility, and so on. Such programs could not only promote interpersonal competence and growth but also an emotionally healthy sense of self.

A second critical factor is that service-learning activity be linked to a period of reflection (Andersen, 1998). The degree of reflection varies from program to program from activities as writing a one-page reflection paper to keeping a daily journal. As noted by literacy researchers (Donaldson, 1978, 1992; Olson, 1994), reflection is important in that it affords learners to share and discuss their emotional experiences and to connect those experiences to their own social values and sense of self (Andersen, 1998).

Overall, the notion of "trust" and psychological and emotional safety is crucial as many researchers have claimed with trust associated with the affective connections of care, regulated by moral and emotional reciprocity, and continuity (Noddings, 2003; Nucci, 2006; Nussbaum, 2000). As Noddings (2003) among others have advocated, an "ethics of care" is an essential component of moral and emotional education. Consistent with the notion of caring for and understanding others, Noddings (2006) suggests that schools need to promote the notion of moral interdependence in that both teachers and learners need to listen intently to one another's values and beliefs, and to share responsibility for treating each other with respect and kindness. In general, as Crain (2007) suggests, in contrast to working toward the future, we need to focus today on creating a child-centered approach to education and parenting for learners of all ages. Such an approach would help to encourage parents and adult educators to ask themselves how can they best contribute to the ethical, emotional, and moral development of the learner. Through activities including the creative arts, play, and connections with nature, educators who are nurturing, emotionally tied to nature, and imaginative can help children to learn the ability to care about others, the world, and themselves.

Teaching and Learning as Intentional Activities: Developmental Frameworks

As Frye and Ziv (2005) note, when both teaching and learning are intentional, the activities become reciprocal and interchange as both teacher and learner experience teaching and learning together. In ToM terms, teachers' and learner' beliefs and emotions play a mutual or reciprocal role in the co-creation of the shared discourse (Gutierrez & Rogoff, 2003; Tomasello, 1999; Ziv & Frye, 2007). Similarly, Olson and Bruner (1996) proposed that teaching and learning take place in the forms of discussion, collaboration, and negotiation in which different ways of construing the subject content are encouraged. Thus, ToM may help children to recognize and engage in the teaching and learning process because it depends on a person's understanding of knowledge differences between at least two learners, and in part, on an intentional attempt to help to minimize these differences (Ziv & Frye, 2007).

Astington and Pelletier (2005) provide evidence to show that ToM contributes to learning and school readiness in the early school grades. More specifically, they found that the relation between ToM and language is at the origin of children's developmental readiness for school and may provide a useful framework for ongoing success in school. Regarding emotional and social competence, Astington and Pelletier (2005) found that the happier children were in school, the higher they scored on the false-belief tasks. Thus, Astington and Pelletier (2005), conclude that children's ToM understanding is related to their emotional well-being, as well as to their social competence. As they claim, both of these factors play significant roles in children's school success. Astington and Pelletier's (2005) ideas to increase the use of metacognitive language in the classroom also could connect with Wierzbicka's (1999) NSM language in that both aspects of language could be used in the classroom to promote the understanding of emotions and mental states, through teacher-child conversations, classroom activities.

To further increase the amount of mental state self-talk, the use of psycho-educational programs could also be integrated within the curriculum to provide children with some tools to create positive self-talk or private speech. For example Stallard's (2002) psycho-educational program entitled, "Think Good/Feel Good" applies the principles of cognitive behavior therapy such as promoting the balance between thoughts, feelings, and behaviors, and encourages children to develop a coherent understanding of the relation between how people think, how they feel, and what they do. For example, one of the learning strategies involves encouraging children to monitor and document their self-speech regarding their thoughts and feelings promotes children's metacognitive and emotional abilities. Such an activity will encourage children to label and recognize their thoughts and emotions and may also lead to further self-growth.

Curriculum: Importance of Inquiry and Critical Dialogue and Reflection (Internal/Self-talk and Social Talk)

Similarly, as mentioned earlier in the chapter, educators could also choose to read books in the classroom which incorporate the use of mental state and emotional language, and encourage children to choose such books to read during their personal reading time, encourage them to illustrate their mental and emotional worlds through text (e.g., journaling, poetry), graphic representation (e.g., painting, drawings, sculpture, etc.), or physical movement. Such follow-up activities could also encourage children to develop a reflective awareness of the language in that the process of writing and/or drawing/creating—or social and/or imaginary play may encourage them to reflect upon the language (Danon-Boileau, 2001; Donaldson, 1978; Jones & Cooper, 2006). This reflection may also encourage awareness of one's own and others' mental states (Olson, 1994).

Although a vast amount of research findings show that play is a complex and paramount phenomenon in the lives of children of all ages (Scarlett et al., 2005), activities incorporated into the classroom helps to develop social problem solving skills, promotes "creativity and divergent thinking skills," appear to focus on the early childhood years and continually play a less significant role as children progress through the grade school years into secondary school. That is, although play is often incorporated in many early childhood education programs (Jones & Cooper, 2006), the concept of play as an academic area often becomes diluted over the years, and takes a backseat to the more academic disciplines such as mathematics, science, language arts, etc. Interestingly, the use of creative, imaginative, and social (cooperative, competitive, solitary) play in learning activities has the potential to address almost all aspects of learning, and can be adapted for any developmental level.

As Jones and Cooper (2006) note, to create a playful, psychologically and emotionally safe learning community within the classroom, educators need to practice what they refer to as "the believing game" (p. 109). That is, as adults, we need to practice what we preach with respect to showing the value of play within the learning context. As Jones and Cooper state, workshops, training classes, and university classes for educators need to incorporate the importance of the play environment across all ages–not just limited to early childhood education. Educators of all ages can learn to adapt the strategies of an early childhood classroom's play environment to create a model for developmentally appropriate active learning classes for learners across the lifespan (Singer, Michnick, Golinkoff, & Hirsh-Pasek, 2006). That is, such classes can promote inquiry, dialogue, critical reflection and divergent thinking and imaginative skills within the context of a caring, supportive and playful learning environment.

However, as educators and play leaders, adults who work with children must believe in what they are teaching in that they are capable players with words, materials and encourage and feel competent and confident in using learning activities in the classroom that encourage divergent thinking and story sharing. As a play leader, educators of all ages should provide a role model for learners as they should show how one can become engaged with playing with words, open-ended play materials (such as play dough, blocks, etc.). As Jones and Cooper (2006) suggest, play activities can cut across all ages, an educators of preschoolers through adults can show the importance of play by engaging in the actives with the learners. Such a co-participation encourages learners to engage in what Csikszentmihalyi refers to as "the politics of enjoyment" in that educators can help children to recognize opportunities for action in an environment and to develop all skills of the body and mind so that they can avoid feeling bored, anxious, or helpless.

For example, to help learners to make sense of new concepts/ideas, I often incorporate the use of open-ended play materials such as puppets, play dough, blocks into various brainstorming learning activities in all learning levels (grade school to graduate). Such an activity promotes cognitive flexibility, multiple perspective-taking, and divergent thinking skills and can be applied to all ages levels, and can also be adapted for either individual or group work. I've used this activity to introduce new concepts in developmental and educational psychology. Regarding some of my graduate education classes that I teach regarding developmental and educational issues in children and adolescents, as a class we then critically reflect on the activity by discussing the main lesson everyone learned from engaging in the activity, describe their thoughts and feelings during and after the activity, what aspect of the activity either worked well or did not work well and why, how could this activity be developed for various ages across development, possible methods of assessment, etc.

Educational Programs for Emotionally Sensitive Children

Combined with Chandler's (1987) assertion that the development of relativistic thought is linked to the emergence of generic self-doubt (implying a decrease in self-worth), one could hypothesize that the development of higher-order cognitive abilities such as recursive and reflective thought may negatively impact a child's sense of self (Dabrowski, 1967). Furthermore, given that some research suggests that girls develop their sense of self through their connections with others, some girls may be more likely to internalize their social problems (e.g., Chernin, 1985), classroom silence may have a more negative effect on adolescent girls' self-concept as compared to boys (Silverstein & Perlick, 1995). For example, a more sophisticated understanding of others' mental states may also be related to a greater psychoemotional sensitivity that may lead one to feel psychologically isolated and vulnerable.

As discussed in Chapter 2, Dabrowski (1967) refers to this experience as "over-excitability," which he claims is often accompanied by feelings of isolation and vulnerability. In turn, such negative emotions may lead to a decrease in one's sense of self-worth and an increased feeling of being silenced from within (McHolm et al., 2005; Park & Park, 1997). As discussed in the previous section on the benefits and limitations of emotional development, the possibility that sensitivity to classroom emotional experiences may have a deleterious influence on a child's sense of self and may lead to thoughts and feelings of being invisible or non-existent to others, requires further exploration.Educational implications regarding children's oversensitivity to classroom situations, particularly concerning emotions and social situations, need to be addressed from a psychocultural as this may also have implications for the development of emotional awareness which would involve the awareness of both positive and negative feelings including the possible experience of suspiciousness (Bodem & Berenbaum, 2007). Thus, to investigate the possibility of maladaptive social-emotional responses as a consequence of developing an advanced understanding of others' thoughts and feelings, more applied research is needed on the role emotion plays in children's cognitive and affective processes, particularly the complex emotions including envy and jealousy (Miceli & Castelfranchi, 2007).

As discussed in Chapter 2, such findings also support the notion that perhaps sophisticated, or advanced emotional competence may have both intrapersonal and interpersonal costs and benefits (Cutting & Dunn, 1999; Sutton et al., 1999). For example, regarding interpersonal implications, children with a highly advanced emotional understanding ability may also use this ability to harm others such as excluding certain peers from a group by developing friendship with someone else (Sutton et al., 1999). As Dunn (1995) reminds us, a child's emotional and moral sensitivity level and ability to understand someone's emotional state does not tell us how that child may behave in a relationship with that person. Given the challenging task of interpreting ambiguous social behaviors, perhaps due to the subtle nature of social interactions throughout grade school including prosocial and aggressive behaviors, educators need to be aware of children's contradictory behaviors exhibited in the classroom, with such interactions containing a combination of social and aggressive behaviors. For example, regarding psychological and relational aggression, a child may choose to smile at someone while writing her/him a derogatory letter. Thus, teachers may also be aware of such contradictory behaviors exhibited by children in the classroom and ways in which to assess and deal with such behaviors (Crick & Nelson, 2002).

Thus, during the grade school years, in addition to parents, teachers also play a crucial role in shaping their students' self-concepts and competencies (Denham, 1998;

Novak & Purkey, 2001; Novak, Rocca, & Dibiase, 2006; Purkey, 2000). For example, educators could serve as socioemotional and linguistic "coaches" by providing a supportive scaffold (in the Vygotskian sense) that could be used to facilitate children's socioemotional and linguistic competence, which in turn may lead to a greater sense of self-worth and emotional presence.

As discussed throughout this book, emotional competence is an interdisciplinary and multifaceted field (Bar-On & Parker, 2000; Goleman, 1995, 2006; Matthews, Zeidner, & Roberts, 2002). However, as a psychological construct, emotional competence has a large body of theoretical and empirical literature to support current efforts in that it is often connected to the concept of social competence, and is rooted in a tradition of psychology including Thornedike (1905), Kelly (1955), and Rogers (1961), Social competence is defined by some researchers as the use of the ability to integrate feeling, thinking, and action to achieve social tasks and outcomes valued in a particular cultural context (Topping, Brenner, & Holmes, 2000). That is, to enact social competence, one must have the ability to achieve personal goals in social interaction while simultaneously maintaining positive relationships with others over time and across situations (Rose-Krasnor, 1997; Rubin & Rose-Krasnor, 1992). By this definition, emotional competence is seen as one dynamic in what is currently being perceived as social and emotional learning and the emotional sophisticate is one who is able master the ability to learn how to balance both personal emotional needs and to simultaneously address the emotional needs of the other (e.g., peer, friend).

This literature of emotional competence furthers our understanding of the emotional lives of children, and Saarni (1999) reviewed the development of emotional competence, which contains three primary aspects: ones' moral sense or character; one's developmental history, and ones self or ego identity. Given the overlap with character education, a moral and ethical sense is suggested to be a source of emotional growth. The components of emotional competence are those skills needed to manage emotions, enhance self-esteem, and become resilient and adaptive.

According to Lazarus (1991), each emotion is associated with a core relational theme and helps to provide a context to help children learn how to develop particular emotional skills. For example, anger, when seen in relational terms comes about through perceived offense against me and mine. Anxiety develops through perceiving an uncertain threat, or the uncertainty of the challenge of a known threat. Building on the work of Lazarus (1991) and Arsenio (1988), programs for children characterized as shy or socially withdrawn may benefit particularly from such programs that focus on these particular emotions. The emotional part of social and emotional learning should help educator children to understand the role emotions play in their lives, their relationships, and in their sense of selves.

Emotional competence in the areas of sympathy (feeling for someone), empathy (feeling with someone), and guilt (accepting responsibility when you have done something bad or wrong) directly impacts moral perception and the likelihood that you will respond to other people when they are in need (Davis, 1980; Eisenberg & Mussen, 1989; Hoffman, 1984, 2000; Saarni, 1999). This complementarity and overlap with character and moral education carries over to social and emotional learning more broadly conceived.

Cohen (2001) defines social and emotional education as referring to "learning skills, understandings, and values that enhance our ability to read others and ourselves and then, to use this information to become flexible problem solvers and creative learners" (p. xiii). In addition, during the time of middle childhood, I suggest that educators promote children's ability to become not only flexible and creative learners, but also healthy skeptics who care about themselves and others, and also learn how to question critically—to ask who creates the rules and definitions that guides societal social and moral norms and actions.

Educational activities to promote these abilities could focus on skills that help us to process, manage, and express the social and emotional aspects of our experience and our lives. These abilities provide the platform for general academic learning, and for moral development through learning to be self-reflective, caring, cooperative, responsibility, and an effective social problem solver. Given that children's social and emotional capacities affect their ability to communicate and listen, concentrate, recognize, understand, and problem solve in the social world, moderate their own emotional states so they are not controlled by them, and resolve conflicts adaptively (Cohen, 2001, pp. 3–4).

One example of an educational program that promotes social and emotional learning is CASEL which was founded in 1994 to provide leadership to researchers, educators, and policy makers regarding social and emotional learning and its place in school curriculum and practice (CASEL, 2002). They define social and emotional learning as "the process of developing the ability to recognize and manage emotions, develop caring and concern for others, make responsible decisions, establish positive relationships, and handle challenging situations effectively" (2002, p. 3). These positive outcomes are supported by the development of five core social and emotional competencies including self-awareness, social awareness, self-management, relationship skills, and responsible decision making. CASEL (2002) emphasizes the need for safe, caring, supportive learning environments and the authors acknowledge the overlap between social and emotional learning and character education, suggesting that effective programs should aim to include both components. Drawing on past empirical evidence, many researchers and educators support the notion that character education programs that incorporate a social-emotional learning component are more effective than programs without a social and emotional learning component (Berkowitz et al., 2006).

5.4. Directions for Future Researchers

Regarding issues for future researchers, in the realm of emotional development there are many areas of inquiry waiting to be explored. First, we need to learn more about how to teach children wisdom and the notion of emotional experts who are wise. Given that Simon (1995) claimed that to explore a phenomenon we must first have a mental representation of the problem area. This notion of mental representation would also include an emotional aspect—and perhaps educators need to develop their ability to create emotional representations of particular educational issues. As explained earlier in the chapter, within the framework of "Positive Psychology," Seligman (2004) have has outlined a range of traits and virtues much of which include emotional and moral strengths, which may help to buffer against psychological and emotional difficulties.

Future research needs to address the complex interplay between emotionality, morality, and a sense of self. Consistent with Nucci (2001), given that it is questionable to separate morality from the construction of the self, researchers need to explore the question of what role does emotionality play in this developmental framework? In particular, how does this framework change and adapt during childhood and adolescence? As previously noted throughout this book, although a large amount of research exists on self-development, a more holistic, psychocultural approach needs to be taken to connect self-development with ethical awareness, morality, and emotionality.

In addition to the holistic education approaches that were mentioned earlier in this chapter, an education model that may be an interesting area for future research involves integrative ethical education which is an outgrowth form the work done during the Minnesota Community Vices and Character Education Project (see the website from the Center of Ethical Education website http://cee.nd.edu). To further extend the work of integrative ethical education, educators and researchers could build on this model to present a model of emotional and character education that integrates applied developmental sociocognitive science with traditional and holistic progressive models of socioemotional and character education models.

A holistic, emotional education program can draw on the Integrative Ethical Education framework by suggesting that the combination of personal and community success, rational and traditional moral education, focusing on the personal and emotional domain (Nucci, 2006), with a psychocultural view of human emotional development and cognition. In comparison to other integrative programs, it provides a more cohesive and systematic framework. Moreover, drawing on the Integrative Ethical Education programs, it views the ancient Greek understanding of ethics as still relevant today: ethics is the practical and moral wisdom learned for community living and under the guidance of community. This emphasis on the past and present is also consistent with Haidt's (2006) emphasis on exploring happiness through modern and ancient works, and Postman's (1999) notion of bridging the gap in the seventeenth and twenty-first centuries.

The Integrative Ethical Education model could be used to explain how an Integrative and Holistic Emotional Education model could be developed in the sense that it focuses on the notion of expertise development or a refined deep understanding that is different from technical competence or intellectual ability (Hansen, 2001), is evident in both action and practices and engages the full capacities of the individual. Experts differ from novices in that they have better organized knowledge thank novices (Chi, Glaser, & Farr, 1988). Expert knowledge is of several kinds that interact in performance, for example, declarative (what), procedural (how), conditional (when and how much). Experts perceive and react to the world different, noticing details and opportunities that novices miss. Third, experts behave differently from novices in that they use conscious, critically reflective methods to solve problems, expert skills are highly automatic and effortless. Expertise requires a great deal of practice that is beyond the usual everyday amount of exposure to a domain (Ericsson & Charness, 1994).

This education model could be applied to children's emotional development and aim to develop children's expertise regarding emotional competence. Emotional competence requires the various processes for successful completion—emotional sensitivity, emotional judgment, emotional focus, and emotional action. Each individual acts the same way in similar situations in that skills form an embodied cognition (Varela, Thompson, & Roach, 1991). Such an educational program could help children to develop a holistic and contextualized understanding that engages the entire brain-mind-body system and its evident in moral and ethical emotional action (Paechter, 2000).

Similar to developing moral expertise, children could be encouraged to develop emotional skills in all of the suggested areas as well as others including emotional sensitivity and awareness including the ability to read and understand the emotions of others, communicate effectively and connect with others. Emotional judgment may help them to understand emotional problems, reason and reflect ethically, and develop coping and resiliency skills. Emotional focus would encourage children to respect others, develop conscience, act responsibly, help others and develop emotional identity and integrity. Finally, emotional action would included the resolving of conflicts and problems, assert respectively, take on initiative as a leader and listener, implement decisions, cultivate courage, and persevere.

As I have argued throughout this book and in agreement with many others (Bosacki, 2005; Csikszentmihalyi, 1990; Noddings, 2003; Saarni, 1999), an integrated, transformational learning model that connects education to therapy could provide a useful foundation within which holistic, constructivist developmentally-appropriate educational models can be developed. Research findings from the areas of developmental social cognitive neuroscience and positive psychology could be used to help create developmentally appropriate educational and clinical programs. As discussed earlier in the chapter, one such example is the application of the ToM research on children to help create a developmentally appropriate curriculum that aims to promote both social and personal competence (Astington & Pelletier, 2005; Ziv & Frye, 2007).

Other examples, as noted earlier this chapter, both service learning and developmental discipline aim to establish trust within classrooms and enlist children's intrinsic motivations of autonomy and socially connection to help students engage in moral conduct for their own reasons (Nucci, 2006). Although Watson (2003) grounds her approach to developmental discipline in attachment theory, at a practical level, it has much in common with the classroom management in practices that DeVries and Zan (1994) advocate for preschool settings based on their reading of Piaget and Kohlberg. Both developmental approaches integrate affective warmth from caring adults with an emphasis on personal connection and relationships, and the uses of moral discourse and reflection as a tool for moral and emotional growth and behavioral change. Thus, these approaches focus on an appreciation that emotional development requires learners' construction of their own understandings of fairness with others, and not simply the compliance to adult norms and values.

Future researchers need to explore recent school practices that investigate the topic of moral or social emotions and suggest ways in which school practices might foster the emotional component of moral functioning. As Nucci (2006) advocates, unfortunately the majority of the research fosters the misconception that cognition and affect operate independently. For example, critics state that emotivist models claim peoples' responses to moral events are directed by a set of inborn affective triggers, and that moral reasoning occurs after the fact that a means to explain our own reactions to ourselves (Green & Haidt, 2002; Izard, 1986). Critics have claimed that such emotivist models fail to adequately account for the ways in which cognitions constructed over a person's lifetime alter or enter inter the regulation of affect, and final appraisal of a social situation which would help children to navigate their social and emotional worlds. Such emotivist theories misrepresent the ways in which cognition and affect are reciprocally mutual and integrated (Damasio, 1996).

In contrast to the emotivist approaches, Arsenio and his colleagues (Arsenio & Lover, 1995), provide a more integrative and comprehensive theory of the role of affect as it relates to children's moral, emotional, and social development. Consistent with Lazarus' (1991) notion of contextual-based emotion (explained earlier in this chapter), Arsenio's work demonstrates that children associate different feelings with different events domains of social events. Issues of social conventions generally elicit "cool" or neutral affect on the part of children. This holds for acts of compliance as well as transgressions (Arsenio, 1988). Children experience "hot" emotions, it is the part of adults who occasionally respond with anger to children's conventional transgressions. Issues of morality, however, are viewed by children as filled with "hot" emotions of anger, fear, and sadness among victims of transgressions, and happiness among all parties in the classes where moral situation turn out fairly (Arsenio, 1988). Drawing further on the current research in developmental social cognitive neuroscience (Carlson, 2007; Lewis, 2007; Thompson, 2006), future researchers need to continue to explore children's experiences regarding these "hot" and "cold" emotions and how hot/cold emotions relate to other variables such as moral reasoning sociability, self-concept, and language particularly within various contexts within the classroom (Carpendale & Sokol, 2007; Turiel, 2007).

As discussed earlier in the book, some researchers suggest that emotions are stored as part of the co-construction of social-cognitive representations and repeated experience events may help children to form generalized social and emotional scripts (Bruner, 1996; Harre, 1986; Karniol, 2002; Saarni, 1999). As outlined in the above chapter, through the use of various educational programs, educators and researchers can work together to create evidence-based educational activities that encourage emotional awareness in children, and may be especially useful for children who experience shyness in the classroom.

Given the possible valuable research tools of various psycho-educational programs (e.g., Stallard, 2002), Wierzbicka's (1999) NSM and ToM language, how do we use such language tools to promote emotional health in children and to help promote children to become wise and caring listeners within the North American and increasingly global cultural mosaic? How do we as educators and developmentalists address the universality as well as the unique diversity of human emotion and the emotion language across the North American cultural landscape? Given the increasing diversity in the school population within Canada alone, how feasible will it be for government and policy makers to integrate language programs to represent all ethnicities in schools? Who will decide which language becomes part of the official curriculum? If such things as linguistic universals exist such as concepts of "good" and "bad" (Wierzbicka, 2006), how can educators use such universals in the classroom to promote the effective and caring communication with one another, and to ensure human connections, perhaps schools can begin to work on such a program. Furthermore, how can teachers and parents draw on these language tools to help children who are sensitive and socially withdrawn in the classroom to learn how to be happy?

In addition to the many areas of future research questions that we can continue to explore, regarding ongoing future questions, given the evidence provided in this book regarding the stories of the six children who are rated as shy or socially withdrawn, particularly within our increasingly diverse student population and the increasing prevalence of educational technologies within our learning contexts, the key questions for future researchers may be around how to connect issues of diversity including moral, emotional, cultural, spiritual diversity, and the role of technology, particularly the electronic media within the classroom. For example, researchers need to explore the underlying reasons why some children may choose to engage in technology and the electronic media as opposed to engaging in alternative learning activities, and ask children to explain their thinking and feelings around their media choices. What role does the family and peer group play in children's emotional experiences with the media? How can researchers and educators work together to investigate how both the use of electronic learning tools and alternative learning activities such as active play outdoors may promote issues of both cultural and emotional competence? How can educators and researchers help children to further develop a sense of an emotional presence within their learning environments (both virtual and physical)?

Future work on emotionality in education also needs to include an elaborate discussion of the influence of technology and the media on children's development. Given the increasingly important role technology and pop culture play in the majority of children's lives (Elliott et al., 2002; Kaiser Family Foundation, 1999), future research needs to explore how both the electronic media and popular culture influences children's sense of selves, and their emotional lives and social relations. For example, Postman (1999) warns that technology and pop culture might have a detrimental affect on the spiritual and moral development of children. Furthermore, it is imperative that educators and parents of youth remain up-to-date on the current status of the notion of emotionality and spirituality within the context of pop culture. For example, in an article in *Teen People* magazine, entitled "Choosing My Religion" outlines interviews with five American teenagers on what spirituality means to them (Adato, 1998/1999).

A growing number of educators and researchers are becoming increasingly engaged in an ongoing conversation regarding the social, moral, and emotional implications of our technologically advanced society (e.g., Anderson, Gentile, & Buckley, 2006; Glazer, 1999; Meehan, 2002; Myers, 2000; Noddings, 2003, 2006). As Noddings suggests, perhaps the information overload is wearing us down emotionally and spiritually. Is it all about time and efficiency or should we be aiming toward teaching for self-knowledge and wisdom? As Noddings notes (2003, 2006), if we are so efficient and productive, why are an increasing number of children in North American so unhappy?

Relatedly, the headline and subsequent article in the Canadian weekly news magazine *Maclean's* (2004) "Teen trouble: Drugs, sex, depression: Canadian experts on how to help kids survive trying times" suggests that we need to look beyond the "behaviors" such as drugs, alcohol, and disordered eating, as these are just masking the difficult emotional difficulties children may experience as they approach adolescence. Thus, adults need to be concerned about the emotional lives of children, but also why children choose to remain silent or listen to what they children are saying, or alternatively, the child who may wish to say something, but for some reason, may not feel ready psychologically or emotionally to speak. As Philp (2007) notes in a recent article in the Canadian national paper *The Globe and Mail*, in Ontario, Canada, mental health difficulties of children and adolescents such as depression, attention deficit hyperactivity disorder (ADHD), anxiety, etc., continues to be a major concern for all those who work with youth, particular regarding the area of prevention and treatment. Given the complexity of these emotional difficulties, holistic, multifaceted approaches need to be developed that address all aspects of the child's experience.

Researchers need to explore the emotional lives of children and explore which aspects of their lives play a role in their adult life silent. Similarly, as Postman (1999) contests, how do we encourage children and adolescents (and adults) to discern meaning from information and create knowledge? How do we encourage children and adolescents to develop wisdom from knowledge? Can faster computers and more advanced websites and Internet servers help children to feel more emotionally secure and promote emotional health? Given the role of the media, future researchers need to explore how popular media can help to encourage quiet and shy children to find a voice that they feel comfortable with. Although past research suggests that the media and popular culture have a shaping influence on children's beliefs, values, and actions (Kraut, Patterson, Lundmark, Kiesler, Mukopahdyay, & Scherlis, 1998; Paik, 2001; Strasburger & Wilson, 2002), much research needs to be conducted on how popular media affects children's emotional health and sense of self-worth (Bensen, Donohue, & Erickson 1989; Heller, 1986; Rintel, & Pittam, 1997; Spilka, Hood, Hunsberger, & Gorsuch, 2003; Tarpley, 2001; Ward, 2004).

Given the increasing violent and sexual content reflected in popular media in today's society (e.g., Strasburger & Wilson, 2002), many educators and researchers question the social, moral, and religious implications of our advanced technology (e.g., Ho, 2001; Kegan, 1994; Kessler, 2000; Postman, 1999; Roberts & Foeher, 2004). A growing number of researchers suggest that more research, particularly longitudinal studies, need to be conducted on how media such as television, Internet, electronic games, and movies influences children's and adolescents' values, beliefs, and behaviors toward human beings (Flory, 2000; Lane, 2007; Ream & Savin-Williams, 2003; Rossiter, 1999; Strasburger & Wilson, 2002; Zimmerman, & Christakis, 2005).

Finally, another key area for future researchers, as mentioned previous chapters, is to explore the possibility that girls and boys differ regarding their emotional experiences. Given the expanding focus on gender and education to include gender-role perceptions and orientations (Leaper, 2000; Noddings, 2006; Weaver-Hightower, 2003), researchers and educators will need to continue to explore the gendered implications language holds for children's emotional-understanding. Such research may help researchers to make sense of the contradictory and inconclusive research that currently exists on children's emotional experiences during middle childhood.

5.5. Summary

Overall, this chapter explored some of the theoretical, practical, and future research implications of exploring shy or socially withdrawn children's emotional experiences within the classroom. That is, this chapter discussed some ideas for theorists, educators, and researchers to continue to discuss some strategies that may help children develop a better sense of emotional awareness within the classroom.

Although the discussion focused on those children in middle childhood who are considered to be shy or socially withdrawn, the ideas presented in this chapter could be adapted to help children of all ages and socioemotional abilities. This chapter aimed to provide educators and researchers with helpful pedagogical and empirical directions that will encourage emotionality to remain an important belief, value, and practice of the elementary school curriculum.

Conclusion: Emotions Speak (The Language of Emotions): Where do we go from Here?

"I shall take the heart," returned the Tin Woodman, "for brains do not make one happy, and happiness is the best thing in the world."

(Baum, 1984/1900, p. 47)

Overall, the goal of this book was to provide a window into the complex emotional lives children experience within the grade school classroom, particularly those who are considered to be shy or socially withdrawn. I aimed to illustrate the importance of emotions and sensitivity in learning and how being sensitive to emotions and social experiences may help children to further understand the emotional experiences of themselves and others. Given the overlap between the conceptual and practical issues concerning social and emotional learning and character development and education—educational programs that promote an emotionally healthy learner will help society in that developing emotional health occurs in tandem with ethical action in that it is respectful, caring, and responsible. This book also emphasized the importance of language and communication in emotional learning, and the importance of connection with others—as well as oneself. We need to promote educational programs that promote emotionally healthy self-talk and private vocabulary that is positive and respectful toward oneself and others. Educational programs that focus on social skills and respectful treatment of others must first begin with how we feel and believe about ourselves. How effective could a social skills or character education program be if children learn how to treat others ethically, but do not believe in, care about, or feel good about themselves?

Some future questions for educators as we continue to embark in this increasingly morally, emotionally, and culturally diverse educational context include how can educators help to foster self-regulation that is both emotionally sensitive and caring. Given that personal agency is formed from our self-regulatory skills and lies at the heart of the sense of self, how can educators promote healthy choices when children are learning how to be the best person they can be. Who defines "best" and are aspects of respect, reasoning, and self-control as important as the human basic needs including autonomy, belongingness, and competence (Deci & Ryan, 1985).

Regarding the issue of developing "emotional expertise"—is this feasible and how do children learn how to become emotional experts? Also, how do adults and those who spend time with children aim to become supportive and caring "emotional coaches?" How do we help educators develop an orientation to the ongoing challenge of building and maintaining good character in themselves? Campbell (2004) offers valuable insight into the working minds and classroom challenges of teacher and their need for ethical and emotional knowledge and coaching. Professional ethics and emotions course for educators might be designed according to Integrative Ethical Education principles incorporating aspects of emotional, social, and moral development (Narvaez, 2006). Thus, perhaps educators and researchers can work toward co-creating an Emotional Education that integrates aspects of ethical education and moral education.

In a democratic, pluralist society, how we cultivate and support virtuous personhood in parents, community members, and each other in ways that supports the connections between emotional and mental health and personal and social success? For example, how can we help children to develop self-regulation within the context of emotional development? According to Alexander, Kulikowich, and Schulze (1994), the development of a domain occurs as result of the interplay of skill (knowledge) and thrill (interest). How can we incorporate the promotion of both skills and interest or engagement within sustainable, cohesive, and mutually supportive and caring communities in today's society? How do we motivate communities to take on a construction of a holistic and psychocultural, transformative approach to children's sense of selves and their emotional experiences from an early age, particularly focusing on the middle childhood years? These and other questions provide a full and exciting agenda for researchers and educators in the years to come. Overall, it is my hope that by providing the reader with a brief summary of a few children's emotional experiences within the grade school classroom, this book has encouraged educators and researchers to become inspired to focus on the crucial role emotions play in learning and our development of ourselves.

As an educator and researcher concerned with the emotional health of Canada's youth, I question North American society's focus on physical health only, and the particular educational focus in Canada on children's physical health. We need to have a balanced educational vision, one that incorporates both mind and body equally. Although the Ontario government (2006) has started a new initiative on Character Education to address both the "head" and the "heart" of the child, the message is still contradictory given that the January 20, 2007 headline "Unhealthy schools" by Andrew Picard and Caroline Alphonso, of the Canadian national newspaper the *Globe and Mail* examines the "health" of Canadian schools including air quality, nutrition, and exercise, stating that "Canada's schools fail the health test" (Picard & Alphonso, 2007, A8). The newspaper series is based on results from a nationwide Globe and Mail survey which was sent to 139 publicly funded school boards across the country toward the end of the 2005–2006 academic year with seventy-four school boards responding. The three part series focused on nutrition, the physical education factor, and environmental hazards. In the January 20, 2007 article, there is no mention of emotional or psychological health.

As Elinor Wilson the chief executive officer of the Canadian Public Health Association states (2007), we need to explore our expectations of the school system and continue public debate. Upon finishing this book, my concern is around what is missing from the text, or what is "silent." That is, why is not emotional and mental health a part of our national educational plan? How can we begin to discuss healthy lifestyle choices such as regular physical activity and healthy eating habits if we do not consider the emotional, social, and mental lives of ourselves and the children? As a pluralist, responsible, and caring, compassionate modern society how can we be concerned about the environment and our physical health to the detriment of our emotional health? Or is the "cost of caring" too high? It is my hope that upon finishing this book, the reader will believe that the cost of caring about the emotional health of children is irrelevant, and that if we are to help children acquire self-knowledge and emotional competence, we need to focus on encouraging children to love and accept themselves.

Thus, I hope that my book will encourage readers to believe that our primary responsibility as researchers and educators is to further develop our emotional health and emotional presence and those we connect with, as we try to ensure that children in our future society may become not only cognitively and culturally competent, but also kind, caring, and compassionate. In collaboration with those who work with children and share the vision of the importance of emotional health, it is my hope that we will find that balance. In the end—if we as educators and researchers are genuinely concerned with, and invested in caring for and nurturing the child's heart, mind, and soul, we need to consider the question of how "competent and confident" will a child who is considered to be an academic "star" become if that child feels invisible and emotionally unwell? Thus if our educational system begins to focus and place importance and value around children's emotional health to the same extent it focuses on physical health and academic excellence, there is great hope for the present and future lives of our children. As the final word, I invite you to ponder the following question: How can we as educators and researchers encourage children to develop and maintain a healthy sense of self and emotional life in the classroom?

References

Adato, A. (1998, December/1999, January). Choosing my religion. *Teen People Magazine*, 138–144.

Akseer, S., Varnish, A., & Bosacki, S. (2007, May). *Gendered socio-moral understandings in middle childhood*. Poster presented at the Annual Conference of the Canadian Society for the Study of Education. Saskatoon, SA.

Alder, P., & Moulton, M. (1998). Caring relationships: Perspectives from middle school students. *Research in Middle Level Quarterly, 21*, 15–32.

Alexander, P., Kulikowich, J., & Schulze, S. (1994). How subject-matter knowledge affects recall and interest. *American Educational Research Journal, 31*, 313–337.

Allport, G. (1960). *Personality and social encounter*. Boston: Beacon.

Anderson, C., Gentile, D., & Buckley, K. (2006). *Violent video game effects on children and adolescents: Theory, research, and public policy*. New York, NY: Oxford University Press.

Anderson, K., & Leaper, C. (1998). Emotion talk between same- and mixed-gender friends: Form and functions. *Journal of Language and Social Psychology, 17*, 421–450.

Anderson, S. (1919). *Winesburg, Ohio*. New York: B. W. Huebsch.

Anning, A., & Ring, K. (2004). *Making sense of children's drawings*. Berkshire, UK: Open University Press.

Arbeau, K., & Coplan, R. (2007). Kindergarten teachers' beliefs and responses to hypothetical Prosocial, asocial, and antisocial Children. *Merrill-Palmer Quarterly, 53*, 291–318.

Aronson, E. (2004). Reducing hostility and building compassion: Lessons from the jigsaw classroom. In A. Miller (Ed.), *The social psychology of good and evil* (pp. 469–488). New York: Guilford Press.

Arsenio, W. (1988). Children's conceptions of the situational affective consequences of sociomoral events. *Child Development, 59*, 1611–1622.

Asher, S., & Coie, J. (Eds.). (1990). *Peer rejection in childhood*. New York: Cambridge University Press.

Astington, J. (1988). Children's understanding of the speech act of promising. *Journal of Child Language, 15*, 157–173.

Astington, J. (1993). *The child's discovery of the mind*. Cambridge, MA: Harvard University Press.

Astington, J. (1996). What is theoretical about the child's theory of mind? A Vygotskian view of its development. In P. Carruthers, & P. Smith (Eds.), *Theories of theory of mind* (pp. 184–199). Cambridge: Cambridge University Press.

Astington, J., & Jenkins, J. (1995). Theory of mind development and social understanding. *Cognition and Emotion, 9*, 151–165.

Astington, J., & Olson, D. (1995). The cognitive revolution in children's understanding of mind. *Human Development, 38*, 179–189.

Astington, J., & Pelletier, J. (1996). The language of mind: Its role in teaching and learning. In D. Olson, & N. Torrance (Eds.), *Handbook of education and human development: New models of learning, teaching, and schooling* (pp. 593–619). Oxford, UK: Blackwell.

Astington, J., & Pelletier, J. (1997, April). *Young children's theory of mind and its relation to their success in school*. Paper presented at the biennial meeting of the Society for Research in Child Development. Washington, DC.

Astington, J., & Pelletier, J. (2005). Theory of mind, language, and learning in the early years: Developmental origins of school readiness. In D. Homer, & C. Tamis-LeMonda (Eds.), *The development of social cognition and communication* (pp. 205–230). Mahwah, NJ: Lawrence Erlbaum Associates.

Austin, J. (1962). *How to do things with words*. Cambridge, MA: Harvard University Press.

Baker, C., & Luke, A. (1991). *Toward a critical sociology of reading pedagogy*. Amsterdam: John Benjamins.

Bakhtin, M. (1981). *The dialogic imagination* (C. Emerson, & M. Holquist, Trans.). Austin: University of Texas Press.

Baladerian, M. (1994). Intervention and treatment of children with severe disabilities who become victims of abuse. *Developmental Disabilities Bulletin, 22*, 93–99.

Baldwin, J. (1902*). Social and ethical interpretations in mental life*. New York: Macmillan.

Baldwin, J. (1913). *History of psychology*. London, UK: Watts.

Banerjee, R., & Henderson, L. (2001). Social-cognitive factors in childhood social anxiety: A preliminary investigation. *Social Development, 10*, 558–572.

Banerjee, R., & Watling, D. (2005). Children's understanding of faux pas: Associations with peer relations. *Hellenic Journal of Psychology, 2*, 27–45.

Banerjee, R., & Watling, D. (2007, June). *Children's understanding of faux pas: Longitudinal associations between socio-emotional understanding and peer relations*. Paper presented at the annual meeting of the Jean Piaget Society. Amsterdam, The Netherlands.

Banerjee, R., & Yuill, N. (1999). Children's understanding of self-presentational display rules: Associations with mental-state understanding. *British Journal of Developmental Psychology, 17*, 111–124.

Barenboim, C. (1981). The development of person perception in childhood and adolescence: From behavioral comparisons to psychological constructs to psychological comparisons. *Child Development, 52,* 129–144.

Baron, R., & Kenny, D. (1986). The moderator-mediator variable distinction in social psychological research: Conceptual, strategic, and statistical considerations. *Journal of Personality and Social Psychology, 51,* 1173–1182.

Bar-On, R., & Parker, J. (2000). *The handbook of emotional intelligence.* San Francisco: Jossey-Bass.

Baron-Cohen, S. (1995). *Mindblindness.* Cambridge, MA: Bradford/MIT.

Barresi, J., & Moore, C. (1995). Intentional relations and social understanding. *Behavioral and Brain Sciences, 18*, 256–279.

Bartlett, F. (1932). *Remembering: A study in experimental psychology.* Cambridge, UK: Cambridge University Press.

Bartsch, K., & Wellman, H. (1995). *Children talk about the mind.* New York: Oxford University Press.

Baska, L. (1989). Characteristics and needs of the gifted. In J. Feldhusen, J. Van Tassel-Baska, & K. Seeley (Eds.), *Excellence in educating the gifted* (pp. 15–28). Denver: Love Publishing.

Basso, K. (1970). "To give up on words": Silence in Western Apache culture. *Southwestern Journal of Anthropology, 26*, 213–230.

Baum, F. (1900/1984). *The wonderful wizard of Oz.* New York: Penguin.

Baumrind, D. (1991). Effective parenting during the early adolescent transition. In P. Cowan, & M. Hetherington (Eds.), *Family transitions* (pp. 111–163). Mahwah, NJ: Lawrence Erlbaum Associates.

Behrens, K. (2004). A multifaceted view of the concept of *amae*: Reconsidering the indigenous Japanese concept of relatedness. *Human Development, 47,* 1–27.

Belenky, M., Clinchy, B., Goldberger, N., & Tarule, J. (1986). *Women's ways of knowing.* New York: Basic Books.

Bellah, R., Madsen, R., Sulllivan, W., Swider, A., & Tipton, S. (1985). *Habits of the heart: Individualism and commitment in American life.* Berkeley, CA: University of California Press.

Bennett, M. (Ed.) (1993). *The child as psychologist: An introduction to the development of social cognition.* New York: Harvester Wheatsheaf.

Bennett, K., & LeCompte, M. (1990). *The way schools work: A sociological analysis of education.* New York: Longman.

Benson, P., Donahue, M., & Erickson, J. (1989). Adolescence and religion: A review of the literature from 1970 to 1986. *Research in the Social Scientific Study of Religion, 1,* 153–181.

Ben-Zur, H. (2003). Happy adolescents: The link between subjective well-being, internal resources, and parental factors. *Journal of Youth and Adolescence, 32*, 67–79.

Berger, P., & Luckmann, T. (1967). *The social construction of reality: A treatment in the sociology of knowledge*. Garden City, NY: Anchor.

Bering, J., Blasi, C., & Bjorklund, D. (2005). The development of 'afterlife' belief in religiously and secularly schooled children. *British Journal of Developmental Psychology, 23*, 587–607.

Berkowitz, M., Sherlbom, S., Bier, M., & Battistich, V. (2006). Educating or positive youth development. In M. Killen, & J. Smetana (Eds.), *The handbook of moral development* (pp. 683–701). Mahwah, NJ: Lawrence Erlbaum Associates.

Best, S., & Thomas, J. (2004). Cultural diversity and cross-cultural perspectives. In A. Eagley, A. Beall, & R. Sternberg (Eds.), *The psychology of gender* (pp. 296–327). New York: Guilford Press.

Bhanot, R., & Jovanovic, J. (2005). Do parents' academic gender stereotypes influence whether they intrude on their children's homework? *Sex Roles, 52*, 597–607.

Block, J., Gjerde, P., & Block, J. H. (1991). Personality antecedents of depressive tendencies in 18-year-olds: A prospective study. *Journal of Personality and Social Psychology, 60*, 726–738.

Bloom, M. (2000). The uses of theory in primary prevention practice: Evolving thoughts on sports and after-school activities as influences of social competence. In S. Danish, & T. Gullotta (Eds.), *Developing competent youth and strong communities through after-school programming* (pp. 17–66). Washington, DC: CWLA Press.

Bloom, P. (2004). *Descartes' baby: How the science of child development explains what makes us human*. New York: Basic Books.

Blos, J. (1979). *The adolescent passage: Developmental issues*. New York: International Universities Press.

Blume, J. (1972). *Tales of a fourth-grade nothing*. New York: Yearling.

Bocchino, R. (1999). *Emotional literacy: To be a different kind of smart*. Thousand Oaks, CA: Corwin Press.

Boden, M., & Berenbaum, H. (2007). Emotional awareness, gender, and suspiciousness. *Cognition and Emotion, 21*, 268–280.

Bohlin, G., Haegkull, B., & Andersson, K. (2005). Behavioral inhibition as a precursor of peer social competence in early school age: The interplay with attachment and nonparental care. *Merrill-Palmer Quarterly, 51*, 1–19.

Boivin, M., & Hymel, S. (1997). Peer experiences and social self-perceptions: A sequential model. *Developmental Psychology, 33*, 135–145.

Bolger, K., & Patterson, C. (2001). Pathways from child maltreatment to internalizing problems: Perceptions of control as mediators and moderators. *Development and Psychopathology, 3*, 913–940.

Bolger, K., Patterson, C., Thompson, W., & Kupersmidt, J. (1995). Psychosocial adjustment among children experiencing persistent and intermittent family economic hardship. *Child Development, 5*, 1107–1129.

Bosacki, S. (1995). Promoting positive attitudes towards aboriginal elementary students. *Canadian Social Studies, 30*, 19–23.

Bosacki, S. (1997). Theory of mind and education: Toward a dialogical curriculum. *Holistic Education Review, 10*, 32–41.

Bosacki, S. (1998). *Theory of mind in preadolescence: Connections among social understanding, self-concept, and social relations.* Unpublished doctoral dissertation, University of Toronto, Toronto, ON.

Bosacki, S. (2000). Theory of mind and self-concept in preadolescents: Links with gender and language. *Journal of Educational Psychology, 92*, 709–717.

Bosacki, S. (2001). "Theory of mind" or "Theory of soul"?: The role of spirituality in children's understanding of minds and emotions. In J. Erricker, C. Ota, & C. Erricker (Eds.), *Spiritual education: Cultural, religious, and social differences: New perspectives for the 21st century* (pp. 156–169). Brighton, UK: Sussex Academic Press.

Bosacki, S. (2003). Psychological pragmatics in preadolescents: Sociomoral understanding, self-worth, and school behavior. *Journal of Youth and Adolescence, 32*, 141–155.

Bosacki, S. (2005a, April). *Social cognitive and emotional competencies in shy young girls and boys.* Paper presented at the annual meeting of the American Educational Research Association, Montreal, Quebec.

Bosacki, S. (2005b). *The culture of classroom silence.* New York: Peter Lang.

Bosacki, S. (2005c). Religious development in children and youth. In C. Frisby, & D. Reynolds (Eds.), *Comprehensive Handbook of Multicultural School Psychology* (pp. 611–650). New York: Wiley & Sons.

Bosacki, S. (2007, March). *Self and social understanding during middle childhood.* Poster presented at the biennial meeting of the Society of Research in Child Development. Boston, MA.

Bosacki, S., & Astington, J. (1999). Theory of mind in preadolescence: Relations between social understanding and social competence. *Social Development, 8*, 237–255.

Bosacki, S., & Astington, J. (1997, April). *"She's such a shy child": Metacognitive underpinnings and teachers' perceptions of shyness in young girls and boys.* Poster presented at the annual meeting of the American Educational Research Association. San Diego, California.

Bosacki, S., Dane, A., Marini, Z., & YLC-CURA. (2007). Peer relationships and internalizing problems in adolescents: Mediating role of self-esteem. *Emotional and Behavioural Difficulties, 12*, 261–282.

Bosacki, S., Innerd, W., & Towson, S. (1997). Field independence-dependence and self-esteem: Does gender make a difference? *Journal of Youth and Adolescence, 26*, 691–703.

Boseovski, J., Marcovitch, S., & Love, J. (2007, March). *When does the thought count: Role of intention and frequency information in young children's personally attributions.* Poster presented at the biennial meeting of the Society for Research in Child Development, Boston, MA.

Bosacki, S., & Moore, C. (2004). Preschoolers' understanding of simple and complex emotions: Links with gender and language. *Sex Roles: A Journal of Research, 50,* 659–675.

Bosacki, S., Sargeson, K., Rose-Krasnor, L., Rubin, K., & Burgess, K. (2007, June). *Psychological language and self-perceptions in aggressive/socially withdrawn and "typical" children.* Paper presented at annual meeting of the Jean Piaget Society, Amsterdam, The Netherlands.

Bosacki, S., Varnish, A., & Akseer, S. (2006, June). *Pictorial and narrative representations of children's sense of self and play.* Paper presented at the annual meeting of the Jean Piaget Society, Baltimore, MD.

Briggs, J. (1995). The study of Inuit emotions: Lessons from a personal retrospective. In J. Russell, J. Fernandez-Dols, A. Manstead, & J. Wellencamp (Eds.), *Everyday conceptions of emotion* (pp. 203–220). Dordrecht, The Netherlands: Kluwer Academic Publishers.

Brewer, J., & Hunter, A. (1989). *Multimethod research: A synthesis of styles.* Newbury Park, CA: Sage.

Brody, L. (2001). *Gender emotion and the family.* Cambridge, MA: Harvard University Press.

Brody, L., & Hall, J. (1993). Gender and emotion. In M. Lewis, & J. Haviland (Eds.), *Handbook of emotions* (pp. 447–460). New York: Guilford.

Bronfenbrenner, U. (1977). Toward an experimental ecology of human development. *American Psychologist, 32,* 513–531.

Brooks-Gunn, J. (1989). Pubertal processes and the early adolescent tradition. In W. Damon (Ed.), *Child development today and tomorrow* (pp. 155–176). San Francisco: Jossey-Bass.

Brown, J., Donelan-McCall, N., & Dunn, J. (1996). Why talk about mental states? The significance of children's conversations with friends, siblings, and mothers. *Child Development, 67,* 836–849.

Brown, L., & Gilligan, C. (1992). *Meeting at the crossroads.* New York: Ballantine.

Bruce, P. (1958). Relationship of self-acceptance to other variables with sixth-grade children oriented in self-understanding. *Journal of Educational Psychology, 49,* 229–237.

Bruchkowsky, M. (1992). The development of empathic cognition in middle and early childhood. In R. Case (Ed.), *The mind's staircase: Exploring the conceptual underpinnings of children's thought and knowledge* (pp. 153–170). Mahwah, NJ: Lawrence Erlbaum Associates.

Bruner, J. (1986). *Actual minds, possible worlds.* Cambridge, MA: Harvard University Press.

Bruner, J. (1990). *Acts of meaning.* Cambridge, MA: Harvard University Press.

Bruner, J. (1996). *The culture of education.* Cambridge, MA: Harvard University Press.

Bruner, J., & Kalmar, D. (1997). Narrative and metanarrative in the construction of self. In M. Ferrari, & R. Sternberg (Eds.), *Self-awareness: Its nature and development* (pp. 1–52). New York: Guilford.

Buber, M. (1970). *I and thou* (W. Kaufmann, Trans.). New York: Charles Scribner's Sons.

Burke, K. (1990). Language and symbolic action. In P. Bizzell, & B. Herzberg (Eds.), *The rhetorical tradition: Reading from classical times to the present* (pp. 1034–1041). Boston: Bedford Books of Martin's Press.

Burkitt, E., Barrett, M., & Davis, A. (2003). The effect of affective characterizations on the size of children's drawings. *British Journal of Developmental Psychology, 21*, 565–584.

Burton, S., & Mitchell, P. (2003). Judging who knows best about yourself: Developmental change in citing the self across middle childhood. *Child Development, 74*, 426–443.

Buss, A. (1980). *Self-consciousness and social anxiety*. San Francisco, CA: Freeman.

Bussey, K., & Bandura, A. (1999). Social cognitive theory of gender development and differentiation. *Psychological Review, 106*, 676–713.

Bussey, K., & Bandura, A. (2004) (2nd Ed.). Social cognitive theory of gender development and functioning. In A. Eagly, A. Beall, & R. Sternberg, (Eds.), *The psychology of gender* (pp. 92–119). New York: Guilford.

Bybee, J. (1998). The emergence of gender differences in guilt during adolescence. In J. Bybee (Ed.), *Guilt and children* (pp. 114–122). San Diego, CA: Academic Press.

Cahan, E. (1997). John Dewey and human development. *Developmental Psychology, 28*, 205–214.

Cairns, R., Cairns, B., Neckerman, H., Ferguson, L., & Gariepy, J. (1989). Growth and aggression: 1. Childhood to early adolescence. *Developmental Psychology, 23*, 320–330.

Campbell, E. (2004). *The ethical teacher*. Maidenhead, PH: Open University Press.

Capps, L., Yirmiya, N., & Sigman, M. (1992). Understanding of simple and complex emotions in non-retarded children with autism. *Journal of Child Psychology and Psychiatry, 33*, 1169–1182.

Carlson, S. (2007, June). *Neural mechanisms underlying executive function and social understanding.* Paper presented at the annual meeting of the Jean Piaget Society. Amsterdam, The Netherlands.

Carpendale, J., & Shelton, K. (1999, April). *"Two kinds of happiness": Relations between interpretive theory of mind and ambivalent emotion understanding.* Paper presented at the Biennial Meeting of the Society for Research in Child Development. Albuquerque, New Mexico.

Carpendale, J., & Sokol, B. (2007, June). *Is neuroscience of morality a possibility?* Paper presented at the annual meeting of the Jean Piaget Society. Amsterdam, The Netherlands.

Case, R., Okamoto, Y., Griffin, S., McKeough, A., Bleiker, C., Henderson, B., & Stephenson, K. (1996). The role of central conceptual structures in the development of children's thought. *Monographs of the Society for Research in Child Development, 61*, (1–2, Serial No. 246).

Cederblom, J. (1989). Willingness to reason and the identification of the self. In E. Maimon, B. Nodine, & F. O'Connor (Eds.), *Thinking, reasoning, and writing* (pp. 147–159). New York: Longman.

Chandler, M. (1987). The Othello effect: Essay on the emergence and eclipse of sceptical doubt. *Human Development, 30*, 137–159.

Chen, X., Rubin, K., & Li, Z. (1995). Social functioning and adjustment in Chinese children. *Developmental Psychology, 31*, 531–539.

Chernin, K. (1985). *The hungry self: Women, eating, and identity.* New York: Harper & Row.

Children and the Internet: A parents' guide (1999). *Family Times, 153* (18), 22–28.

Chodorow, N. (1978). *The reproduction of mothering.* Berkeley, CA: University of California Press.

Clark, B. (1988). *Growing up gifted: Developing the potential of children at home and at school* (3rd Ed.), New York: Macmillan.

Cohen, J. (Ed.) (2001). *Caring classrooms/intelligent schools: The social emotional education of young children.* New York: Teachers' College Press.

Coie, J., & Dorval, B. (1973). Sex differences in the intellectual structure of social interaction skills. *Developmental Psychology, 8*, 261–267.

Coles, R. (1990). *The spiritual life of children.* Boston: Houghton Mifflin.

Coles, R. (1997). *The moral intelligence of children: How to raise a moral child.* New York: Plume.

Collin, A. (1996). Re-thinking the relationship between theory and practice: Practitioners as map-readers, map-makers–or jazz players? *British Journal of Guidance and Counselling, 24*, 67–81.

Cooley, C. (1912). *Human nature and social order.* New York: Scribner.

Coopersmith, S. (1967). *The antecedents of self-esteem.* San Francisco, CA : Freeman.

Coplan, R., & Armer, M. (2005). Talking yourself out of being shy: Shyness, expressive vocabulary, and socioemotional adjustment in preschool. *Merrill-Palmer Quarterly, 51*, 20–41.

Cowley, G., & Springen, K. (April 17, 1995). Rewriting life stories. *Newsweek*, 70–74.

Crain, W. (2006). On preparing children for the future. *Encounter: Education for Meaning and Social Justice, 2*, 2–4.

Cremin, L. (1976). *Public education.* New York, NY: Basic Books.

Creswell, J. W. (2005). *Educational research: Planning, conducting, and evaluating quantitative and qualitative research.* Upper Saddle River, NJ: Merrill Prentice Hall.

Crick, N., & Dodge, K. (1994). A review and reformulation of social information-processing mechanisms in children's social adjustment. *Psychological Bulletin, 115*, 74–101.

Crick, N., Nelson, D., Morales, J., Cullerton-Sen, C., Casas, J., & Hickman, S. (2001). Relational victimization in childhood and adolescence: I hurt you through the grapevine. In J. Juvonen, & S. Graham (Eds.), *School-based peer harassment: The plight of the vulnerable and victimized* (pp. 196–214). New York: Guilford Press.

Cross, T. (2005). *The social and emotional lives of gifted kids: Understanding and guiding their development.* Waco, TX: Prufrock Press, Inc.

Csikszentmihalyi, M. (1990). *Flow.* New York: Harper & Row.

Cutting, A., & Dunn, J. (1999). Theory of mind, emotion understanding, language, and family background: Individual differences. *Child Development, 70,* 853–865.

Cutting, A., & Dunn, J. (2002). The cost of understanding other people: Social cognition predicts young children's sensitivity to criticism. *Journal of Child Psychology and Psychiatry, 43,* 849–860.

D'Andrade, R. (1984). Cultural meaning systems. In R. Shweder, & R. LeVine (Eds.), *Culture theory: Essays on mind, self, and emotion* (pp. 92–108). Cambridge: Cambridge University Press.

Dabrowski, K. (1967). *Personality shaping through positive disintegration.* Boston: Little, Brown.

Dabrowski, K. (1972). *Psychoneurosis is not all an illness.* London: Gryf.

Dabrowski, K., & Piechowski, M. (1977). *Theory of levels of emotional development* (Vols. 1 & 2). Oceanside, New York: Dabor Science.

Dahl, R. (2007, May). *Adolescent brain development: A developmental periods of vulnerability and opportunity.* Paper presented at the annual meeting of the Jean Piaget Society. Amsterdam, The Netherlands.

Damasio, A. (1996). *The feeling of what happens: Body and emotion in the making of consciousness.* New York: Harcourt.

Damon, W., & Hart, D. (1988). *Self-understanding in childhood and adolescence.* New York: Cambridge University Press.

Danish, S., Taylor, T., & Fazio, R. (2003). Enhancing adolescent development through sports and leisure. In G. Adams, & M. Berzonsky (Eds.), *Blackwell handbook of adolescence* (pp. 92–108). Malden, MA: Blackwell.

Danon-Boileau, L. (2001). *The silent child: Exploring the world of children who do not speak.* New York: Oxford University Press.

Davis, G., & Rimm, S. (1998). *Education of the gifted and talented* (4th Ed.). Needham Heights, MA: Allyn & Bacon.

Davis, M. (1980). Measuring individual differences in empathy: Evidence for a multidimensional approach. *Journal of Personality and Social Psychology, 44,* 113–126.

Debold, E., Tolman, D., & Brown, L. (1996). Embodying knowledge, knowing desire: Authority and split subjectives in girls' epistemological development. In N. Goldberger, J. Tarule, B. Clinchy, & M. Belenky (Eds.), *Knowledge, difference and power* (pp. 85–125). New York: Basic Books.

Deci, E., & Ryan, R. (1985). *Intrinisc motivation and self-determiniation in human behavior.* New York: Academic Press.

Denham, S. (1998). *Emotional development in young children.* New York: Guilford Press.

Denham, S., Blair, K., DeMulder, E., Levitas, J., Sawyer, K., Auerbach-Major, S., & Queenan, P. (2003). Preschool emotional competence: Pathway to social competence? *Child Development, 74,* 238–256.

Denham, S., Cook, M., & Zoller, D. (1992). Baby looks very sad: Implications of conversations about feelings between mother and preschooler. *British Journal of Developmental Psychology, 10,* 301–315.

Denham, S., von Salisch, M., Olthof, T., Kochanoff, A., & Caverly, S. (2002). Emotional and social development in childhood. In P. Smith, & C. Hart (Eds.), *Blackwell handbook of childhood social development* (pp. 307–328). Oxford, UK: Blackwell.

De Villiers, P. (1999, April). *Language and thought: False complements and false beliefs.* Paper presented at the biennial meeting of the Society for Research in Child Development. Albuquerque, New Mexico.

DeVries, R., & Zan, B., (1999). *Moral classrooms, moral children: Creating a constructivist atmosphere in early education.* New York: Teachers College Press.

Dewey, J. (1902/1966). *The child and the curriculum.* Chicago, IL: University of Chicago.

Dewey, J. (1933/1966). *How we think: A restatement of the relation of reflective thinking to the educative process.* Boston: D.C. Heath.

DiBiase, A., Gibbs, J., & Potter, G. (2005). *EQUIP for Educators: Teaching youth (Grades 5–8) to think and act responsibly.* Champaign, IL: Research Press.

Dockett, S. (1997, April). *Young children's peer popularity and theories of mind.* Poster presented at the Biennial Meeting of the Society for Research in Child Development. Washington, DC.

Dockett, S., & Perry, R. (2007). Trusting children's accounts in research. *Journal of Early Childhood Research, 5*, 47-63.

Dodge, K., & Feldman, E. (1990). Issues in social cognition and sociometric status. In S. Asher, & J. Coie (Eds.), *Peer rejection in childhood* (pp. 119–155). New York: Cambridge University Press.

Dodge, K., & Frame, C. (1982). Social cognitive biases and deficits in aggressive boys. *Child Development, 53*, 620–635.

Donaldson, M. (1992). *Human minds: An exploration.* Harmondsworth, UK: Allen Lane.

Donelan-McCall, N., & Dunn, J. (1996). School work, teachers, and peers: The world of first grade. *International Journal of Behavioral Development, 21,* 155–178.

Drake, S. (1992). *Developing an integrated curriculum using the story model.* Toronto, ON: OISE Press.

Dunn, J. (1988). *The beginning of social understanding.* Oxford, UK: Blackwell.

Dunn, J. (1995). Children as psychologists: The later correlates of individual differences in understanding of emotions and other minds. *Emotion and Cognition, 9*, 187–201.

Dunn, J. (2000). Mind-reading, emotion understanding, and relationships. *International Journal of Behavioral Development, 24*, 142–144.

Dunn, J. (2004). *Children's friendships: The beginning of intimacy.* Malden, MA: Blackwell.

Dunn, J. (2006). Moral development in early childhood and social interaction in the family. In M. Killen, & J. Smetana (Eds.), *The handbook of moral development* (pp. 331–374). Mahwah, NJ: Lawrence Erlbaum Associates.

Dunn, L., & Dunn, L. (1997). *Peabody picture vocabulary test* (3rd Ed.). Circle Pines, Minnesota: American Guidance Service.

Dyson, R. (2000). *Mind abuse: Media violence in an information age*. Montreal, Quebec: Black Rose Books.

Eisenberg, N., & Mussen, P. (1989). *The roots of prosocial behavior in children*. New York: Cambridge University Press.

Elliott, A., Woloshyn, V., Richards, M., Bosacki, S., & Golden, L. (2002, April). *Grade six students' experiences with traditional and interactive technological media*. Paper based on a larger study by Elliott, A., Bosacki, S., Murray, N., Richards, M., Woloshyn, V., Mindorff, D., Golden, L., & Pollon, D. Presented at the annual meeting of the American Educational Research Association. New Orleans, LA.

Engel, S. (1999, April). *Children's first autobiographies*. Poster presented at the Biennial Meeting of the Society for Research in Child Development. Albuquerque, New Mexico.

Erwin, P. (1993). *Friendship and peer relations in children*. Chichester, UK: Wiley.

Filoppova, E., & Astington, J. (2008). Further development in social reasoning revealed in discourse irony understanding. *Child Development, 79,* 126–138.

Finders, M. (1997). *Just girls: Hidden literacies and life in junior high*. New York: Teachers College Press.

Finn, J. (1989). Withdrawing from school. *Review of Educational Research, 59,* 117–142.

Fiske, A., Kitayama, S., Markus, H., & Nisbett, R. (1998). The cultural matrix of social psychology. In D. Gilbert, A. Fiske, & G. Lindzey (Eds.), *The handbook for social psychology*: Vol. 2 (pp. 915–981). New York: McGraw Hill.

Fivush, R. (1989). Exploring sex differences in the emotional content of mother-child conversations about the past. *Sex Roles, 20,* 675–691.

Fivush, R. (2000). Accuracy, authority, and voice: Feminist perspectives on autobiographical memory. In P. Miller, & E. Scholnick (Eds.), *Toward a feminist developmental psychology* (pp. 85–106). New York: Routledge.

Fivush, R. (2004). Voice and silence: A feminist model of autobiographical memory. In J. Lucariello, J. Hudson, R. Fivush, & P. Bauer (Eds.), *The development of the mediated mind: Sociocultural context and cognitive development* (pp. 79–100). Mahwah, NJ: Lawrence Erlbaum Associates.

Flapan, D. (1968). *Children's understanding of social interaction*. New York: Teachers College Press.

Flavell, J. (2000, June). *Development of intuitions about the mental experiences of self and others*. Paper presented at the 30th annual conference of the Jean Piaget Society. Montreal, Quebec.

Flavell, J., & Miller, P. (1998). Social cognition. In W. Damon (Series Ed.), D. Kuhn, & R. Siegler (Vol. Eds.), *Handbook of child psychology: Vol. 2. Cognition, perception and language development* (5th Ed.) (pp. 851–898). New York: Wiley.

Flory, R. (2000). Toward a theory of Generation X religion. In R. Flory, & D. Miller (Eds.), *Gen X religion* (pp. 231–250). New York: Routledge.

Fodor, J. (1975). *The language of thought*. New York: Cromwell.

Fontana, A., & Frey, J. (1994). Interviewing. In N. Denzin, & Y. Lincoln (Eds.), *Handbook of Qualitative Research*. Thousand Oaks, CA: Sage.

Ford, M. (1982). Social cognition and social competence in adolescence. *Developmental Psychology, 18*, 323–340.

Fox, R. (1991). Developing awareness of mind reflected in children's narrative writing. *British Journal of Developmental Psychology, 9*, 281–298.

Fraser, S., & Strayer, J. (1997). *Guilt and shame in middle childhood: Relationships with empathetic responsiveness*. Poster presented at the biennial meeting of the Society for Research in Child Development. Washington, DC.

Freedman, J., & Combs, G. (1996). *Narrative therapy: The social construction of preferred realities*. New York: Norton.

Freymann, S., & Elffers, J. (1999). *How are you peeling? Foods with moods*. New York: Arthur S. Levine Books.

Fridja, N. (1986). *The emotions*. Cambridge, UK: Cambridge University Press.

Fridlund, A. (1994). *Human facial expression: An evolutionary review*. San Diego, CA: Academic Press.

Frith, U. (1989). *Autism: Explaining the enigma*. Oxford, UK: Basil Blackwell.

Frye, D., & Ziv, M. (2005). Teaching and learning as intentional activities. In D. Homer, & C. Tamis-LeMonda (Eds.), *The development of social cognition and communication* (pp. 231–258). Mahwah, NJ: Lawrence Erlbaum Associates.

Gardner, H. (1982). *Art, mind, and brain*. New York: Basic Books.

Gardner, H. (1985). *Frames of mind*. New York: Basic Books.

Gardner, H. (1991). *The unschooled mind*. New York: Basic Books.

Gardner, H., Csikszentmihalyi, M., & Damon, W. (2001). *Good work: When excellence and ethics meet*. New York: Basic Books.

Geary, D. (1998). *Male, female: The evolution of human sex differences*. Washington, DC: APA.

Geertz, C. (1973). *The interpretation of cultures*. New York: Basic Books.

Gelman, S., & Heyman, G. (1999). Carrot-eaters and creature-believers: The effects of lexicalization on children's inferences about social categories. *Psychological Science, 10*, 489–493.

Gergen, K., & Walrhus, L. (2001). *Social construction in context*. London: Sage Publications.

Gibbs, J., Potter, G., & Goldstein, A. (1995). *The EQUIP program: Teaching youth to think and act responsibly through a peer-helping approach*. Champaign, IL: Research Press.

Gilligan, C. (1993). Adolescent development rediscovered. In A. Garrod (Ed.), *Approaches to moral development* (pp. 103–132). New York: Teachers' College Press.

Glazer, S. (Ed.) (1999). *The heart of learning: Spirituality in education*. New York: Penguin Putnam.

Goffman, I. (1959). *The presentation of self in everyday life*. New York: Doubleday.

Goldberg, M. (1997). *Arts and learning: An integrated approach to teaching and learning in multicultural and multilingual settings.* New York: Longman.

Goldberger, N. (1996). Cultural imperatives and diversity in ways of knowing. In N. Goldberger, J. Tarule, B. Clinchy, & M. Belenky (Eds.), *Knowledge, differences, and power: Essays inspired by women's ways of knowing* (pp. 335–371). New York: Basic Books.

Goldberger, N., Tarule, J., Clinchy, B., & Belenky, M. (1996). *Knowledge, differences, and powers: Essays inspired by women's ways of knowing.* New York: Basic Books.

Goldman, R. (1964). *Religious thinking from childhood to adolescence.* London: Routledge & Kegan Paul.

Goldstein, L. (1997). *Teaching with love: A feminist approach to early childhood.* New York: Teachers College Press.

Goleman, D. (1995). *Emotional intelligence.* New York: Bantam Books.

Goleman, D. (2006). *Social intelligence: The new science of human relationships.* New York: Bantam Books.

Gollnick, D., & Chinn, P. (2002). *Multicultural education in a pluralistic society* (6th Ed.). Upper Saddle River, New Jersey: Merrill/Prentice Hall.

Golomb, C. (1990). *The child's creation of a pictorial world.* Berkely, CA: University Press.

Gottfredson, D. (2001). *Schools and delinquency.* Cambridge, UK: Cambridge University.

Greenberg, M., Domotrovich, C., & Bumbarger, B. (2001). Toward a concept of psychological maturity. *Journal of Youth and Adolescence, 3,* 329–358.

Greenberger, E., & Sorenson, A. (1974). Toward a concept of psychosocial maturity. *Journal of Youth and Adolescence, 3,* 329–358.

Grice, H. (1968). Utterer's meaning, sentence-meaning and word-meaning. *Foundations of Language, 4,* 1–18.

Griffin, S. (1995). A cognitive-developmental analysis of pride, shame, and embarrassment in middle childhood. In J. Tangney, & K. Fischer (Eds.), *Self-conscious emotions: The psychology of shame, guilt, embarrassment, and pride* (pp. 219–236). New York: Guilford.

Griffith, J., & Griffith, M. (1994). *The body speaks: Therapeutic dialogues for mind-body problems.* New York: Basic Books.

Grossman, L. (November 24, 2003). Old school, new tricks. *Time Magazine* (Canadian edition), 36–40.

Group for the Advancement of Psychiatry, Committee on Adolescents. (1996). *Adolescent suicide* (Report No. 140). Washington, DC: American Psychiatric Press.

Gruter, M., & Masters, R. (1986). Ostracism as a social and biological phenomenon: An introduction. *Ethology and Sociobiology, 7,* 149–158.

Guralnick, M. (1999). Family and child influences on the peer-related social competence of young children with developmental delays. *Mental Retardation and Developmental Disabilities Research Reviews, 5,* 31–29.

Guralnick, M., Connor, R., Hammond, M., Gottman, J., & Kinnish, K. (1996). The peer relations of preschool children with communication disorders. *Child Development, 67,* 471–489.

Guralnick, M., & Neville, B. (1997). Designing early intervention programs to promote children's social competence. In M. Guralnick (Ed.), *The effectiveness of early intervention* (pp. 579–610). Baltimore, MD: Paul H. Brookes.

Gutierrez, K., & Rogoff, B. (2003). Cultural ways of learning: Individual traits or repertoires of practice. *Educational Researcher, 32,* 19–25.

Haden, C., Haine, R., & Fivush, R. (1997). Developing narrative structure in parent-child reminiscing across the preschool years. *Developmental Psychology, 33,* 295–307.

Haidt, J. (2006). *The happiness hypothesis: Finding modern truth in ancient wisdom: Why the meaningful life is closer than you think.* New York: Perseus.

Haines, B., & Bartels, F. (1997, April). *Shyness and academic performance: Mediating or moderating roles of self-esteem, attributional style, and ethnicity.* Poster session presented at the biennial meeting of the Society for Research in Child Development. Washington, DC.

Hall, N. (1980). *The moon and the virgin.* New York: Harper and Row.

Hall, R. (1986). What nursery school teachers ask us about: Psychoanalytic consultations in preschools: Living with Spiderman et al.: Mastering aggression and excitement. *Emotions and Behavior Monographs* (Monograph No. 5), 89–99.

Halpern, D. (1992). *Sex differences in cognitive abilities* (2nd Ed.). Hillsdale, NJ: Lawrence Erlbaum Associates.

Hammack, P. (2005). The life course development of human sexual orientation: An integrative paradigm. *Human Development, 48,* 267–290.

Hankin, B., & Abramson, L. (2001). Development of gender differences in depression: An elaborated cognitive vulnerability-transactional stress theory. *Psychological Bulletin, 127,* 773–796.

Harkness, S. (2002). Culture and social development: Explanations and evidence. In P. Smith, & C. Hart (Eds.), *Blackwell handbook of childhood social development* (pp. 60–77). Oxford, UK: Blackwell.

Harre, R. (1986). *The social construction of emotions.* Oxford, UK: Blackwell.

Harris, P. (1989). *Children and emotion.* Cambridge, MA: Basil Blackwell.

Harris, P. (2000). On not falling down to earth: Children's metaphysical questions. In K. Rosengren, C. Johnson, & P. Harris (Eds.), *Imagining the impossible: The development of magical, scientific, and religious thinking in contemporary society* (pp. 157–178). Cambridge: Cambridge University Press.

Harris, P., Johnson, C., Hutton, D., Andrews, G., & Cooke, T. (1989). Young children's theory of mind and emotion. *Cognition and Emotion, 3,* 379–400.

Hart, D., & Fegley, S. (1995). Prosocial behavior and caring in adolescence: Relations to self-understanding and social judgement. *Child Development, 66,* 1346–1359.

Harter, S. (1999). *The construction of the self: A developmental perspective.* New York: Guilford Press.

Harter, S., & Buddin, B. (1987). Children's understanding of the simultaneity of two emotions: A five-stage developmental acquisition sequence. *Developmental Psychology, 23*, 388–399.

Harter, S., Waters, P., Whitesell, N., & Kastelic, D. (1997, April). *Predictors of level of voice among high school females and males: Relational context, support, and gender orientation.* Paper presented at the biennial meeting of the Society for Research in Child Development. Washington, DC.

Hasting, P., Utendale, U., Sullivan, C., & McShane, K. (2007, March). *Testing a bio-psychosocial model of preschool-aged children's risk for social wariness and internalizing problems.* Paper presented at the biennial meeting of the Society for Research in Child Development. Boston, MA.

Hatcher, R., & Hatcher, S. (1997). Assessing the psychological mindedness of children and adolescents. In M. McCallum, & W. Piper (Eds.), *Psychological mindedness: A contemporary understanding* (pp. 59–75). Mahwah, NJ: Lawrence Erlbaum Associates.

Hatcher, R., Hatcher, S., Berlin, M., Okla, K., & Richards, J. (1990). Psychological mindedness and abstract reasoning in late childhood and adolescence: An exploration using new instruments. *Journal of Youth and Adolescence, 19*, 307–325.

Hay, D., & Nye, R. (1998). *The spirit of the child.* London: Fount.

Haynes, J. (2002). *Children as philosophers: Learning through enquiry and dialogue in the primary classroom.* London: Routledge Falmer.

Haynes, N., & Marans, S. (1999). The cognitive, emotional, and behavioral (CEB) framework for promoting acceptance of diversity. In J. Cohen (Ed.), *Educating minds and hearts: Social emotional learning and the passage into adolescence* (pp. 158–170). New York: Teachers College Press.

Hazel, K., & Mohatt, G. (2001). Cultural and spiritual coping in sobriety: Informing substance abuse for Alaskan Native communities. *Journal of Community Psychology, 29*, 541–562.

Henggeler S. (2003). Advantages and disadvantages of multisystemic therapy and other evidence-based practices for treating juvenile offenders. *Journal of Forensic Psychology and Practice, 1,* 53–59.

Heyman, G., Dweck, C., & Cain, K. (1992). Young children's vulnerability to self-blame and helplessness: Relationships to beliefs about goodness. *Child Development, 63*, 401–415.

Hiatt, L. (1978). *Australian aboriginal concepts.* Canberra: Australian Institute of Aboriginal Studies.

Hill, J., & Lynch, M. (1983). The intensification of gender-related role expectations during early adolescence. In J Brooks-Gunn, & A. Peterson (Eds.), *Girls at puberty: Biological and psychosocial perspectives* (pp. 201–228). New York: Plenum.

Hinde, R. (1997, December). *Religion and Darwinism: The Voltaire Lecture, 9.* London: British Humanist Association.

Hinde, R. (2002). *Why good is good: The sources of morality.* London/New York: Wiley.

Ho, W. (2001). The prospects of spirituality in a globalized, technologized world. In J. Erricker, A. Ota & C. Erricker (Eds.), *Spiritual education: Cultural, religious, and social differences: New perspectives for the 21st century* (pp. 170–183). Brighton, UK: Sussex Academic Press.

Hobson, P. (1991). Against the theory of "Theory of Mind." *British Journal of Developmental Psychology, 9,* 33–51.

Hoffman, H. (2000). *Empathy and moral development: Implications for caring and justice.* Cambridge, UK: Cambridge University Press.

Hoffman, M. (1984). Interaction of affect and cognition in empathy. In C. Izard, J. Kaagn, & R. Zajonc (Eds.), *Emotions, cognitions and behavior* (pp. 103–121). New York: Cambridge University Press.

Homer, B., & Nelson, K. (2005). Seeing objects as symbols and symbols as objects: Language and the development of dual representation. In B. D. Homer, & C. Tamis-LeMonda (Eds.), *The development of social cognition and communication* (pp. 29–54). Mahwah, NJ: Lawrence Erlbaum Associates.

Honess, T. (1981). Girls' and boys' perceptions of their peers: Peripheral versus central and objective versus interpretive aspects of free descriptions. *British Journal of Psychology, 70,* 485–497.

Hughes, C., Deater-Deckard, K., & Cutting, A. (1999). "Speak roughly to your little boy"? Sex differences in the relations between parenting and preschoolers' understanding of mind. *Social Development, 8,* 143–160.

Hughes, C., & Dunn, J. (1998). Theory of mind and emotion understanding: Longitudinal associations with mental-state talk between young friends. *Developmental Psychology, 34,* 1026–1037.

Hughes, C., Dunn, J., & White, A. (1998). Trick or treat? Uneven understanding of mind and emotion and executive dysfunction in "hard-to-manage" preschoolers. *Journal of Child Psychology and Psychiatry, 39,* 981–994.

Huges, C., Jaffe, S., Happe, F., Taylor, A., Caspi, A., & Moffitt, T. (2005). Origins of individual differences in theory of mind: From nature or nurture? *Child Development, 76,* 356–370.

Hughes, F. (1999). *Children, play, and development.* Boston: Allyn & Bacon.

Hutchison, D. (1998). *Growing up green: Education for ecological renewal.* New York: Teachers College Press.

Hutchison, D. (2007). *Playing to learn: Video games in the classroom.* Westport, CT: Teacher Ideas Press.

Izard, C. (1992). Basic emotions, relations among emotions, and emotion-cognition relations. *Psychological Review, 99,* 561–565.

Jacobsen, T., Edelstein, W., & Hofmann, V. (1995). A longitudinal study of the relation between representations of attachment in childhood and cognitive functioning in childhood and adolescence. *Developmental Psychology, 30,* 112–124.

Jacques, S., & Zelazo, P. (2005). On the possible roots of cognitive flexibility. In B. D. Homer, & C. Tamis-LeMonda (Eds.), *The development of social cognition and communication* (pp. 53–81). Mahwah, NJ: Lawrence Erlbaum Associates.

Jahnke, H., & Blanchard-Fields, F. (1993). A test of two models of adolescent egocentrism. *Journal of Youth and Adolescence, 22*, 313–327.

Jahoda, G. (1959). The development of children's ideas about country and nationality, Pt. I: The conceptual framework. *British Journal of Educational Psychology, 33*, 47–60.

Jenkins, J., & Astington, J. (1996). Cognitive factors and family structure associated with theory of mind development in young children. *Developmental Psychology, 32*, 70–78.

Johnson, E. (1997). Children's understanding of epistemic conduct in self-deception and other false belief stories. *Child Development, 68*, 1117–1132.

Jones, E., & Cooper, R. (2006). *Playing to get smart.* New York: Teachers College Press.

Jones, M., & Gerig, T. (1994). Silent sixth-grade students: Characteristics, achievement and teacher expectations. *The Elementary School Journal, 2*, 169–182.

Junger-Tas, J. (1999). The Netherlands. In P. Smith et al. (Eds.), *The nature of school bullying* (pp. 205–223). London: Routledge.

Juvonen, J., & Bear, G. (1992). Social adjustment of children with and without learning disabilities in integrated classrooms. *Journal of Educational Psychology, 84*, 322–330.

Kagan, J. (1981). *The second year: The emergence of self-awareness.* Cambridge, MA: Harvard University Press.

Kagan, J. (1984). *The nature of the child.* New York: Basic Books.

Kagan, J. (2005). Human morality and temperament. In G. Carlo (Ed.), *Moral motivation through the lifespan. Nebraska Symposium on Motivation* (Vol. 15). Lincoln, Nebraska: University of Nebraska Press.

Kaiser Family Foundation (1999). *Kids and media at the new millenium.* Menlo Park, CA: Author.

Kamawar, D., Ridgeway, D., Holock, A., & Glennie, E. (2007, April). *He didn't mean to do it, but punish him anyway: ascribing intention, assigning penalty, and moral judgment in children and adults.* Poster presented at the biennial meeting of the Society for Research in Child Development. Boston, MA.

Kashima, Y., Yamaguchi, S., Kim, U., Choi, S., Gelfand, M., & Yuki, M. (1995). Culture, gender, and self: A perspective from individualism-collectivism research. *Journal of Personality and Social Psychology, 69*, 925–937.

Kazdin, A. (2003). Psychotherapy for children and adolescents. *Annual Review of Psychology, 54*, 253–276.

Kazdin, A., Siegel, T., & Bass, D. (1992). Cognitive problem-solving skills training and parent management training in the treatment of antisocial behavior in children. *Journal of Consulting and Clinical Psychology, 60*, 733–747.

Keating, D. (1990). Adolescent thinking. In S. Feldman, & G. Elliott (Eds.), *At the threshold: The developing adolescent* (pp. 56–89). Cambridge, MA: Harvard University Press.

Keenan, T. (1995). *The role of echoic information in young children's comprehension of sarcasm.* Unpublished doctoral dissertation. University of Toronto, Toronto, ON.

Kegan, R. (1994). *In over our heads: The mental demands of modern life.* Cambridge, MA: Harvard University Press.

Kelley, S., Brownell, C., & Campbell, S. (2000). Mastery motivation and self-evaluative affect in toddlers: Longitudinal relations with maternal behavior. *Child Development, 7*, 1061–1071.

Kelly, D. (2007, January 27). Childhood, unplugged. *The Globe and Mail*, M1, 5.

Kelly, G. (1955). *A theory of personality: The psychology of personal constructs.* New York: W.W. Norton.

Kerr, B. (1994). *Smart girls two: A new psychology of girls, women and giftedness.* Dayton, OH: Ohio Psychology Press.

Kessler, R. (2000). *The soul of education: Helping students find connection, compassion, and character at school.* Alexandria, VA: ASCD.

Killen, M., & Fox, N. (2007, June). *Developmental science and social neuroscience: Integrative approaches.* Paper presented at the annual meeting of the Jean Piaget Society. Amsterdam, The Netherlands.

King, C., Akiyama, M., & Elling, K. (1996). Self-perceived competencies and depression among middle school students in Japan and the United States. *Journal of Early Adolescence, 16*, 192–210.

Kirkpatrick, L. (1997). A longitudinal study of changes in religious belief and behavior as a function of individual differences in adult attachment style. *Journal for the Scientific Study of Religion, 36*, 207–217.

Kitayama, S., Markus, H., & Matsumoto, H. (1995). Culture, self, and emotion: A cultural perspective on "self-conscious" emotions. In J. Tangney, & K. Fischer (Eds.), *Self-conscious emotions: The psychology of shame, guilt, embarrassment, and pride* (pp. 439–464). New York: Guilford.

Kitchener, K., & King, K. (1981). Reflective judgement: Concepts of justification and their relationship to age and education. *Journal of Applied Psychology, 2*, 89–116.

Kochanska, G. (1994). Maternal reports of conscience development and temperament in young children. *Child Development, 65*, 852–868.

Kochanska, G., Casey, R. J., & Fukumoto, A. (1995). Toddlers' sensitivity to standard violations. *Child Development, 66(3)*, 643–656.

Kohlberg, L. (1963). *The psychology of moral development: The nature of and validity of moral stages.* San Francisco, CA: Harper & Row.

Kopp, C. (1989). Regulation of distress and negative emotions: A developmental review. *Developmental Psychology, 25*, 343–354.

Koppitz, E. (1969). Emotional indicators of human figure drawings of boys and girls from lower and middle-class backgrounds. *Journal of Clinical Psychology, 25*, 432–434.

Kraut, R., Patterson, M., Lundmark, V., Kiesler, S., Mukopahdyay, T., & Scherlis, W. (1998). Internet paradox: A social technology that reduces social involvement and psychological well-being? *American Psychologist, 53*, 1017–1031.

Kroger, J. (1996). *Identity in adolescence: The balance between self and other.* London: Routledge.

Kruger, A. (1992). The effect of peer and adult-child transactive discussions on moral reasoning. *Merrill-Palmer Quarterly, 38*, 191–211.

Kuhn, D. (1989). Making cognitive development research relevant to education. In W. Damon (Ed.), *Child development today and tomorrow* (pp. 261–287). San Francisco: Jossey-Bass.

Lagattuta, K. (2007). Thinking about the future because of the past: Young children's knowledge about the causes of worry and preventative decisions. *Child Development, 5*, 1492–1509.

Laible, D., & Thompson, R. (1998). Attachment and emotional understanding in preschool. *Developmental Psychology, 34*, 1038–1045.

Laing, R. (1961). *Self and others*. London: Penguin Books.

Lalonde, C., & Chandler, M. (1995). False belief understanding goes to school: On the social-emotional consequences of coming early or late to a first theory of mind. *Cognition and Emotion, 9*, 167–185.

Lalonde, C., & Chandler, M. (1997, April). *The development of an interpretive theory of mind*. Paper presented at the biennial meeting of the Society for Research in Child Development. Washington, DC.

Lalonde, C., & Chander, M. (2002). Children's understanding of interpretation. *New Ideas In Psychology, 20*, 163–198.

Lamb, S. (1993). First moral sense: An examination of the appearance of morally related behaviours in the second year of life. *Journal of Moral Education, 22*, 97–109.

Lamb, S. (2001). *The secret lives of girls: What good girls really do–Sex play, aggression, and their guilt*. New York: Free Press.

Lane, C. (2007). *Shyness: How normal behavior became a sickness*. New Haven, CT: Yale University Press.

Lather, P. (1986). Issues of validity in openly ideological research: Between a rock and a soft place. *Interchange, 17*, 63–84.

Lather, P. (1991). *Getting smart: Feminist research and pedagogy with/in the postmodern*. New York: Routledge.

Layard, P. (2005). *Happiness: Lessons from a new science*. New York: Penguin Press.

Lazarus, R. (1991). *Emotion and adaptation*. New York: Oxford University Press.

Leahy, R. (1981). Development of the conception of economic inequality: Descriptions and comparisons of rich and poor people. *Child Development, 52*, 523–532.

Leaper, C. (2000). The social construction and socialization of gender during development. In P. Miller, & E. Scholnick (Eds.), *Toward a feminist developmental psychology* (pp. 127–152). New York: Routledge.

Lee, C. (2003). Why we need to re-think race and ethnicity in educational research. *Educational Researcher, 32*, 3–5.

Leech, G. (1980). *Explorations in semantics and pragmatics*. Amsterdam: Johns Benjamins B. V.

Leekam. S. (1993). Children's understanding of mind. In M. Bennett (Ed.), *The child as psychologist: An introduction to the development of social cognition* (pp. 26–61). New York: Harvester Wheatsheaf.

Leiser, D., Sevon, G., & Levy, D (1990). Children's economic socialization: Summarizing the cross-cultural comparison of ten countries. *Journal of Economic Psychology, 11,* 591–614.

Levin, J., Taylor, R., & Chatters, L. (1994). Race and gender differences in religiosity among older adults: Findings from four national surveys. *Journal of Gerontology, 49,* 137–145.

Levinas, E. (1989). Ethics as first philosophy. In S. Hand (Ed.), *The Levinas reader* (pp. 31–54). Oxford, UK: Blackwell.

Levine, S. (1999). Children's cognitive capacities: The foundation for creative healing. *Journal of Poetry Therapy, 12,* 135–153.

Levinson, S. (1995). Interactional biases in human thinking. In E. Goody (Ed.), *Social intelligence and interaction* (pp. 221–260). New York: Cambridge University Press.

Levitt, M., & Selman, R. (1996). The personal meaning of risk behavior in G. Noam & W. Fischer (Eds.), *Development and vulnerability in close relationships* (pp. 201–233). Hillsdale, NJ: Erlbaum.

Lewis, C., & Carpendale, J. (2002). Social cognition. In P. Smith, & C. Hart (Eds.), *Blackwell handbook of childhood social development* (pp. 375–393). Oxford, UK: Blackwell.

Lewis, M. (1995). Embarrassment: The emotion of self-exposure and evaluation. In J. Tangney, & K. Fischer (Eds.), *Self-conscious emotions: The psychology of shame, guilt, embarrassment, and pride* (pp. 198–218). New York: Guilford Press.

Lewis, M. (2007, June). *Cortical and subcortical regulation of emotional development.* Paper presented at the annual meeting of the Jean Piaget Society. Amsterdam, The Netherlands.

Lewis, M., Sullivan, M., Stanger, C., & Weiss, M. (1989). Self-development and self-conscious emotions. *Child Development, 60,* 146–156.

Lightfoot, C. (1997). *The culture of adolescent risk-taking.* New York: Guilford Press.

Lillard, A. (1997). Other folks' theories of mind and behavior. *Psychological Science, 8,* 268–274.

Linn, S. (2005). *Consuming kids: Protecting our children from the onslaught of marketing and advertising.* New York: Anchor Books.

Lionni, L. (1970). *Fish is fish.* New York: Dragonfly Books.

Lord, C., & Magill-Evans, J. (1995). Peer interactions of autistic children and adolescents. *Development and Psychopathology, 7,* 611–626.

Lovecky, D. (1992). Exploring social and emotional aspects of giftedness in children. *Roeper Review, 15,* 18–25.

Lovecky, D. (2004). *Different minds: Gifted children with AD/HD, Asperger Syndrome, and other learning deficits.* London: Jessica Kingsley Publishers.

Luttrell, W. (1993). "The teachers, they all had their pets": Concepts of gender, knowledge, and power. *Signs: Journal of Women in Culture and Society, 18,* 505–546.

Lutz, C. (1988). *Unnatural emotions: Everyday sentiments on a Micronesian atoll and their challenge to Western theory.* Chicago: University of Chicago Press.

Lutz, C., & White, G. (1986). The anthropology of emotions. *Annual Reviews in Anthropology, 15*, 405–435.

Maccoby, E. (1998). Gender and relationships: A developmental account. *American Psychologist, 45*, 513–520.

Malchiodi, C. (1990). *Breaking the silence: Art therapy with children from violent homes.* New York: Bruner/Mazel.

Malchiodi, C. (1998). *Understanding children's drawings.* New York: Guildford Press.

Mansfield, A., & Clinchy, B. (1997, April). *Toward the integration of objectivity and subjectivity: A longitudinal study of epistemological development between the ages of 9 and 13.* Poster presented at the biennial meeting of the Society for Research in Child Development. Washington, DC.

Mant, C., & Perner, J. (1988). The child's understanding of commitment. *Developmental Psychology, 24*, 343–351.

Marini, Z., Dane, A., Bosacki, S., & YLC-CURA (2005). Direct and indirect bully-victims: Differential psychosocial risk factors associated with adolescents involved in bullying and victimization. *Aggressive Behavior, 32*, 1–19.

Markway, B., & Markway, G. (2005). *Nurturing the shy child: Practical help for raising confident and socially skilled kids and teens.* New York: Thomas Dunne Books/St. Martin's Press.

Markus, H., & Kitayama, S. (1994). The cultural construction of self and emotion: Implications for social behavior. In S. Kitayama, & H. Markus (Eds.), *Emotion and culture: Empirical studies of mutual influence* (pp. 89–132). Washington, DC: APA.

Markus, H., & Wurf, E. (1987). The dynamic self-concept: A social psychological perspective. *Annual Review of Psychology, 38*, 299–337.

Marsh, H., & Shavelson, R. (1985). Self-concept: Its multifaceted, hierarchical, structure. *Educational Psychologist, 20*, 107–125.

Maslow, A. (1971). *The farther reaches of human nature.* New York: Viking.

Matousek, M. (1998, July–August). Should you design your own religion? *UTNE Reader,* 44–48.

Matthews, G., Zeidner, M., & Roberts, R. (2002). *Emotional intelligence: Science and myth.* Cambridge, MA: MIT Press.

Matthews, K., & Keating, D. (1995). Domain specificity and habits of mind: An investigation of patterns of high-level development. *Journal of Early Adolescence, 15*, 319–343.

McCormick, P. (1994). *Children's understanding of mind: A case for cultural diversity.* Unpublished doctoral dissertation, University of Toronto, Toronto, ON.

McGinn, M., & Bosacki, S. (2004, March). Research ethics and practitioners: Concerns and strategies for novice researchers engaged in graduate education [52 paragraphs]. *Forum Qualitative Sozialforschung/Forum: Qualitative Social Research* [Online Journal], *5(2)*. Retrieved November 11, 2007, from http://www.Qualitative-research.net/fqs-texte/2-04/2-04mcginnbosacki-e.html

McGrath, E., Keita, G., Strickland, B., & Russo, N. (1990). *Women and depression.* Washington, DC: American Psychological Association.

McHolm, A., Cunningham, C., & Vanier, C. (2005). *Helping your child with selective mutism: Practical steps to overcome a fear of speaking.* Oakland, CA: New Harbinger Publications, Inc.

McKeough, A. (1992). A neo-structural analysis of children's narrative and its development. In R. Case (Ed.), *The mind's staircase: Exploring the conceptual underpinnings of children's thought and knowledge* (pp. 171–188). Mahwah, NJ: Lawrence Erlbaum Associates.

McKeough, A., Templeton, L., & Marini, A. (1995). Conceptual change in narrative knowledge. Psychological understandings for low-literacy and literate adults. *Journal of Narrative and Life History, 5,* 21–49.

Mead, G. (1934). *Mind, self and society.* Chicago: Chicago University Press.

Meehan, C. (2002, March). Promoting spiritual developing in the curriculum. *Pastoral Care,* 16–24.

Mendaglio, S. (1995). Sensitivity among gifted persons: A multi-faceted perspective. *Roeper Review, 17,* 169–172.

Menyuk, P., & Menyuk, D. (1988). Communicative competence: A historical and cultural perspective. In J. Wurzel (Ed.), *Toward multiculturalism: A reader in multicultural education* (pp. 131–152). Yarmouth, ME: Intercultural Press.

Miller, A. (1997). *The drama of the gifted child: The search for the true self* (Rev. Ed.). New York: Basic Books.

Miller, J (1993). *The holistic curriculum.* Toronto, ON: OISE Press.

Miller, J. (2000). *Education and the soul: Toward a spiritual curriculum.* New York: State University of New York Press.

Miller, P., & Scholnick, E. (2000). Introduction: Beyond gender as a variable. In P. Miller, & E. Scholnick (Eds.), *Toward a feminist developmental psychology* (pp. 3–10). New York: Routledge.

Miller, P., Kessel, F., & Flavell, J. (1970). Thinking about people thinking about people thinking about …: A study of social cognitive development. *Child Development, 41* 613–623.

Miller, P. H., & Aloise, P. A. (1989). Young children's understanding of the psychological causes of behavior: A review. *Child Development, 60(2),* 257–285.

Moore, C. (1996). Theories of mind in infancy. *British Journal of Developmental Psychology.*

Moore, C. (2006). *The development of commonsense psychology.* Mahwah, NJ: Lawrence Erlbaum Associates.

Morrison, T. (1994). *The bluest eye.* New York: Plume.

Morton, J., & Trehub, S. (2001). Children's understanding of emotion in speech. *Child Development, 72,* 834–843.

Myers, D. (2000). *The American paradox: Spiritual hunger in an age of plenty.* New Haven, CT: Yale University Press.

Narvaez, D. (2006). Integrative ethical education. In M. Killen, & J. Smetana (Eds.), *The handbook of moral development* (pp. 703–732). Mahwah, NJ: Lawrence Erlbaum Associates.

Nasir, N., & Saxe, G. (2003). Ethnic and academic identities: A cultural practice perspective on emerging tensions and their management in the lives of minority students. *Educational Researcher, 32*, 14–18.

Neisser, U. (1988). Five kinds of self-knowledge. *Philosophical Psychology, 1*, 35–39.

Nelson, K. (1996). *Language in cognitive development: Emergence of the mediated mind.* New York: Cambridge University Press.

Nelson, K., Henseler, S., & Plesa, D. (2000). Entering a community of minds: Theory of mind from a feminist standpoint. In P. Miller, & E. Scholnick (Eds.), *Toward a feminist developmental psychology* (pp. 61–83). New York: Routledge.

Nesbitt, E. (1998). British, Asian, and Hindu: Identity, self-narration and the ethnographic interview. *Journal of Beliefs and Values, 19*, 189–200.

Nesbitt, E. (2001). Religious nurture and young people's spirituality: Reflections on research at the university of Warwick. In J. Erricker, C. Ota, & C. Erricker (Eds.), *Spiritual education: Cultural religious, and social differences: New perspectives for the 21st century* (pp. 130–142). Brighton, UK: Sussex University Press.

Noddings, N. (1984). *Caring: A feminine approach to ethnic and moral education.* Berkeley, CA: University of California.

Noddings, N. (2003). *Happiness and education.* New York: Cambridge University Press.

Noddings, N. (2006). *Critical lessons: What our schools should teach.* New York: Cambridge University Press.

Novak, J., & Purkey, W. (2001). *Invitational education.* Bloomingtom, Indiana: Phi Delta Kappa Educational Foundation.

Novak, J., Rocca, W., & Dibiase, A. (Eds.) (2006). *Creating inviting schools.* San Francisco: Caddo Gap Press.

Nucci, L. (2001). *Education in the moral domain.* New York: Cambridge University Press.

Nucci, L. (2006). Education for moral development. In M. Killen, & J. Smetana (Eds.), *The handbook of moral development* (pp. 657–681). Mahwah, NJ: Lawrence Erlbaum Associates.

Nussbaum, M. (2000). Emotions and social norms. In L. Nucci, G. Saxe, & E. Turiel (Eds.), *Culture, thought, and development* (pp. 41–63). Mahwah, New Jersey: Lawrence Erlbaum Associates.

Oatley, K., & Duncan, E. (1994). The experience of emotions in everyday life. *Cognition and Emotion, 8*, 369–381.

Ochs, E., & Schieffelin, B. (1984). Language acquisition and socialization: Three developmental stories. In R. Shweder, & R. LeVine (Eds.), *Culture theory: Mind, self and emotion* (pp. 276–320). Cambridge, UK: Cambridge University Press.

Offer, D., Ostrov, E., Howard, K., & Atkinson, R. (1988). *The teenage world: Adolescents' self-image in ten countries.* New York: Plenum.

Olson, D. (1994). *The world on paper.* New York: Cambridge University Press.

Olson, D. (1997). Critical thinking: Learning to talk about talk and text. In G. Phye (Ed.), *Handbook of academic learning* (pp. 493–510). New York: Academic Press.

Olson, D. (2003). *Psychological theory and educational reform: How school remakes mind and society.* Cambridge, UK: Cambridge University Press.

Olson, D., & Bruner, J. (1996). Folk psychology and folk pedagogy. In D. Olson, & N. Torrance (Eds.), *Handbook of education and human development: New models of learning, teaching and schooling* (pp. 9–27). Oxford, UK: Blackwell.

Ontario Ministry of Education (2006, October). *Finding common ground: Character development in Ontario schools, K-12.* Toronto, ON: Ministry of Education.

Oyserman, D., & Markus, H. (1993). The sociocultural self. In J. Suls (Ed.), *Psychological perspectives on the self,* (Vol. 4, pp. 187–220). Hillsdale, NJ: Erlbaum.

Paechter, C. (2000). *Changing school subjects: Power, gender, and curriculum.* Buckingham, UK: Open University Press.

Paik, H. (2001). The history of children's use of electronic media. In D. Ginger, & J. Singer (Eds.), *Handbook of children and the media* (pp. 7–27). Thousand Oaks, CA: Sage.

Pajares, F., Miller, D., & Johnson, M. (1999). Gender differences in writing self-beliefs of elementary school students. *Journal of Educational Psychology, 91,* 50–61.

Paley, V. (1999). *The kindness of children.* Cambridge, MA: Harvard University Press.

Paley, V. (2004). *A child's work.* Chicago, IL: University Press of Chicago.

Palmer, P. (1999, January). Evoking the spirit. *Educational Leadership,* 6–11.

Parent, S., Normandeau, S., Cossett-Richard, M., & Letarte, M. (1999, April). *Preschoolers' emotional competence and social behavior within the family: May gender differences be in the eye of the beholder?* Poster presented at the biennial meeting of the Society for Research in Child Development. Albuquerque, New Mexico.

Parker, J., Taylor, G., & Bagby, R. (2003). The 20-Item Toronto Alexithymia Scale III. Reliability and factorial validity in a community population. *Journal of Psychomatic Research, 55,* 269–275.

Parkhurst, J., & Asher, S. (1992). Peer rejection in middle school: Subgroup differences in behavior, loneliness, and interpersonal concerns. *Developmental Psychology, 28,* 231–241.

Park, L., & Park, T. (1997). Personal intelligence. In M. McCallum, & W. Pipher (Eds.), *Psychological mindedness: A contemporary understanding* (pp. 133–168). Mahwah, NJ: Lawrence Erlbaum Associates.

Patterson, C., Kupersmidt, J., & Griesler, P. (1990). Children's perceptions of self and of relationships with others as a function of sociometric status. *Child Development, 61,* 1335–1349.

Pearce, L., & Van Ryn, M. (2007, March). *In their own words: How youth talk about religiosity and spirituality across early and late adolescence.* Paper presented at the biennial meeting of the Society for Research in Child Development. Boston, MA.

Peevers, F., & Secord, P. (1973). Developmental changes in attribution of descriptive concepts of persons. *Journal of Personality and Social Psychology, 27,* 120–128.

Pellegrini, D. (1985). Social cognition and competence in middle childhood. *Child Development, 56,* 253–264.

Pellegrini, D. (2005). *Recess: Its role in education and development.* Mahwah, NJ: Lawrence Erlbaum Associates.

Pepler, D., & Craig, W. (1995). A peek behind the fence: Naturalistic observations of aggressive children with remote audiovisual recording. *Developmental Psychology, 31*, 348–553.

Perner, J. (1991). *Understanding the representational mind.* Cambridge, MA: Bradford/ MIT.

Perner, J., & Wimmer, H. (1985). "John thinks that Mary thinks that…" Attribution of second-order beliefs by 5- to 10-year-old children. *Journal of Experimental Child Psychology, 39*, 437–471.

Peshkin, A. (1988). In search of subjectivity–one's own. *Educational Researcher, 14*, 17–22.

Peterson, G., & Leigh, G. (1990). The family and social competence in adolescence. In T. Gullotta, G. Adams, & R. Montemayor (Eds.), *Developing social competency in adolescence* (pp. 97–138). Newbury Park, CA: Sage Publications.

Philp, M. (2007, June 9). Nearly half of children in Crown care are medicated. *The Globe and Mail*, A1, A6.

Phinney, J. (1990). Ethnic identity in adolescents and adults: A review of the research. *Psychological Bulletin, 108*, 499–514.

Piaget, J. (1963). *The origins of intelligence in children.* New York: Norton.

Piaget, J. (1965). *The moral judgement of the child.* New York: Free Press.

Piaget, J. (1981). *Intelligence and affectivity: Their relationship during children development.* Palo Alto, CA: Annual Reviews.

Piaget, J., & Inhelder, B. (1956). *The child's conception of space.* London, UK: Routledge & Kegan Paul.

Picard, A., & Alphonso, C. (2007, January 20). Unhealthy schools. *The Globe and Mail*, A8.

Piechowski, M. (2006). *"Mellow out," they say. If I only could. Intensities and sensitivities of the young and bright.* Madison, WI: Yunasa Books.

Piechowski, M. (1997). Emotional giftedness: The measure of intrapersonal intelligence. In N. Colangelo, & G. Davis (Eds.), *Handbook of gifted education* (2nd Ed.) (pp. 366–381). Boston: Allyn & Bacon.

Piechowski, M. (1979). Developmental potential. In N. Colangelo, & R. Zaffrann (Eds.), *New voices in counseling the gifted* (pp. 25–27). Dubuque, IA: Kendall/Hunt.

Pinker, S. (2007). *The stuff of thought: Language as a window into human nature.* New York: Viking.

Plath, S. (1996). *The it-doesn't-matter suit.* New York: St. Martin's Press.

Pomerantz, E., & Eaton, M. (2001). Maternal intrusive support in the academic context: Transactional socialization processes, *Developmental Psychology, 37*, 175–186.

Pons, F., Lawson, J., Harris, P. L., & de Rosnay, M. (2003). Individual differences in children's emotion understanding: Effects of age and language. *Scandinavian Journal of Psychology, 44*, 347–411.

Pope, C. (2001). *"Doing school." How are we creating a generation of stressed out, materialistic, and miseducated students.* London: Yale University Press.

Postman, N. (1995). *The end of education: Redefining the value of school.* New York: Vintage Books.

Postman, N. (1999). Information. *Building a bridge to the 18th century* (pp. 82–98). New York: Vintage Books.

Potter, S. (1988). The cultural construction of emotion in rural Chinese social life. *Ethos, 16,* 181–208.

Prakash, K., & Coplan, R. (2007). Socio-emotional characteristics and school adjustment of socially-withdrawn children in India. *International Journal of Behavioural Development, 31,* 123–132.

Purkey, W. (2000). *What students say to themselves: Internal dialogue and school success.* Thousand Oaks, CA: Corwin Press, Inc.

Quinn, N., & Holland, D. (1987). Culture and cognition. In D. Holland, & N. Quinn (Eds.), *Cultural models in language and thoughts* (pp. 3–40). Cambridge, UK: Cambridge University Press.

Rabin, A. (1986). Concerning projective techniques. In A. Rabin (Ed.), *Projective techniques for adolescents and children* (pp. 3–13). New York: Springer.

Radford, M. (2006). Spirituality and education; inner and outer realities. *International Journal of Children's Spirituality, 11,* 385–396.

Ream, G., & Savin-Williams, R. (2003). Religious development in adolescence. In G. Adams, & M. Berzonsky (Eds.), *Blackwell handbook of adolescence* (pp. 51–59). Malden, MA: Blackwell.

Reinharz, S. (1992). *Feminist methods in social research.* New York: Oxford University Press.

Reinharz, S. (1997). Who am I? The need for a variety of selves in the field. In R. Hertz (Ed.), *Reflexivity and voice.* Thousand Oaks, CA: Sage.

Rich, G. (2003). The positive psychology of youth and adolescence. *Journal of Youth and Adolescence, 32,* 1–3.

Richer, S. (1990). *Boys and girls apart: Children's play in Canada and Poland.* Ottawa: Carleton University Press.

Rigby, K. (2002). Bullying in childhood. In P. Smith, & C. Hart (Eds.), *Blackwell handbook of childhood social development* (pp. 549–568). Oxford, UK: Blackwell.

Rinaldi, C., & Heath, N. (2006). An examination of the conflict resolution strategies and goals of children with depressive symptoms. *Emotional and Behavioral Difficulties, 11,* 187–204.

Rintel, E., & Pittam, J. (1997). Strangers in a strange land: Interaction management on Internet relay chat. *Human Communication Research, 23,* 507–534.

Roberts, D., & Foeher, U. (2004). *Kids and media in America.* Cambridge, UK: Cambridge University Press.

Roeper, A. (1982). How the gifted cope with their emotions. *Roeper Review, 5,* 21–24.

Rogers, A. (1993). Voice, play, and practice of courage in girls and women's lives. *Harvard Educational Review, 63,* 265–295.

Rogers, A. (2000). When methods matter: Qualitative research issues in psychology. *Harvard Educational Review, 70,* 75–85.

Rogers, C. (1961). *On becoming a person.* New York: Houghton Mifflin.

Rogoff, B. (1990). *Apprenticeship in thinking: Cognitive development in social context.* New York: Oxford University Press.

Rogoff, B. (2003). *The cultural nature of human development.* New York: Oxford University Press.

Rose-Krasnor, L. (1997). The nature of social competence: A theoretical review. *Social Development, 6,* 111–135.

Rose-Krasnor, L., & Rubin, K. (1992). Interpersonal problem-solving and social competence in children. In V. B. van Hasselt, & M. Hersen (Eds.), *Handbook of social development: A lifespan perspective* (pp. 283–323). New York: Plenum.

Rosenberg, M. (1989). *Society and the adolescent self-image* (Rev. Ed.). Middletown, CT: Wesleyan University Press.

Rossiter, G. (1999). The shaping influence of film and television on the spirituality and identity of children and adolescents: An educational response–part 3. *International Journal of Children's Spirituality, 4,* 207–224.

Rozak, T. (1992). *The voices of the earth.* New York: Simon & Schuster.

Rubin, K. (1972). Relationship between egocentric communication and popularity among peers. *Developmental Psychology, 7,* 364.

Rubin, K., & Asendorpf, J. (1993). Social withdrawal, inhibition, and shyness in childhood: Conceptual and definitional issues. In K. Rubin, & J. Asendorf (Eds.), *Social withdrawal, inhibition and shyness in childhood* (pp. 3–17). Mahwah, NJ: Lawrence Erlbaum Associates.

Rubin, K., & Burgess, K. (2001). Social withdrawal and anxiety. In M. Vasey, & M. Dadds (Eds.), *The developmental psychopathology of anxiety* (pp. 407–434). New York: Oxford University Press.

Rubin, K., Burgess, K., & Coplan, R. (2002). Social withdrawal and shyness. In P. Smith, & Hart (Eds.), *Blackwell handbook of childhood social development* (pp. 329–352). Oxford, UK: Blackwell.

Rubin, K., LeMare, L., & Lollis, S. (1990). Social withdrawal in childhood: Developmental pathways to peer rejection. In S. Asher, & J. Coie (Eds.), *Peer rejection in childhood* (pp. 217–249). Cambridge, UK: Cambridge University Press.

Rudolph, K., & Conley, C. (2005). The socioemotional costs and benefits of social-evaluative concerns: Do girls care too much? *Journal of Personality, 73,* 116–137.

Rudolph, K., Caldwell, M., & Conley, C. (2005). Need for approval and children's well-being. *Child Development, 76,* 309–323.

Saarni, C. (1999). *The development of emotional competence.* New York: Guilford Press.

Sacks, O. (2007). *Musicophilia: Tales of music and the brain.* New York: Alfred A. Knopf.

Sadker, M., & Sadker, D. (1994). *Failing at fairness: How America's schools cheat girls.* New York: Charles Scribner.

Salovey, P., & Sluyter, D. (1997). *Emotional development and emotional intelligence: Educational implications.* New York: Basic Books.

Santrock, J. (1993). *Adolescence: An introduction.* Dubuque, IA: Brown & Benchmark.

Scarlett, G., Naudeau, S., Salonius-Pasternak, D., & Ponte, I. (2005). *Children's play.* Thousand Oaks, CA: Sage Publications.

Schaffer, R. (1996). *Social development.* Oxford, UK: Blackwell.

Schultz, L., & Selman, R. (1989). Bridging the gap between interpersonal thought and action in early adolescence: The role of psychodynamic processes. *Development and Psychopathology, 1,* 133–152.

Searle, J. (1969). *Speech acts: An essay in the philosophy of language.* Cambridge, UK: Cambridge University Press.

Seligman, M. (2002). *Authentic happiness: Using the new positive psychology to realize your potential for lasting fulfillment.* New York: Free Press.

Seligman, M., & Csikszentmihalyi, M. (2000). Positive psychology: An introduction. *American Psychologist, 55,* 5–15.

Selman, R. (1980). *The growth of interpersonal understanding.* New York: Academic Press.

Selman, R. (2003). *The promotion of social awareness: Powerful lessons from the partnership of developmental theory and classroom practice.* New York: Russell Sage Foundation.

Selman, R. (2007, May). *A case conference on an adolescent's thoughts and actions in an incident of ostracism.* Paper presented at the annual meeting of the Jean Piaget Society. Amsterdam, The Netherlands.

Seroczynski, A., Jacquez, F., & Cole, D. (2003). Depression and suicide during adolescence. In G. Adams, & M. Berzonsky (Eds.), *Blackwell handbook of adolescence* (pp. 550–573). Malden, MA: Blackwell.

Shantz, C. (1983). Social cognition. In P. Mussen (Ed.), *Handbook of child psychology: Vol. 3* (pp. 495–555). New York: Wiley.

Sheridan, S., Kratochwill, T., & Elliott, S. (1990). Behavioral consultation with parents and teachers: Delivering treatment for socially withdrawn children at home and school. *School Psychology Review, 19,* 33–52.

Shields, S. (2002). *Speaking from the heart: Gender and the social meaning of emotion.* Cambridge, UK: Cambridge University Press.

Shilling, A. (1986). *The Ojibway dream.* Montreal, Quebec: Tundra.

Shweder, R. (1991). *Thinking through cultures: Expeditions in cultural psychology.* Cambridge, MA: Harvard University Press.

Shweder, R. (1993). The cultural psychology of the emotions. In M. Lewis, & J. Haviland (Eds.), *Handbook of emotions* (pp. 417–431). New York: Guilford Press.

Silver, R. (1997). Sex and age differences in attitudes towards the opposite sex. *Art Therapy: Journal of the American Art Therapy Association, 14,* 286–272.

Silverman, L. (1989). Invisible gifts, invisible handicaps. *Roeper Review, 12*, 37–42.

Silverman, L. (1993a). Understanding giftedness. In L. Silverman (Ed.), *Counseling the gifted and talented* (pp. 3–28). Denver: Love Publishing.

Silverman, L. (1993b). A developmental model for counseling the gifted. In L. Silverman (Ed.), *Counseling the gifted and talented* (pp. 51–78). Denver: Love Publishing.

Silverstein, B., & Perlick, D. (1995). *The cost of competence: Why inequality causes depression, eating disorders, and illness in women.* New York: Oxford University Press.

Simon, H. (1995). The information-processing theory of mind. *American Psychologist, 50*, 507–508.

Simmons, R., Rosenberg, F., & Rosenberg, H. (1973). Disturbance in the self-image at adolescence. *American Sociological Review, 38*, 535–568.

Singer, D., Michnick Golinkoff, & Hirsh-Pasek, K. (Eds.) (2006). *Play-learning: How play motivates and enhances children's cognitive and social-emotional growth.* New York: Oxford University Press.

Slomkowski, C., & Dunn, J. (1996). Young children's understanding of other people's beliefs and feelings and their connected communication with friends. *Developmental Psychology, 32*, 442–447.

Spatz, J., & Wright Cassidy, K. (1999). *Theory of mind and prosocial behavior in preschool children.* Poster presented at the biennial meeting of the Society for Research in Child Development. Albuquerque, New Mexico.

Sperber, D., & Wilson, D. (1986). *Relevance: Communication and cognition.* Cambridge, MA: Harvard University Press.

Spilka, B., Hood, R., Hunsberger, B., & Gorsuch, R. (2003). *The psychology of religion* (3rd Ed.). New York: Guildford.

Steiner, R. (1976). *Education of the child in the light of anthroposophy* (G. Adams, & M. Adams, Trans.). London: Rudolph Steiner Press.

Steinhausen, H., & Juzi, C. (1996). Elective mutism: An analysis of 100 cases. *Journal of the American Academy of Child and Adolescent Psychiatry, 35*, 606–614.

Sternberg, R. (2007). Who are the bright children? The cultural context of being and acting intelligent. *Educational Researcher, 36*, 148–155.

Stipek, D., Recchia, S., & McClintic, S. (1992). Self-evaluation in young children. *Monographs of the Society for Research in Child Development, 57* (1, Serial No. 226), 1–84.

Stallard, P. (2002). *Think good-feel good: A cognitive behaviour therapy workbook for children and young people.* Chichester, UK: John Wiley and Sons.

Strasburger, V., & Wilson, B. (2002). *Children, adolescents, and the media.* Thousand Oaks, CA: Sage Publications.

Strauss, S., & Shiloney, T. (1994). Teachers' models of children's minds and learning. In L. Hirschfeld, & S. Gelman (Eds.), *Mapping the mind: Domain specificity in cognition and culture* (pp. 455–473). New York: Cambridge University Press.

Sullivan, H. (1953). *The interpersonal theory of psychiatry.* New York: Norton.

Sullivan, K., Zaitchik, D., & Tager-Flusberg, H. (1994). Preschoolers can attribute second-order beliefs. *Developmental Psychology, 30,* 395–402.

Sullivan, S., Yuill, N., & Slade, L. (2007, June). *The relationship between emotion recognition and theory of mind abilities in middle childhood and its relation to earlier measures of belief and emotion understanding.* Poster presented at the annual meeting of the Jean Piaget Society. Amsterdam, The Netherlands.

Sulloway, F. (1996). *Born to rebel: Birth order, family dynamics and creative lives.* New York: Vintage Books.

Super, C., & Harkness, S. (1997). The cultural structuring of child development. In J. Berry, P. Dasen, & T. Saraswathi (Eds.), *Handbook of cross-cultural psychology: Vol. 2. Basic processes and human development* (pp. 1–39). Boston: Allyn & Bacon.

Sweet, L. (1997). *God in the classroom: The controversial issue of religion in Canada's schools.* Toronto, ON: McClelland & Stewart.

Tager-Flusberg, H., Sullivan, K., Barker, J., Harris, A., & Boshart, J. (1997, April). *Theory of mind and language acquisition: The development of cognition verbs.* Poster presented at the biennial meeting of the Society for Research in Child Development. Washington, DC.

Talwar, V., Murphy, S., & Lee, K. (2007). White lie-telling in children and politeness purposes. *International Journal Behavioural Development, 31,* 1–11.

Tangney, J. (1991). Moral affect: The good, the bad and the ugly. *Journal of Personality and Social Psychology, 61,* 598–607.

Tannen, D. (1994). *Gender and discourse.* New York: Oxford University Press.

Tarpley, T. (2001). Children, the Internet, and other new technologies. In D. Singer, & J. Singer (Eds.), *Handbook of children and media* (pp. 547–556). Thousand Oaks, CA: Sage Publications.

Tatum, B. (2003). *Why are all the black kids sitting together in the cafeteria: And other conversations about race.* New York: Basic Books.

Tavris, C. (1992). *The mismeasure of women.* New York: Simon & Schuster.

Taylor, M., & Carlson, S. (2000). The influence of religious beliefs on parental attitudes about children's fantasy behavior. In K. Rosengren, C. Johnson, & P. Harris (Eds.), *Imagining the impossible: The development of magical, scientific, and religious thinking in contemporary society* (pp. 247–268). Cambridge UK: Cambridge University Press.

Teen trouble: Drugs, sex, depression: Canadian experts on how to help kids survive trying times. (2004, March 1). *Maclean's: Canada's Weekly Magazine,* 26–33.

Thomas, G., & Silk, A. (1990). *An introduction to the psychology of children's drawings.* Hemel Hamsptead, UK: Harvester Wheatsheaf.

Thompson, R. A. (2006). The development of the person: Social understanding, relationships, conscience, self. In W. Damon, & R. M. Lerner (Eds.) & N. Eisenberg (Vol. Ed.), *Handbook of child psychology: Vol. 3. Social, emotional, and personality development* (6th Ed., pp. 24–98). New York: Wiley.

Thompson, R., & Lagattuta, K. H. (2006). Feeling and understanding: Early emotional development. In K. McCartney, & D. Phillips (Eds.), *Blackwell handbook of early childhood development* (pp. 317–337) Oxford, UK: Blackwell.

Thornedike, E. (1905). *The elements of psychology*. New York: A. G. Seiler.

Tilley, S. (1998). Conducting respectful research: A critique of practice. *Canadian Journal of Education, 23*, 316–328.

Tomasello, M. (1999). *The cultural origins of human cognition*. Cambridge, MA: Harvard University Press.

Topping, K., Bremner, W., & Holmes, E. (2000). Social competence: The social construction of the concept. In R. Bar-On, & J. Holmes (Eds.), *The handbook of emotional intelligence* (pp. 28–39). San Francisco: Jossey-Bass.

Torrance, D. (1997). "Do you want to be in my gang?" A study of the existence and effects of bullying in a primary school class. *British Journal of Special Education, 24*, 158–162.

Trawick-Smith, J. (2003). *Early childhood development: A multicultural perspective* (3rd Ed.). Upper Saddle River, NJ: Merrill-Prentice Hall.

Tremblay, N. (2000). The development of aggressive behaviours during childhood: What have we learned in the past century? *International Journal of Behavioural Development, 24,* 129–141.

Trulear, H. (2000). *Faith-based institutions and high-risk youth: First report to the field*. Philadelphia, PA: Public/Private Ventures.

Turiel, E. (2007, June). *The relevance of moral epistemology and psychology for neuroscience*. Paper presented at the annual meeting of the Jean Piaget Society. Amsterdam, The Netherlands.

Underwood, M. (2002). Sticks and stones and social exclusion: Aggression among boys and girls. In P. Smith, & C. Hart (Eds.), *Blackwell handbook of childhood social development* (pp. 533–348). Oxford, UK: Blackwell.

Underwood, M., Galen, B., & Paquette, J. (2001). Top ten methodological challenges for understanding gender and aggression: Why can't we all just get along? *Social Development, 10*, 248–267.

Van Manen, M. (1990). *Researching lived experience: Human science for an action sensitive pedagogy*. Albany, NY: SUNY Press.

Varela, F. (1992; 1999 Trans). *Ethical know-how: Action, wisdom, and cognition*. Stanford, CA: Stanford University Press.

Varela, F., Thompson, E., & Rosch, E. (1991). *The embodied mind: Cognitive science and human experience*. Cambridge, MA: MIT Press.

Vecchio, J., & Kearney, C. (2005). Selective mutism in children: Comparison to youths with and without anxiety disorders. *Journa of Psychopathology and Behavioral Assessment, 27*, 31–27.

Vernon, A. (1997). *Thinking, feeling and behaving: An emotional education curriculum for adolescents*. Waterloo, ON: Colwell Systems/Research Press.

Vinden, P., & Astington, J. (2000). Culture and understanding other minds. In S. Baron-Cohen, H. Tager-Flusberg, & D. Cohen (Eds.), *Understanding other minds: Perspectives from developmental cognitive neuroscience* (pp. 503–519). Oxford, UK: Oxford University Press.

Vygotsky, L. (1978). *Mind in society: The development of higher psychological processes.* Cambridge, MA: Harvard University Press.

Wallander, J., & Varni, J. (1998). Effects of pediatric chronic physical disorders on child and family adjustment. *Journal of Child Psychology and Psychiatry, 39,* 29–46.

Wang, Q. (2004). The emergence of cultural self-constructs: Autobiographical memory and self-description in European American and Chinese children. *Developmental Psychology, 40,* 3–15.

Ward, M. (2004). Wading through stereotypes: Positive and negative associations between media use and black adolescents' conceptions of self. *Developmental Psychology, 40,* 284–294.

Watson, A., Nixon, C., Wilson, A., & Capage, L. (1999). Social interaction skills and theory of mind in young children. *Developmental Psychology, 35,* 386–391.

Watson, M. (2003). *Learning to trust.* San Francisco: Jossey-Bass.

Watt, M. (2006). *Scaredy squirrel.* Toronto, ON: Kids Can Press.

Watts, A. (1944). *The language and mental development of children.* London, UK: George G. Harrap & Company.

Watts, F., & Williams, M. (1988). The psychology of religious knowing. Cambridge, UK: Cambridge University Press.

Weaver-Hightower, M. (2003). The "boy turn" in research on gender and education. *Review of Educational Research, 73,* 471–498.

Wellman, H. (1990). *The child's theory of mind.* Cambridge, MA: MIT Press.

Wellman, H., & Lagattuta, K. (2004). Theory of mind for learning and teaching: The nature and role of explanation. *Cognitive Development, 19,* 479–497.

Wentzel, K., & Asher, S. (1995). The academic lives of neglected, and rejected, popular, and controversial children. *Child Development, 66,* 754–763.

Werner, R., & Cassidy, K. (1997, April). *Children's psychological understanding and its relationship to social information processing and social competence.* Poster presented at the biennial meeting of the Society for Research in Child Development. Washington, DC.

Wertsch, J. (1989). A sociocultural approach to mind. In W. Damon (Ed.), *Child development today and tomorrow* (pp. 14–33). San Francisco: Jossey Bass.

White, G. (1994). Affecting culture: Emotion and morality in everyday life. In S. Kitayama, & H. Markus (Eds.), *Emotion and culture: Empirical studies of mutual influence* (pp. 219–239). Washington, DC: APA Publishing.

Wichmann, C., Coplan, R., & Daniels, T. (2004). The social cognitions of socially withdrawn children. *Social Development, 13,* 377–392.

Wierzbicka, A. (1989). Soul and mind: Linguistic evidence for ethnopsychology and cultural history. *American Anthropologist, 91,* 41–58.

Wierzbicka, A. (1994). Emotion, language, and cultural scripts. In S. Kitayama, & H. Markus (Eds.), *Emotion and culture: Empirical studies of mutual influence* (pp. 133–196). Washington, DC: APA.

Wierzbicka, A. (1999). *Emotions across languages and cultures: Diversity and universals.* Cambridge, UK: Cambridge University Press.

Wierzbicka, A. (2006). *English: Meaning and culture.* New York: Oxford University Press.

Wilgosh, L. (1994). The underachievement of girls: A societal rather than a gender issue. *Education in Canada, Spring,* 18–23.

Willats, J. (2005). *Making sense of children's drawings.* Mahwah, NJ: Lawrence Erlbaum Associates.

Williams, K. (2001). *Ostracism: The power of silence.* New York: Guilford Press.

Willoughby, T., Chalmers, H., & Busseri, M. (2006). Where is the syndrome? Examining co-occurrence among multiple problem behaviors in adolescence. *Journal of Consulting and Clinical Psychology, 72,* 1022–1037.

Wimmer, H., & Perner, J. (1983). Beliefs about beliefs: Representation and constraining function of wrong beliefs in young children's understanding of deception. *Cognition, 13,* 103–128.

Winner, E. (1988). *The point of words: Children's understanding of metaphor and irony.* Cambridge, MA: Harvard University Press.

Winner, E. (2000). The origins and ends of giftedness. *American Psychologist, 55,* 159–169.

Winner, E., & Leekam, S. (1991). Distinguishing irony from deception: Understanding the speaker's second-order intention. *British Journal of Developmental Psychology, 9,* 257–270.

Winston, J. (2002). Drama, spirituality and the curriculum. *International Journal of Children's Spirituality, 7,* 241–255.

Wojslawaowicz Bowker, J., Rubin, K., Rose-Krasnor, L., & Both-LaForce. (2007, March). *Social withdrawal, negative emotion, and peer difficulties during late childhood.* Paper presented at the biennial meeting of the Society for Research in Child Development. Boston, MA.

World Health Organization. (1999). *WHO Statistical Information System.* Geneva, Switzerland.

Yon, D. (2000). *Elusive culture: Schooling, race, and identity in global times.* New York: State of University of New York Press.

Young, E. (1992). *Seven blind mice.* New York: Philomel Books.

Youniss, J., McLellan, J., & Yates, M. (1999). Religion, community service, and identity in American youth. *Journal of Adolescence, 22,* 243–253.

Yuill, N. (1993). Understanding of personality and dispositions. In M. Bennett (Ed.), *The child as psychologist: An introduction to the development of social cognition* (pp. 87–110). New York: Harvester Wheatsheaf.

Yuill, N., & Coultas, J. (2007, June). *The relation between emotion recognition and social experience in early adolescence.* Poster presented at the annual meeting of the Jean Piaget Society. Amsterdam, The Netherlands.

Zahn-Waxler, C., & Robinson, J. (1995). Empathy and guilt: Early origins of feelings of responsibility. In J. Tangney, & K. Fischer (Eds.), *Self-consciousness emotions: The psychology of shame, guilt, embarrassment, and pride* (pp. 143–173). New York: Guilford Press.

Zimbardo, P., & Radl, S. (1981). *The shy child: Overcoming and preventing shyness from infancy and to adulthood.* Cambridge, MA: Malor Books.

Zimmerman, E., & Christakis, D. (2005). Children's television viewing and cognitive outcomes: A longitudinal analysis of national data. *Archives of Pediatric Adolescent Medicine, 159,* 619–625.

Ziv, M., & Frye, D. (2007, June). *Children's theory of mind and understanding of teaching.* Paper presented at the annual meeting of the Jean Piaget Society. Amsterdam, The Netherlands.

Index

media
influence of, need for research on, 169–71
and need for critical literacy, 145–46
Mendaglio, S., 46, 53
mental state language, 27–28
mental state understanding. *see* understanding, mental state
mental state verbs, 27–28
Miller, J., 23
Miller, P., 56
mindfulness/awareness, 141–44
Mitchell, P., 12
Mohatt, G., 148
Moore, C., xi
moral behavior, 33
. *see also* morality
moral education, 153, 156–58
morality
and emotions, 110
and hot/cold emotions, 168
judgments in stories, 110
moral behavior, 33
moral education, 153, 156–58
research of, 165
moral language, 110–11
moral reasoning, 168
moral sensitivity of gifted individuals, 53–55
Moulton, M., 69
mutism, selective, 52–53

name, as self-labeling concept, 86–87
narratives, interpretive, 27
natural semantic meta-language (NSM), 139, 141–44, 159
Nesbitt, E., 83
neuroscience, social-cognitive, 136–37
Noddings, N., 139, 158, 170
normative behavior, 31–32
norms, toddlers' awareness of, 54

Novak, J., xi
Nucci, L., 165, 167

Oatley, K., 30
Ochs, E., 98
OE (overexcitability), 43, 44, 45, 161–62
Offer, D., 58
Olson, D., 158
Ostrov, E., 58
others, understanding of. *see* ToM; understanding, mental state
overexcitability (OE), 43, 44, 45, 161–62

parents
children's reaction to unsolicited interventions by, 38
and children's theories about abilities, 38
expectations of and self-conscious emotions, 37–38
expectations of gender roles, 63, 64, 65
interventions for, 151–52
reminiscing, 65
participants
assessment of self-continuity of, 86–88, 90–91
assessment of self-distinctiveness of, 88–90, 91
assessment of sense of self of, 88
passion, 44
Peabody Picture Vocabulary Test (PPVT-III), 76–77
peer acceptance and self-concept, 36
peer relationships
and communication, 121–22, 123, 125, 126, 128–29
and development of social cognition, 15
influence on girls, 49–50, 93
lack of research on, 28–29
link with emotional understanding, 40–41
link with self-concept, 41–42